I DARE YOU

EMBRACE LIFE WITH PASSION

JOYCE MEYER

HODDER

British Library Cataloguing in Publication Data
A record for this book is available from the British Library

ISBN 978 0340 954492

Offset by Avon DataSet Ltd, Bidford on Avon, Warwickshire

Printed and bound in Great Britain by
Clays Ltd, St Ives plc

The paper and board used in this paperback are natural recyclable products
made from wood grown in sustainable forests. The manufacturing processes
conform to the environmental regulations of the country of origin.

Hodder & Stoughton
A Division of Hodder Headline Ltd
338 Euston Road
London NW1 3BH
www.madaboutbooks.com

CONTENTS

Passionate Pursuits

'God loves with a great love the man whose heart is bursting with a passion for the IMPOSSIBLE.'

– William Booth

A lot of people are talking about purpose these days. It's an important topic – knowing and understanding our purpose is essential to knowing and understanding what it is God wants to do with us. When we understand our purpose, we have a road map in front of us that's a useful and necessary guide. However, if purpose is our journey and destination, then passion is the fuel that's going to get us there and it's vital for us to keep that fuel in well-stocked supply.

Life without purpose and passion is a life not worth living. We all need a reason to get up every day and we need to find the passion – the spark that keeps us motivated and moving. We need to be enthusiastic! Too many of us walk around with long faces looking and feeling indifferent, bored or just plain worn-out. But the human heart was made for passion, for strong desire to reach for something beyond ourselves. We need to be able to celebrate each day of our lives, no matter the circumstances.

We get up; we go to work; we take care of the kids; we go to church; we come home; we go to bed, and start it all over again tomorrow. We're losing both our passion and our purpose, and we're passing that lack of enthusiasm to our children. Maybe a holiday or a big win from our favourite sports team might rouse us out of our

> We are here to enjoy God and do His will.

slumber for a little bit, but pretty soon we're back to having no real enthusiasm about life.

Over the centuries millions of people have asked, 'What am I here for? What is my purpose?' There's a simple answer for this, but not everyone is willing to accept it. We are here to enjoy God and do His will. We were created for His pleasure. He is the Alpha and the Omega, the beginning and the end. Therefore, He must also be everything in between. This is a lot for some people to accept. They want to know what God is going to do *for them*, but they should be asking what God is going to do *through them*.

That's something Paul thought about every day. Look at how many times he uses these words:

I will not venture to speak of anything except what Christ has accomplished through me . . .
– ROMANS 15:18 (NIV)

But the Lord stood at my side and gave me strength, so that through me the message might be fully proclaimed . . .
– 2 TIMOTHY 4:17 (NIV)

But whatever I am now, it is all because God poured out his special favor on me – and not without results. For I have worked harder than all the other apostles; yet it was not I but God who was working through me by his grace.
– 1 CORINTHIANS 15:10 (NLT)

We are born, we live, and we die. We cannot do anything about being born or about dying, but we can do a lot about how we live. Paul understood that. So did Peter. He was an eager disciple who made a lot of mistakes in his ministry and as one of Christ's followers, and yet God used him because he was willing to step out boldly when Jesus called. Peter was filled with zeal, passion and enthusiasm.

Taking responsibility for how we live is a brave thing. It takes courage to accept life as it comes to us and it also takes courage to be determined to make the most we can out of it. Life is too short to waste it by always erring on the cautious side or playing it safe instead of pursuing all you can be. It's time to take action and make your life count: step out of the boat and start working towards leaving a legacy when you are gone.

Passion Is More Than a Feeling

When most people think about passion, they may think about sex or bursts of emotion that come and go. They see passion as unstable, maybe unsatisfying and even unnecessary, and as a result they typically respond to life and signs of enthusiasm this way: *Let's not get worked up about this . . . Let's just take one day at a time and see what happens . . . I don't let things get to me one way or another.*

When we feel less, we risk less. I'm here to tell you, though, the passion I'm talking about – enthusiastic enthusiasm – is not a feeling that comes and goes or a mood you wait to have in order to act on something. Passion is the way you approach life.

Look how God uses passion. Everything He does is done with a purpose, and He does it passionately. He does it with His whole heart. We are to love God with *our* whole hearts, and do all we do with enthusiasm and drive. No half-hearted effort on our part will ever please God, nor will it produce true joy in our lives.

There is an innate desire deep inside each of us to reach for goals that seem unreachable. I'm talking about those hopes and dreams we all have; some are lying just below the surface, but some have been so deeply buried for so long it will take time to dig them out. It's our nature to have something to be moving towards at all times. We all need something to strive for, to work towards, and to dream about. We need a reason to get out of bed in the morning, and one that is greater than merely existing for another day. I believe we all have a deep desire to be daring, to get out of the box and live on the edge. If someone asked us, we would readily acknowledge we want life to be exciting, but some of us have got too comfortable and coy sitting on our respective couches of life. We need a challenge, but only a few of us ever dare to follow our hearts. I have decided to be one of the few. Will you join me? Will you dare to be different? Will you dare to live life like you mean it?

Will you dare to live life like you mean it?

Like some of you, I spent many years not enjoying life's journey. I fought with life, always wishing to have something different than what I had. I finally learned that life is more about the journey than the destination and I made a commitment to enjoy it all. I thank God He taught me to face life boldly, knowing He is with me and that I can do whatever I need to do with Him by my side, and I can do it with joy. I now know I have a purpose, God has a plan and I have decided to live out my days with passion and enthusiasm. I believe this book will have a profound effect on you. It will add a quality to your life that may have been missing, and I'm praying God will show you the purpose and the passion He wants you to have.

Our Greatest Example of Passion

As Christians, when we talk about passion, many of us will think of the passion plays we've seen at Easter and, of course, the 2004 film, *The Passion of the Christ,* which depicts the last twelve hours of Jesus' life on earth.

Jesus was passionate about His purpose. And He didn't just show it through intense emotional moments, such as becoming angry when He saw people selling their wares in the temple or weeping when He saw the unbelief of people. His passion could be seen in His concern for the sick, the poor, and those being treated unjustly. He always stopped to help and comfort hurting people who came to Him. He prayed passionately and showed great endurance while on the cross. He loved His Father passionately. We can safely say that everything Jesus did was done wholeheartedly, and we should follow His example.

When we think about passion, we need to think about the passion of Christ. We need to remember His focus, His determination, and how engaged He was with life and with His Father's plan. We need to adopt His passion for our own. We need to be as engaged with life as He was and is.

If you want to make the most of your life and live it with enthusiasm and zeal the way Jesus did, just reading this book will not be enough. You will need to make decisions along the way. Your approach to life may need to change. Your attitude and how you allocate your time may need to change. However, the results will be rewarding. Getting up every day with purpose and living out each day passionately is a reward in itself. There's more value to life, and at the end of each day we can sense accomplishment and fulfilment. We can look forward to the next day expectantly.

> Living out each day passionately is a reward in itself.

When we embrace life with passion we won't experience as much dread or regret. Our lives become filled with zeal for the present and we are what I like to call a 'NOW' person. Someone who is fully living in the present and getting all they can out of each day. Even the 'bumps' in the road on life's journey have a purpose and you can learn to find value in them rather than dreading and despising them.

Take this journey with me. Let's learn together how we can be more passionate about the life God has given us. Let's be determined to fulfil our purpose.

PART I

The Complements of Passion and Purpose

CHAPTER 1

Where Passion and Purpose Start

The life of Jesus Christ was an absolute failure from every
standpoint except God's. But what seemed to be failure from
man's standpoint was a triumph from God's standpoint, because
God's purpose is never the same as man's purpose.

– Oswald Chambers, *My Utmost for His Highest*

On 24 December 1968, while families around the world celebrated
the arrival of Christmas, a quite different perspective was being seen
a couple of hundred thousand miles above the earth's surface. Astronauts Frank Borman, Jim Lovell and William Anders, aboard *Apollo 8*
for the historical first manned mission to the moon, looked down in
awe and wonder from their lunar orbit at the world below. In a live
television broadcast where they showed pictures of the earth and the
moon as seen from their spacecraft, the crew ended their transmis-
sion with a reading from Genesis.

'For all the people on Earth, the crew of *Apollo 8* has a message
we would like to send you,' said William Anders. '*In the beginning
God created the heaven and the earth. And the earth was without form,
and void; and darkness was upon the face of the deep. And the Spirit
of God moved upon the face of the waters. And God said, Let there be
light: and there was light . . .*'[1]

It was a powerful moment for a powerful statement. Though it
lasted just an instant, these astronauts, along with the rest of the
world watching their television sets, caught just a glimpse of what
God saw when He first created the world. It brings to mind the might

and the authority of God and it makes us realise how little we really understand about our Creator.

'In the beginning God . . .' (Genesis 1:1). These are the first four words of the Bible recorded in Genesis, and what William Anders read. I think sometimes we speed by those first few words to get to the creation part, but we need to back up a moment and take a look because they are profound. God was not created. He was already there at the beginning and He does not have an end. *God is!* He created everything and He did it out of nothing. Our finite minds have trouble understanding that, but one thing we can be sure of: we will never understand God, so there is no point in trying. Let me put it another way. Let's spend less energy trying to read God's mind on why He does what He does and more on doing what He wants us to do.

> His ways, methods and paths are untraceable, mysterious and undiscoverable.

The truth is, if we could understand Him, He would not be our God. The Bible says in Romans 11:33 that His judgments and decisions are unfathomable, inscrutable and unsearchable. His ways, methods and paths are untraceable, mysterious and undiscoverable. Yet we also know from Scripture that God has a purpose in everything He does. 'The Lord has made everything [to accommodate itself and contribute] to its own end and His own purpose . . .' (Proverbs 16:4).

Can you feel the excitement of mystery stirring in your heart even as you read the words attempting to describe an indescribable God? No one knows the mind of God or can understand Him or His thoughts. No one can counsel God.

Have you ever noticed how often we try to give God advice? How many times we try to tell God what it is we're going to do and then we ask Him to help us work it out? Thankfully, He doesn't pay much attention to our whims and our strategising and plotting. God knows best, and His intention for us is always better than anything we could devise.

When it comes to our purpose, we should pray and then make plans. Not make plans and then pray that God will take our advice and make our plans work out. That's not what knowing God's purpose for our lives is all about. It's about living in His will each and every day and it's the only way we will ever truly know peace and joy.

The Bible teaches us that our minds hold many of our own plans, but it is the Lord's purposes for us that will stand (see Proverbs 19:21). And we should be glad of it. Think about it: if all of our own plans came to pass, we would have very miserable lives. How many times have you wished for something, did not get it, and then discovered later it would have made your life worse, not better?

We have no idea how often we ask for things that aren't good for us. God, in His mercy and wisdom, does not give them to us, but He continues working His will and purpose in our lives. It seems frustrating and confusing to us because we keep trying to make things work out the way we want. But I agree with A. W. Tozer who said people crucified with Christ have three distinct marks: they are facing only one direction, they can never turn back, and they no longer have plans of their own. We will not enjoy life until we accept God's will with joy and stop trying to understand everything that happens contrary to our own desires.

I recently planned a getaway at the Lake of the Ozarks to spend some time with my daughters and some close friends. I had it all planned out: we would stay two nights, go to the spa, shop, eat out, play games, laugh, and just have a wonderful time. I invited everyone three months ahead of time to be sure they didn't already have plans and yet, one by one, they informed me they could not go for one reason or another. I must admit I was disappointed because I felt God had been telling me to spend more time with my friends and take the time to do things like this trip. I didn't understand why things weren't working out until three months later, when a friend reminded me that the party I planned turned out to be on the day I buried my father.

When I started planning that trip, I didn't know my father would die, but God did. On one occasion when Jesus' disciples were confused about something He did, He said, 'You do not understand now what I am doing, but you will understand later on.' (John 13:7). God sees the end from the beginning. We only know what we know, but God knows everything.

> We only know what we know, but God knows everything.

Acceptance with Joy

I think we often get caught up in trying to work out the meaning of things and never quite accept the fact that trusting God means we will always have unanswered questions. But until we accept that, our joy and our passion in life and in our purpose can't really begin.

Most of us remember the film *Indiana Jones and the Last Crusade*. Indy was an adventurer and an explorer whose quest to find the Holy Grail almost took over his life. In the climax of the film, Indy loses his footing and is knocked off the edge of a crevasse of rock. As his father, Professor Jones, tries to pull him up by one arm, Indy stretches his other to try and get to the Grail, just out of his reach. His father tells him firmly: 'Indiana, let it go.' Indy reluctantly listens to his father, and as they escape the collapsing structure, the Grail is lost for good. In our quest to work out God, we often fall short in realising there are many things about Him that aren't to be worked out. And like Indiana Jones, we have to learn to let it go.

I've learned to enjoy knowing that someone is in charge of my life who has more wisdom than me. When I find myself behind a car going ten miles an hour below the speed limit because of heavy traffic, I like to think that maybe there's a car accident I'm avoiding by going slower than I intended. Or when I have made plans to do something and something else happens to prevent me from following my original plan, I remind myself that God is in control and I try to accept the change with joy. We must accept God's Word and what He does at face value and not question it. Trusting God when we don't understand brings a lot of peace to our lives. My motto is, 'Ask God for anything you want, but be content with what He gives you.' Trust that His choice is always the best!

There are many things in the Bible that raise the 'why' question in our minds. God's Word says He loves us because He wants to, not because we give Him any good reason to. The Bible says He chose us for Himself in Christ before the foundation of the world. He adopted us as His own children through Jesus Christ, in accordance with the purpose of His will because it pleased Him (see Ephesians 1:4–5).

I must admit there are times when I don't know why God would want to love me or be in relationship with me, but I have accepted what He says as truth. We don't have to work out the 'why' behind God's love, we just need to accept it. As humans we want to understand everything, but there are some things that only God understands. Perhaps if we don't waste our time and energy trying to work out what only God knows, we will have the energy to live passionate and purposeful lives.

Putting an End to the Why

Why is 'why' always the big question in life? It seems like everyone wants to ask why about everything and it starts when we are children. We ask our parents why the moon is so far away and why we have to go to school and why we can't have a pony in our bedroom. Then, as we get older, we start asking harder questions. Like, why do good people have problems? Why do innocent children die while mean old people live on and on? What about child abuse or world hunger? If

God is good, then why is there so much suffering in the world? Why are some people rich and others poor? Why did this tragedy happen to me? Why do I look the way I do? Why can't I sing or play the piano? Why was it so hard for me to get through school while my sister excelled at everything without even trying? Why? Why? Why?

As human beings, it's natural for us to ask why. God made us inquisitive and curious. However, there's a fine line in seeking to understand and demanding to know as much as God. We have to realise that not every question will have an answer; that there are many things we will never fully understand, and we have to be willing to accept it. For instance, if we begin to compare our lives and situations with those of other people, we will probably see injustice everywhere we look, usually because we always compare ourselves with those who have better lives than us. We fail to look at the multitudes of people whose lives are much worse than ours. If we did, we could be thankful instead of confused and bitter.

I grew up in a dysfunctional home filled with violence, alcoholism and incest. I asked 'why' for about forty years and only ended up miserable with no answers. I finally decided to accept that my life 'is what it is' and determined I would try to discover what might be done with the remainder of my life.

Although I felt I had nothing to give, I gave my nothingness to God and just as He created everything we see out of nothing, He gave me a future and a life worth living. He showed me I had a purpose all along and even though Satan tried to destroy me, God has redeemed me and His purpose for me will stand and be fulfilled.

The purpose for which Jesus came was to destroy the works of the devil (see 1 John 3:8). If you will invite Him into your life to be your Saviour and Lord, He will bring justice and give you double blessing for your former trouble (see Isaiah 61:7–8).

Most people try to give God what they are, but I firmly believe we should also give Him what we are not. He does more with nothing than He does with something! If you feel like nothing, you are just what God is looking for. You are someone He can work with. Give yourself to Him. Accept your life so far, even though you don't have one ounce of understanding about it and you will sense a peace that is wonderful! You cannot go back and change it, so why not let God do something with it? He can turn your pain into gain and your mess into a miracle.

I still don't have all the answers to child abuse. I don't understand the pain of my childhood, but I have decided to leave it with God where it belongs and trust Him to make the life I have left better than it could have been had I not been hurt so badly. Does that sound ridiculous? It may, but God is capable of doing it and He is the only One capable of doing it.

Stop asking why you are alive and what your purpose is and realise right now that you are alive for God's pleasure. You are here because God wants you here and He wants your fellowship. He wants to pour His goodness out on you and delight you with surprises and blessings. He not only wants to bless you, He wants to make you a blessing to others. You are His representative on earth. You are God's ambassador.

Instead of asking 'why, God why?' just tell God you trust Him. Meditate on how big He is. He has created everything we see. The mountains, oceans, trees, birds, animals, insects, people – everything.

The Bible says if we stop relying on our own insight and under-standing God will direct our paths and it will be health to our nerves and moistening to our bones (see Proverbs 3:7–8). In other words, we will be much healthier if we stop asking 'why' about everything and just learn to trust.

As parents we realise that it is natural and even healthy for children to ask questions, but there are times when we get weary of being asked to explain everything we do. There's been many a parent who has dealt with a child asking why this and why that so much that the mum or dad finally erupts with the classic 'Because I said so!' God may be saying the same thing to you at this time of your life. Have you got yourself confused trying to understand things only God knows? You can change your attitude right now if you are willing. Give yourself permission not to know and be satisfied knowing the One who does.

> Give yourself permission not to know and be satisfied knowing the One who does.

i dare you

Stop Asking Why

Don't Ask: Why did God let this happen?
Ask: What can I learn from this that will make me a better person?

Don't Ask: Why is there so much hurt in the world?
Ask: How can God use me to help the hurting?

Knowing God

The Apostle Paul said his determined purpose was to progressively come to know Christ more fully and accurately, and the power of His resurrection (see Philippians 3:10). If you are willing to make knowing God your lifelong pursuit, you will be fulfilling your main purpose.

I believe knowledge is progressive. Everything in life works according to the law of gradual growth. As a child goes through school, he progressively learns. We learn the same way when it comes to spiritual knowledge. To know God, we need to know His Word. We are taught in Luke 1:4 that God's purpose is that we may know the full truth and understand the doctrines of our faith. Truth is what makes us free. It removes deception in our lives. It takes time and effort, but if we continue studying, little by little, we increase in knowledge. Studying God is wise because:

> For from Him and through Him and to Him are all things. [For all things originate with Him and come from Him; all things live through Him, and all things center in and tend to consummate and to end in Him.] To Him be glory forever! Amen (so be it).
> – ROMANS 11:36

> Truth is what makes us free.

Paul was inspired to write this scripture because he realised the importance of it and the fact that it establishes the purpose for each of our lives. Please don't rush past it without taking time to meditate on it. Notice what it's telling us: *everything* begins and ends with God. Everything is from Him, through Him and to Him. In other words, everything comes from Him and all that we do must be done through His ability. We must do it all for Him. He must be the centre of our lives. Until this is accomplished there is no satisfaction to be found in life. Like Rick Warren writes in his book *The Purpose Driven Life,* 'You were made by God and for God and until you understand that, life will never make sense.' Until we accept and embrace that God is everything and we are nothing without Him, we will stay frustrated and unfulfilled and we will struggle with finding joy.

God Is Not Boring

When we talk about embracing passion and engaging life, many people will enthusiastically nod their heads in agreement until we connect God to it. Then they scratch their heads – passion and God in the same sentence? Isn't that an oxymoron? Even some Christians associate God with boredom, not excitement. Take for instance the older sister who was sitting next to her younger brother in church one Sunday morning, unsuccessfully trying to keep him still and quiet. Finally, she whispered, 'I wish you would calm down.' 'I can't,' the boy whispered back. 'It's just so boring.' With that, his sister turned and snapped, 'It's supposed to be boring.' Friends and religion can be boring, but God is never boring.

> Even some Christians associate God with boredom, not excitement.

Men crave adventure and women crave romance and God provides both in abundance. He loves us passionately and serving Him is certainly an adventure that will amaze anyone. The Christian life is not supposed to be dull! He tells us in His Word He has come to give us life that we may enjoy it and 'have it in abundance' (see John 10:10). God loves to invade everyday life and He is full of surprises. He is the only One who can satisfy the deep longings everyone feels in their hearts. He has a life for you beyond anything you could ever imagine. Get excited about knowing and serving God and look forward to every day. Live with passionate expectation that something good is going to happen to you!

CHAPTER 2

Understanding Why You Do What You Do

I once heard a story about a lighthouse keeper who worked on a rocky stretch of coastline. Once a month he would receive a new supply of oil to keep the light burning so ships could safely sail near the rocky coast. One night, though, a woman from a nearby village came and begged him for some oil to keep her family warm. Another time a father asked for some to use in his lamp. Another man needed to lubricate a wheel. Since all the requests seemed legitimate, the lighthouse keeper tried to please everyone and grant the requests of all.

Towards the end of the month, the man noticed his supply of oil was dangerously low. Soon it was gone, and one night the light on the lighthouse went out. As a result, that evening several ships were wrecked and countless lives were lost. When the authorities investigated, the man was very apologetic. He told them he was just trying to be helpful with the oil. Their reply to his excuses, however, was simple and to the point: 'You were given oil for one purpose, and one purpose only – to keep that light burning!'[1]

When was the last time you took a minute to think about why you do what you do? What is it that guides your choices and makes your decisions and carries out your actions? Are you doing what you're

> When was the last time you took a minute to think about why you do what you do?

supposed to be doing? And are you doing it with eagerness and dedication?

It's sad to say but most people never stop long enough to ask themselves why they are doing what they are doing, but it is one of God's main concerns. Actually He is not impressed by what we do, but rather He's interested in 'why' we do it. Good works done with wrong motives will not receive any reward when we stand before God on Judgment Day.

> . . . for He will both bring to light the secret things that are
> [now hidden] in darkness *and* disclose and expose the [secret]
> aims (motives and purposes) of hearts. Then every man will
> receive his [due] commendation from God.
> – 1 CORINTHIANS 4:5b

On that day, every man and woman will give an account of themselves (see Romans 14:12). This is a sobering thought and one we should contemplate seriously. Those who have placed their faith in and received Jesus as Saviour will not be judged concerning salvation – their names are already written in the Lamb's Book of Life – but they will be judged concerning their works done during their time on earth and they'll be rewarded accordingly.

The Bible teaches us that all works done from a wrong motive (evil, selfish) will be burned up and the reward of them will be lost (see 1 Corinthians 3:13–15). We should make sure that we know our motives.

It is possible to know your life's purpose and spend your life doing it with a wrong motive in your heart. For example, I know that part of my purpose in life is to teach God's Word all over the world. In the early years of my ministry, God had to severely chastise me because although I was pursuing my purpose, my motives were not right. I wanted to be important, well thought of and admired. I was seeking to find my worth in what I did when I should have found it in being God's child and knowing who I was in Christ.

Things were not working right in my life. My ministry was not progressing, and I was not happy. I was frustrated most of the time and had no peace or joy. I didn't know what was wrong. I thought the devil was hindering me and then God showed me it was my motives hindering me. I was praying long and strong every day, but God could not answer my prayers because my motives were not right.

> . . . you do ask [God for them] and yet fail to receive, because you ask with wrong purpose and evil, selfish motives. Your intention is [when you get what you desire] to spend it in sensual pleasures.
> – JAMES 4:3

When I realised my heart was wrong, I made a decision to live for God and His glory, not for myself and my glory. It is possible to change our motives by simply making a decision, but we must first know what our motives and purposes are. This requires some deep soul searching that few people take the time to do. Quite often we are afraid to really know ourselves. It is a brave person who faces truth about himself or herself and does whatever is necessary to line up with God's will. I dare you to be bold enough to honestly examine all your motives and be willing to do nothing if you cannot do something for the right reasons.

i dare you

Check Your Motives

One of the best things we can do for our spiritual walk is to sit down and take the time to think about why we do what we do. The more we understand what our true motives are, the better we can work to ensure our purpose aligns with God's. Ask yourself these questions and as you think about your answers, write them down in a notebook or a journal so you can come back and review them periodically. Ask God to help you fine-tune your motives so He can use you fully.

1 When you think about doing something for God, what do you hope to get out of it?

2 When you tell others what you are doing for God, are you secretly hoping they will admire you?

3 How much are you willing to sacrifice to do God's will?

4 Do you find yourself doing more than it seems you can handle just to please people?

5 Do you pray first and then make plans, or plan first and then pray that your plans will work out?

6 Are you willing to stop doing something if God shows you it is time to move on to something else?

To be honest, I was appalled when I realised many of my purposes and motives were wrong. It was hard for me to face but by God's grace I did, and it was a major changing point in my life. God taught me early on in my walk with Him why it's so important to know and understand our motives and I strongly recommend you take some time for soul-searching and learn the 'why' behind your what.

Motivators

Name some of the motivators you have for doing what you do. Everyone has them – those forces or people propelling us forward or causing us to take action on something. Maybe it's the hope for a promotion at work or the love of our children keeping us going. Some people are motivated by applause or approval by friends, family or work colleagues. Unfortunately, not all motivators are good or pleasing to God. Greed is a powerful motivator for many people, but God warns us of the danger of greed (see Luke 12:15). It steals the life of those who are motivated by it.

Some people are motivated by jealousy and envy. Others are motivated by hatred and bitterness. Some are motivated by revenge and others by insecurity and fear. Our motivators are like fuel in a car – it is the force that drives us. We need something to motivate us, to move us to action, but it needs to be something that will produce good fruit in our lives and the lives of others. When a child is not performing well in school, his teacher often says he has no motivation. Perhaps the child can never please his parents no matter what he does, so he has lost his motivation to even try. Perhaps he has not been taught good work ethics and is basically lazy. Perhaps the teaching methods being used at his school don't nurture the way he learns. Some people learn easily from books while others need more hands-on application. The point is when people have no motivation or wrong motivation, there is usually a root cause that needs to be located.

Bitter, angry people who seek revenge have been hurt, and they haven't learned that God is their Vindicator. They don't know He will bring justice in their lives if they will just wait on Him. Those motivated by jealousy and envy are insecure individuals who compare themselves and their lives with other people. They think their worth and value is found in staying ahead of everyone else. Those motivated by greed are seeking power from a wrong source. Those motivated by materialism have forgotten they came into the world with nothing and they will leave with nothing.

So what are some *good* motivators to have in your life? Use this list to get started and see what others you can add to it:

1 God's Spirit. 'My counsel is this: Live freely, animated and motivated by God's Spirit. Then you won't feed the compulsions of selfishness' (Galatians 5:16, The Message). When we truly listen to God's Spirit in us, we have the single best motivator possible to guide our steps because truth cannot mix with anything less than truth. We should be able to say we are motivated by the Spirit of God in what we do. We do what we do because we believe it is the will of God.

2 Pure love. Paul's letter to the Philippians indicates that his imprisonment revealed the true motivations of people, both good and bad. 'It's true that some here preach Christ because with me out of the way, they think they'll step right into the spotlight. But the others do it with the best heart in the world. One group is motivated by pure love, knowing that I am here defending the Message, wanting to help. The others, now that I'm out of the picture, are merely greedy, hoping to get something out of it for themselves . . .' (Philippians 1:15–17, The Message). Genuine love is an important motivator for our purpose and passion because, with it, hate and envy and greed are hard to hold on to. We should be able to say that we do what we do out of pure love.

3 Faith. Like Moses when he led the Israelites out of Egypt, we can be motivated by our faith, our deep belief allowing us to hold to our purpose with unwavering loyalty as 'one who gazed on Him Who is invisible' (see Hebrews 11:27). Whatever is not of faith is sin (see Romans 14:23); therefore, let all that we do be done out of faith.

4 To be a blessing. God told Abraham He would bless him and make him a blessing (see Genesis 12:2). I believe a desire to be a blessing is a great motivator and one that pleases God greatly. I love to put smiles on faces. The Bible says that Jesus went about doing good (see Acts 10:38). Let's strive to be like Him!

5 For the sake of righteousness. I believe a good motivator is very simply doing a thing because it is the right thing to do. Jesus told John to baptise Him in order to fulfil all righteousness (see Matthew 3:15). He did it because it was the right thing to do. There are times in life when 'duty' must be our motivator. The Apostle Paul reminds us that it is our duty to take care of elderly parents and grandparents (see 1 Timothy 5:4). The elderly are often ignored simply because their family members are not doing their duty. I believe doing something because it is our duty is a motive that God accepts.

6 The Word of God. Being obedient to the Word of God is one of the best motivators I know of. We don't have to feel like doing a thing, or think it is fair, or even want to. But if we are willing to do what God says to do in His Word, God will be pleased with our motives and we will not lose our reward.

Once again I urge you to know your purpose and motives. What or who motivates you? A passion to serve God, or a desire to be noticed? Don't be afraid to answer those kinds of questions honestly. The truth will make you free! I can assure you that you are no different than anyone else. Even if you discover that some of your motives are impure, you are not alone. You are just one of the brave people willing to face reality and make the changes you need to make.

Keeping our motives pure is a lifelong process that must be pursued passionately. It is very easy to be self-deceived, so let us commit regularly to examining our motives before God, asking Him to reveal any wrong ones we have.

Passion with Purity

The Bible tells us in Matthew 5:8 that those who are pure in heart will see God. I believe that means people with pure hearts have a clear awareness and understanding from God – they hear Him with great clarity and are confident in His will.

Talk to any engineer and you will learn that the only way metal can safely be used is after testing it repeatedly under very high standards and requirements. The desired metal to be used must be pure, and in order for it to be pure it has to go through fire – it must be melted down and then moulded to fit. Before we can fulfil our purpose, we must be willing to be tested under God's standards and purified so we are ready to be used.

You may have started reading this book because you want to know what your purpose is in life, and I believe you will find it. However, it's vital that you know your own heart's intent before you can understand and realise the rest of what God has for you.

The Bible teaches us God's general will for all people. Some of these things we have already mentioned. God's purpose is that we enjoy Him, obey Him, enjoy life, live passionately, and represent Him well. These things are the same for everyone. But there are other things specific to individuals. God gives unique gifts, talents and abilities to each of us. To one is given the ability to manage and administrate (see Romans 12:6–8). Another person might have the ability to teach and lead, another has the ability to sing or paint, and on and on it goes. Together we make up what the Bible calls the body of Christ. He is our head and we are His body. He takes the lead and we follow. We must train ourselves to keep our motives pure and follow God's will at all times.

Have you ever trained for something strenuous? Maybe for a marathon? What if you were to set out on that race without ever having worked on developing those muscles? What if, instead, you sat around all day and ate junk food? Once you're in the race – as much as your mind might will your body to work – if those muscles of yours aren't trained, if they're not as healthy and physically whole as possible, you're not going to do well. It's the same way with our relationship with God. We choose to practise doing what is right and as we do so again and again we form good habits that become part of our character. We become well trained for the purposes of God.

As we work together corporately, His full will and purpose is accomplished on earth. That's why it is so important to understand why we do what we do and to ensure our motives are pure because our purpose ultimately is to serve God's purpose – not our own.

Give It All You Have Got

God's Word gives us simple instructions regarding how we are to handle our unique abilities. It simply says to give yourself to your abilities (see 1 Timothy 4:15). To me, that means we should get busy doing what we are good at and not attempt to do what we either are not good at or unable to do. Many people try to do what someone else is good at instead of doing what they are good at. They compare and compete and lose their joy in the process.

The Bible says:

[He whose gift is] practical service, let him give himself to serving; he who teaches to his teaching; He who exhorts (encourages), to his exhortation; he who contributes, let him do it in simplicity *and* liberality; he who gives aid *and* superintends, with zeal *and* singleness of mind; he who does acts of mercy, with genuine cheerfulness *and* joyful eagerness.
  – ROMANS 12:7–8

> Years may wrinkle your skin, but to give up enthusiasm wrinkles your soul.

Not only do we need to find God's purpose and do it with right motives, but we are to do it with passion, zeal and enthusiasm. Years may wrinkle your skin, but to give up enthusiasm wrinkles your soul. It dries you up on the inside and everything feels dead. God does not want us to obey Him merely out of obligation. He wants us to serve Him from desire and to thoroughly enjoy Him. To attempt to serve God from duty without also delighting in Him is actually an insult. We are not puppets, we are people created by God with free will. He has chosen us and He wants us to choose Him joyfully.

I am reminded of the wedding in John 2 where Jesus is asked by

His mother for help when it's discovered all the wine has gone. He tells the servants to take six large stone water pots and fill them with water. I wonder what the servants thought of His instructions, knowing their master was at risk of embarrassment in front of his guests and now this man named Jesus was asking them to fill water pots with water. But it doesn't appear they question Him; in fact, the Bible says they filled those water pots 'up to the brim' (John 2:7). Immediately, the water turned into wine.

This was the first recorded miracle of Jesus' ministry on earth and I want to remind you that His miracles did not stop there. He will also do miracles in your life if you obey Him, and offer yourself as a clean pot He can fill.

Just as Jesus worked in partnership with the servants to turn water into wine, He works in partnership with us today. I feel passion stirring in my soul when I remind myself that I am in partnership with the all powerful, all knowing, ever-present God. Just think about it – you are God's partner!

> Just as Jesus worked in partnership with the servants
> to turn water into wine, He works in partnership with
> us today.

Nothing energises us like having a clear vision of what we are supposed to be doing. We have to work in order to survive, but meaningless work wears us out. The world is filled with tired, worn-out people, and most of it is due to people who 'go through the motions'of life, yet they have not found their purpose. They spend their lives doing what they hate and are not courageous enough to do what they really want to do. Sadly, one of the biggest motivators for people is often the salary cheque. You would be better off earning less money and being passionate about what you're doing, than

> Will you dare to follow your heart all the way to fulfilment?

making a lot of money doing something you despise. Will you dare to follow your heart all the way to fulfilment?

Eternity will far outlast any time we have here on Earth, so we should make the most of the years we do have and realise that what we do today, and especially 'why' we do it, affects not only now but later. The here and the hereafter. To have passion means to feel, to risk, to dream and to live. We only have one life in our lifetime – let's not waste it.

CHAPTER 3

Putting Smiles on Faces

There are temporal things and there are eternal things. Unfortunately, we have made the mistake of paying too much attention to temporal things. We get caught up in stuff instead of in service and it's just one of the ways we can be our own worst enemies when it comes to keeping a fire going for the Kingdom.

The Bible says everything we see is currently passing away (see 2 Corinthians 4:18). When we buy something and bring it home, it is already decaying. Go to a car dealership, drive off the garage forecourt with a new car, and your brand-new purchase is already worth less than what you just paid for it five minutes before! I know a couple who bought one of those new digital video recorders that are all the rage now. They were so excited to get it home until the next day when they discovered another model just released with features their machine didn't have. Their new purchase was already outdated. *Things* are temporal. My husband, Dave, and I often drive by junk-yards and comment that those piles of junk were once somebody's dream. People probably went into debt and may have even ruined relationships to own what is now lying in a junkyard, rusted and decayed.

The physical, mental and even spiritual energy we sometimes use in 'keeping up with the Joneses' could be put to much better use. When we serve others, we're being God's hands and feet. We are using our energy for an eternal purpose. We're making a difference in the lives of His children, and often our reward is a smile from someone. It's a reminder that we have given someone joy, and what we sow into the lives of others we can expect to reap in our own. Give joy and you will always have plenty of joy. The Bible teaches us that it is more blessed to give than to receive. I don't know about you, but something that gets me excited every time is the good feeling I get inside when I've helped someone. Being a blessing to others is a key to keeping enthusiasm in your life. It's acting with eternal significance instead of temporal purposelessness, which we'll talk more about in the next chapter.

> Being a blessing to others is a key to keeping enthusiasm in your life.

As it is written, He [the benevolent person] scatters abroad;
He gives to the poor; His deeds of justice and goodness and
kindness and benevolence will go on and endure forever.
– 2 CORINTHIANS 9:9

We serve God by serving people – by making things happen for them that they are not able to do for themselves. By using our energies to make their lives easier and more pleasant, we are being servants to our Creator. These are the things that endure for ever. These things have eternal value.

I know serving other people is not a very popular topic. It gives us a mental picture of doing things for everyone else while they take advantage of us. We tend to think of serving as a job that is not very impressive, but Jesus didn't think of it that way at all. As a matter of fact, He said if we really wanted to be considered great in the Kingdom of God we would have to serve (see Matthew 5:19).

What kind of a mental image do you get when you hear the word 'servant'? Do you see a maid in a little black and white uniform cleaning up after people and doing dishes? Do you see a butler opening the door of a mansion for guests who are arriving? Or do you see Jesus joyfully and enthusiastically washing His disciples' feet and telling them to do the same thing?

Selfishness Leads to Unhappiness

Serving God and others is the pathway to joy, but very few people realise it. Most individuals think having someone serve them is the way to go. They think getting what they want will bring fulfilment, but they are mistaken. Doctor, theologian and philosopher Albert Schweitzer once said, 'The purpose of human life is to serve, and to show compassion and the will to help others.'[1] Some people are blessed to realise the truth before they waste their entire lives.

> Serving God and others is the pathway to joy.

I heard a story about a woman who went to her pastor for counseling because she was terribly depressed. He was a pastor with many years of experience and knew right away what her problem was, but did not feel she was ready to hear the truth. Instead of taking a risk in offending her, he gave her a homework assignment. He knew from past experience she liked to cook so he asked her to go home and bake some cakes and give them away during the week and then come back for another appointment the following week when he would have more time. The woman never returned for her next appointment and when several weeks passed, the pastor noticed the woman at church and asked her why she hadn't come back. She replied, 'Oh, I got so excited when I started baking cakes and giving them to people that I forgot all about being depressed.' The pastor knew her depression was rooted in selfishness and too much idle time to think about everything she didn't like about her life. He believed if he could get her active doing something for others, God's joy would be released in her and, sure enough, it worked.

I lived many years trying to make myself happy by taking care of me first, only to have happiness evade me completely. I discovered in God's Word that Jesus called us as His disciples to forget about ourselves and follow Him (see Mark 8:34). Following Him means we study His ways and do what He did. Jesus obeyed His Father (God), and He went about helping people (see Acts 10:38). Jesus washed His disciples' feet and told them to do what they saw Him do and then they would be happy.

This is sometimes a hard thing for us to understand – the act of giving to someone else over our own needs. We live in a self-serving world these days where there's self-service for petrol, meals, and now even supermarket checkout queues. That's right, in some supermarkets you can check out your own groceries using a barcode machine instead of waiting to be checked out by the cashier on the till. The idea of service has been diluted and washed away in the world we live in, and yet the act of service stimulates so much inside our hearts and spirits. It simply helps us get our minds off of ourselves and onto helping others. There are needs all around us, but we are often too rushed to notice. Let's slow down and make a commitment to help everyone we can. We will be putting a smile on not only their faces, but Jesus' face as well. I strongly suspect we will even end up with a smile on our own faces.

Jesus was never in a hurry; yet, He accomplished more in three years of earthly ministry than thousands of us put together will accomplish in a lifetime. Jesus was not merely busy, He was fruitful. He had a purpose and He pursued it passionately. I believe Jesus put smiles on faces everywhere He went. He always had time to stop and listen to people and help them. Most of us are hurrying around trying to get the things we want in life, and in the process we may completely miss the principles God wants us to live by. Things like, 'It is more blessed to give than to receive' (Acts 20:35, NIV). And, 'Give and it shall be given unto you, good measure, pressed down, shaken together, and running over . . .' (Luke 6:38, KJV).

The Bible says we will not only do the things Jesus did, but even greater things shall we do (see John 1:50, 5:20, 14:12). Why don't we see more of the greater works? I believe it is because our culture today is almost totally self-absorbed. Our advertising pushes people to have more. At the end of 2005, the average household credit card debt in the United States stood at $9,159, according to CardWeb. com, which publishes card statistics and best deals in the industry. All told, households in the United States had a total of $711 billion in credit card debt.[2]

It doesn't matter if we need it or can afford it, we are taught we deserve it. But true happiness does not consist of having more and more. Actually, the more we have the more we not only have to pay for, but we also must take care of it. If you are going to keep bringing more and more stuff home, at least begin giving away some of what you already have to people who don't have as much as you do.

> True happiness does not consist of having more and more.

Anytime I start to get unhappy, I can ask myself what I have been doing for other people and I usually locate the root of my unhappiness. God created us to reach out to others and He promised that if we would, He would reach out to us and give us a joy we cannot find anywhere else. What we make happen for others, God will make happen for us in abundance. If you want to be happier, start sowing seed by making someone else happy. You can serve. You can be the one to put smiles on faces.

The Dumbest Man in the Bible

Greed is the cause of a great deal of unhappiness and a definite detriment to our passion and purpose. In the United States the companies Enron and WorldCom were giants and their leaders were once looked up to, but they were broken by greed. The Bible teaches us to guard against greed and keep ourselves free from all covetousness (the immoderate desire for wealth and the greedy longing to have more) (see Romans 7:7). It is interesting to note that we must keep ourselves from greed. We can ask for God's help, but ultimately we must guard our hearts and guard our emotions from the dangers that greed can hold. We must say no to ourselves as well as yes. How do we do that living in such a self-absorbed society? I believe the only way to fight greed is to be an aggressive giver.

Jesus wanted the people to understand what He was saying about greed, so He told a story about a man who was already wealthy and had yet another harvest coming in that promised to be abundant. This man already had so much he could not work out where he would store his new harvest. So he thought about it and decided to tear down his current storehouses and build bigger and better ones. Then the man said, 'And I will say to my soul, Soul, you have many good things laid up, [enough] for many years. Take your ease; eat, drink, *and* enjoy yourself merrily. But God said to him, You fool! This very night they [the messengers of God] will demand your soul of you; and all the things that you have prepared, whose will they be?' (Luke 12:19–20).

This man missed a great opportunity to not only be blessed himself, but to be a great blessing to others. I call him the dumbest man in the Bible because he had the means to give and all he did was become more and more selfish. Instead of using his resources to be a smile giver, he lost everything.

When we are on our deathbeds, not one of us will ask for our bank balance. We will want our family and friends. We will want to feel we are leaving a good legacy, and feel we made a deposit here on earth that will leave people happy we were alive and sorry we are gone.

The man could have had both. God is not asking us to have nothing and give everything away. However, He is asking us to use part of our resources to serve Him and other people.

God is a giver and His will is that we follow His example. One thing is for sure: God is happy, and if we want to share in His joy, we need to do things His way.

God is a giver and His will is that we follow His example.

Billy Graham is one of the most admired and respected men in the world and he said, 'My one purpose in life is to help people find a personal relationship with God, which, I believe, comes through knowing Christ.' He has given his life to helping other people find life. He lives to make their lives better. Billy Graham did not spend his life trying to be admired and yet he is. He is a true servant of God. He pursues his purpose passionately with a pure heart and God rewards him. If we do what God asks us to by living to serve Him and others, He will do more for us than we could ever do for ourselves.

Treat Others Like You Want to Be Treated

We reap what we sow! How we treat others is the way we will be treated. If we believe that statement and live accordingly, we will have much better lives. George Washington Carver said, 'How far you go in life depends on your being tender with the young, compassionate with the aged, sympathetic with the striving, and tolerant of the weak and the strong – because someday you will have been all of these.' So often in life we don't end up with what we want or think we deserve, but we forget that when we had an opportunity to provide those things for other people, we didn't see it as being important.

Mother Teresa was a woman who gave her life to be a smile giver. She was probably one of the most greatly admired and respected women in the world. People will read and talk about her life for centuries to come; yet she led a very simple existence. Her philosophy was 'Let no one ever come to you without leaving better and happier.' She lived by this principle and gave more of herself than she ever expected of others. Are you courageous enough to lay down your life to help others find life? When we ponder that question, our first thoughts are usually, 'What about me?' 'Who will take care of me and my desires and dreams?' The answer is – God will! When we give our lives away for His sake, He always gives back much more than we were willing to give up.

> Live to give, don't live to get.

Start treating people the way you want to be treated and you will fulfil one of God's highest purposes for your life. Live to give, don't live to get. Focus on giving smiles away and you will always discover that your own smiles will always be in great supply.

i dare you

Make Other People Smile

So many times we wait until we're ready to help others, but unfortunately that may be a long time. Make the effort to reach out to others using the gifts and the abilities God has equipped you with today. Ask yourself the following questions and write your answers down in a notebook or journal you can go back and review later:

1 Name three things you do well.
2 Name three things you enjoy doing.
3 Take one thing from your list of things you do well and brainstorm as many ways as possible for you to use that skill or talent to serve other people.
4 Ask God to give you a servant's heart and help you embrace more passion in your service for Him.

Use What Is in Your Hand

God is calling each of us to do great things, but great things are accomplished by doing a lot of small things. I have a worldwide ministry, but I started by teaching twenty-five people every Tuesday evening in my living room and I was faithful to that for five years before God gave me an opportunity to do something greater. Talk to a lot of people who have big ministries or large organisations or successful businesses and they will share similar stories. If you are faithful in little things, God will make you ruler over much.

When God called Moses to deliver the Israelites from bondage in Egypt, He asked him what was in his hand. It was a rod, a tool that shepherds used while guiding their flock. God told Moses to throw it down on the ground and He filled it with power; then He told him to pick it up again. This is the same rod Moses used to part the Red Sea and help bring the Israelites to safety from the Egyptians.

Ruth used her hands to glean wheat from Boaz's field to feed her and her mother-in-law, Naomi. At any time she could have given up and gone back to her family, but she chose to stay with the woman she admired and loved so much and she worked hard to care for Naomi and do all she could for her (see Ruth 2:2).

Jael was a woman God used to help deliver the Israelites from Jabin, the king of Canaan. She killed one of their enemies by simply using what was in her hand, a tent peg and a hammer, which she drove into his temple while he was sleeping (see Judges 4:21).

A woman who is not named used a millstone she happened to have at hand to kill wicked Abimelech (see Judges 9:53). She could have easily said, 'I can't do anything, I don't have any weapons.'

It is really not what we have in our hand that gets the job done, but it is God's power filling what we have in our hand.

Perhaps you have influence or a position in society God might use like Deborah, who was a mighty judge and she used her influence and position to help people (see Judges 4 and 5).

It is really not what we have in our hand that gets the job done, but it is God's power filling what we have in our hand. It does not matter what we don't have, as long as we do have God. His strength is made perfect in our weaknesses. Don't make the mistake of thinking you don't have enough to fulfil God's purpose for you. Just start using what you do have and God will do the rest.

Many people miss God's plan for them because they feel ill equipped to step out. They are afraid of failing. Sir Winston Churchill said, 'Success is the ability to go from one failure to another with no loss of enthusiasm.' If any person decides to pursue God's purpose, they will make some mistakes along the way. Mother Teresa said, 'God doesn't require us to succeed; He only requires that you try.'

Don't concentrate on what you think you cannot do, just do what you can do. Mother Teresa also said, 'If you can't feed a hundred people, then feed just one.' This is great advice. I think sometimes we don't feel like our purpose or our passion is big enough if we're not reaching lots of people or if our impact isn't as big as we think it should be. I always say I had a mouth and I gave it to God. He is using it all over the world. I had a living room and I gave it to God and it is where my ministry began. Keep your eyes on God, not yourself. After all, it isn't about you, anyway!

Don't Put Off Until Later
What You Can Do Today

'Maybe when I'm older.' 'Maybe when we're more settled.' 'Maybe when the kids have grown up.' 'Maybe when I'm ready to retire.'

Procrastination is a great thief of God's purpose for His people. You might intend to do something one day, but what's stopping you from doing it now? You may think you have too many problems of your own to be helping someone else. The truth is, until you start helping someone else, you may never get your problems solved. Only God can solve your problems anyway, and He will if you give Him something to work with by taking faith-filled action to reach out to others. We cannot expect a harvest if we are not willing to sow seeds.

When we commit to embracing life with passion, the first thing Satan tries to do is defeat us with any means necessary. One of the easiest ways he tries to do this is by suggesting we wait until another time. He convinces us we have plenty of time to get excited about God's call, to get passionate about our purpose and what it is God is asking us to do. So we put it off until tomorrow, and then tomorrow comes; then we put it off until the next day. We procrastinate about many things in life: exercise, prayer, Bible study, getting out of debt, losing weight, and yes, we do it even when it comes to making a commitment to give ourselves to our purpose.

'But I'm just not *feeling* like it's time, Joyce,' you're saying. You may not feel like you are ready, but God does not give us the luxury of *feeling* ready. Stepping out in faith means we usually do it with fear and trembling, knowing that if God doesn't come through and help us, we will make fools of ourselves. There are times when we know deep in our hearts it's not yet time, but we must make sure the feeling is one of the heart and not the head or emotions.

God does not give us the luxury of *feeling* ready.

Recently God asked me to do something and I certainly didn't feel like doing it. At first I rejected the idea entirely, but deep inside I felt it was something I actually should do. Obeying God meant I would have to disappoint someone else. I waited, hoping I would hear something else from God, but all I got was confirmation at every turn. Just because we don't feel like doing a thing does not mean God doesn't want us to do it. We must live by the spiritual discernment we have inside, not the feeling we have in our flesh.

Today matters! Take action today. Don't put off until tomorrow what you can do today. The world is filled with sad, hurting people. You can put smiles on faces. You can be a smile giver. Use what you have in your hand to make someone else's life get better. It will enrich your life and you will find you are smiling too.

CHAPTER 4

Purposelessness

Gwen Gavin is a thirty-eight-year-old wife and mother of three who knows what it takes to have purpose. She found her own purpose when she started working with youngsters at her church and discovered she had a talent for connecting with teenagers and understanding how to talk with them. She spends time each week volunteering with after-school programmes, helping young people learn how to build self-esteem and how to make good choices.

'I try to help young people realise they do have a purpose,' Gwen says. 'And that it takes vision to get there.'[1]

Vision. What a great word and an important one to think about when we're talking about passion and purpose. I don't see a lot of vision being tapped into these days. Rather, there seems to be more purposelessness taking hold of our culture. People are getting caught up in the 'make it better, faster, cheaper, easier' attitude, a disease in our society that's threatening to turn into an epidemic. We are so used to new technologies doing everything for us it's easy to lose the passion and the drive for excellence that's necessary to do things well. Quality is not as important to most as quantity. It is rare to find a person who gives his whole heart to what he is doing and strives to do it with excellence. While good morals and passion for holiness may be disappearing, the world is waiting for someone who will take a stand. Someone who will say, 'I will dare to live with purpose and passion. I will dare to live with excellence and commitment. I will do my very best to be the best me I can be. I will have the courage to be one of the few!'

To live with purpose means to strive towards something – to aim for a goal, to be intentional and determined. What are you aiming towards? What are you striving for?

Lack of purpose isn't just a problem for adults. It hits young people as well. Suicide is currently the third leading cause of death for our teenagers.[2] They see no point in living. Nothing makes sense to the younger generation and they are both curious and concerned about their future, with only three out of ten feeling well prepared for adulthood.[3] They are looking for sincere, genuine, excellent people who will be role models for them and there aren't many around. In many cases their parents have disappointed them by floating downstream with the rest of society. They have lived in homes filled with compromise, broken promises and mediocrity. They don't see anything to reach for. Nothing makes them feel motivated, and as a result they wonder why they're even here. This is a tragedy, but the statistics can be changed if enough people will decide to turn away from the way they *have been* living to the way they *should* be living.

We must realise that we are setting an example for the next generation, and they will do more of what they see us do than what they hear us say. To tell others what to do – and then not do it yourself – is worse than saying nothing at all.

> To tell others what to do – and then not do it yourself – is worse than saying nothing at all.

Do It Right or Don't Do It at All

Think about what might happen if all of us woke up tomorrow and decided that whatever we did, we would do it with excellence. We would give it our all and do our best with nothing less than 100 per cent. Would it change our impact? Would it change our relationships? Would it change the world? You bet it would! Doing things with excellence means you don't take shortcuts. You don't take the easy way just for the sake of it being easy.

Doing things with excellence means you don't take shortcuts.

Noah certainly didn't take the easy way. When God asked him to build the ark, he was about five hundred years old. It took a hundred years for him to complete the ark to God's specifications, while also collecting two of every animal and living creature on earth. His passion and dedication to following God's instructions were necessary for his family's future, as well as the world's, and we know he did it with excellence because we know the outcome was successful. The ark, everything, and everyone in it survived while the rest of the world did not.

Make a decision to be an excellent person. Perhaps if we did less, we could do more things with excellence. Part of our problem in society is most people are trying to do so much they can't do any of it right. Slow down, think seriously about what you are doing, and ask yourself if you're doing any of it with your whole heart. Are you giving it your best?

Is there anything you love enough to dedicate your entire being to it? The heroes, legends, leaders and champions who fill our history books were all people who loved what they did enough to dedicate themselves to it.

Is there anything you love enough to dedicate your entire being to it?

In the late 1800s, Nellie Bly was one of the first investigative news reporters, and the stories she wrote helped change laws and brought social and government plights to the surface. Despite the criticism and rejection she experienced for being a woman reporter, she went on to leave a lasting legacy, but it was her passion and sense of purpose and dedication that helped her keep going.[4]

George Washington Carver was born a slave and grew up during the Reconstruction era of the United States. He faced numerous challenges including exclusion from a university simply on the basis of his skin colour. However, he refused to give up, and eventually went on to earn a master of science degree and is responsible for helping save and restore the South's agricultural industry by conducting research on the peanut and sweet potato. His enthusiasm and devotion ultimately helped him develop more than four hundred additional products including cheese, soap, plastics and cosmetics.[5]

> In order to love what you do, you must do what you love.

Clara Barton was known for her willingness to take initiative when she saw a need. When civil war broke out in the United States, in 1861, Clara organised medicine and supplies for wounded soldiers and travelled with the army throughout the four-year war. Her efforts resulted in the formation of the Red Cross and she continued to lead it and solicit contributions for it until she was eighty-three.[6]

People who are dedicated to something have a reason to get out of bed. They have something to reach for, something to motivate them. In order to love what you do, you must do what you love. Stop putting all of your time into something you don't love enough to give your dedication. You won't find a successful person who wasn't dedicated to what he wanted to be successful at.

i dare you

Do What You Love

Jesus said, 'Love the Lord your God with all your passion and prayer and intelligence.' (Matthew 22:37, The Message). Our first pursuit in life is to love God: passionately, prayerfully and thoughtfully. We can take these same life instruments and apply them towards doing what God wants us to do.

Be Passionate About What You Love: Don't let fear or worries of what others think hold you back from being excited about what you're doing. If you are truly happy in the place God has put you, keep that enthusiasm burning bright because your passion can be the match that lights a spark under someone else.

Be Prayerful About What You Love: Always seek God's guidance as you pursue your purpose. You may enjoy art or music or perhaps you love crunching numbers, but you must always ask, not yourself, but God, if you are staying on course to follow His direction and not your own. Stay prayed up and you will know and can be confident and assured you are in His will.

Be Thoughtful About What You Love: Sometimes the worst problem we can have is *too many things* we love to do. Maybe you're one of those blessed individuals to whom God has given many talents, or many passions you would enjoy pursuing. Think about what you enjoy and ask yourself which of those makes a difference in the lives of others?

Do Something on Purpose

Look carefully then how you walk! Live purposefully and worthily and accurately, not as the unwise and witless, but as wise (sensible, intelligent people).
  – EPHESIANS 5:15

This has always been one of my favourite scriptures. I have never had a problem being a person of purpose. My purpose was not always what it should have been, but I got up every day with a purpose. Purposeless people tend to frustrate me. I see a lot of wasted potential and I know waste always leads to regret. I know people who have wasted their lives and now they are old and have nothing but regret. It is sad!

Have a plan for each day and work your plan.

I believe since you're reading this book it is a good time to take a serious inventory of what you are doing with your life, talents, energy, finances, time, and everything in between. If you find you are not doing your best at what you're doing, then make a decision to change.

Have a plan for each day and work your plan. Don't be legalistic and unwilling to bend if you need to alter your plan, but don't be purposeless. Solomon knew what it was to seek out things that didn't necessarily have meaning. Read what he says in Ecclesiastes 2:4–10:

> I made great works; I built myself houses, I planted vineyards.
>
> I made for myself gardens and orchards and I planted in them all kinds of fruit trees.
>
> I made for myself pools of water from which to water the forest *and* make the trees bud.
>
> I bought menservants and maidservants and had servants born in my house. Also I had great possessions of herds and flocks, more than any who had been before me in Jerusalem.
>
> I also gathered for myself silver and gold and the treasure of kings and of the provinces. I got for myself men singers and women singers, and the delights of the sons of men – concubines very many.
>
> So I became great and increased more than all who were before me in Jerusalem. Also my wisdom remained with me and stood by me.
>
> And whatever my eyes desired I kept not from them;

I withheld not my heart from any pleasure, for my heart rejoiced in all my labor, and this was my portion and reward for all my toil.

On the surface it sounds like Solomon is doing just fine, doesn't it? He's busy, active, wealthy; he's making deals and spinning wheels, you could say. But let's read on:

Then I looked on all that my hands had done and the labor I had spent in doing it, and behold, all was vanity and a striving *after* the wind *and* a feeding on it, and there was no profit under the sun.
    – ECCLESIASTES 2:11

The Message translation describes it this way: 'Then I took a good look at everything I'd done, looked at all the sweat and hard work. But when I looked, I saw nothing but smoke. Smoke and spitting into the wind. There was nothing to any of it. Nothing.'

Solomon realised you can be busy but running on the spot; you can have a full schedule but be empty inside at the same time. The book of Ecclesiastes in the Bible closes with instructions to seek and obey God above all else. Solomon found that it was the foundation of all happiness and the whole purpose for man.

Be a Person of Purpose

Successful people are always disciplined and undisciplined people are always unsuccessful. Success does not just fall on people; they must be disciplined, dedicated and committed. Are you a person of purpose or do you just get up every day and wait to see how you feel before you make any plans? Are you easily swayed by what others want to do, or do you have a plan and stick to your plan? Are you doing what you love or just doing masses of stuff that keeps you busy, but does not satisfy you?

> It is not hard to be dedicated to what you love.

Mark Twain said the secret of success was to be able to make your vocation your vacation. I like that thought. I have experienced that feeling with my work. I love what I am doing so much that even when I am on a so-called vacation, I have trouble not pursuing my vocation. It is not hard to be dedicated to what you love. When you love something and you're passionate about it, discipline comes easily.

> Are you daring enough to follow your heart rather than the crowd?

I wrote a book called *Approval Addiction* and in it I explain that a lot of people never get around to fulfilling God's purpose for them because they are busy keeping everyone else happy. The world is filled with people who think they know what you should be doing with your life. But the bottom line is it is your life, and when you stand before God, He will not ask anyone about your life but you. You will give an account to God of how you've lived, and if you're not already doing so, you must start living in a way that will enable you to stand before God without being ashamed. Are you daring enough to follow your heart rather than the crowd? Are you staying focused even when many voices try to draw you away from your purpose?

There's an interesting phenomenon that happens when someone is purposeless. They get very irritated with people of purpose. I have frequently been told I am too intense, and perhaps to some degree that is true. But I would rather be too intense about what I am trying to accomplish than to be so easy-going I miss God's best for my life.

A popular term these days, especially among teenagers, is 'whatever'. When I ask a direct question and get the answer 'whatever', that tells me the person really does not care at all. Indifference is perhaps the greatest tragedy of all.

I have also noticed that if they don't agree with me, instead of standing up for what they believe is right, they often cave in and say, 'whatever'. That is not a good attitude either. I don't want to see young people being rebellious, but neither do I want to see them not caring about what they feel is right.

You cannot wait to feel motivated, dedicated and committed; you must make the choice to do something on purpose. You have to be intentional. Live life on purpose. Don't just wait to see what everyone else is going to do and then follow the crowd. Take a stand and set a standard that others will strive to achieve. There are two kinds of people in the world. Those who wait for something to happen and those who take the initiative and make something happen. Don't say, 'I wish *they* would do something about this problem.' *You* are *they* – you do something!

Don't Let Your Feelings Vote

We are all going to have an abundance of feelings as long as we are alive, but we must learn they are ever changing. Feelings are not at all dependable. You can have feelings, but don't let them cast the final vote in your decision-making. As I said earlier, there is a time-tested principle called 'duty' that is not really outdated as far as God is concerned. Sometimes we just need to do our duty.

Those who serve in the armed forces know what this means. When they enter whatever branch of military service they join, they take an oath to 'bear true faith and allegiance' to support and defend. They do what they're told – they do their duty – because it's what they're supposed to do. They put their possible feelings of fear, uncertainty, concern and just plain weariness away. They do their duty because it's the right thing to do. We need to do what is right because it is right. I don't even think we should do what is right merely to get a right result, I believe our commitment should be to live life right and let God take care of the results. If we are not committed fully, we might start to compromise if we don't get results fast enough.

> We need to do what is right because it is right.

You cannot be vague and indecisive just because you feel vague and indecisive. Stir yourself up, make a decision, and get going in a direction. You cannot drive a parked car. Double-mindedness and indecision can become a real problem in many people's lives. It is almost addictive. The more vague people are, the more vague they become, until eventually their decision is to make no decisions. According to the Apostle James double-minded people become indecisive, unsure, and uncertain about everything they think, feel and decide.

[For being as he is] a man of two minds (hesitating, dubious, irresolute), [he is] unstable *and* unreliable *and* uncertain about everything [he thinks, feels, decides].
    – JAMES 1:8

I don't always feel like making decisions, especially important ones. After all, what if I am wrong? But, I realise that part of being a leader is being decisive. If I don't give people direction, the only thing any of us will be doing is nothing. If I make mistakes (which I do), at least I will know not to do that thing again. Some of the biggest lessons I have learned in life have been through making mistakes.

> I realise that part of being a leader is being decisive.

I believe the reason why many people don't press towards excellence is because their feelings give up on them before the job is finished. Your feelings are often excited by something new, but before you're finished, you may have to go forward simply because you're determined to do so. It's like buying a home. Any homeowner has experienced the euphoria of finding a wonderful new place to live and then the realisation of the stressful process they have to go through before they can actually live in the house. However, if you want the home badly enough, you will be willing to stay the course. It's the same way with excellence. Dedicate yourself to excellence and don't let your feelings run your life. Remember, you will always have them, but they don't have to have you.

Jesus Was a Success

If there is any successful role model we should look to, it should be Jesus. I know what you're thinking – well, Jesus was successful because He was Jesus. Not exactly. He had all the same temptations you and I face, but He still did the will of His Father in heaven. He knew why He was here and what His mission was. He pursued the will of God relentlessly. When others gave up, He kept going. He asked His disciples to pray with Him while He was suffering in the Garden of Gethsemane, but they fell asleep and, like many of us, He had to face His most difficult time in life alone. He did not run, though. He had already determined that even if He had to stand alone, He would do so. Successful people don't run from hard things. They face issues and deal with them.

> Successful people don't run from hard things.

Character is the key to success. Jesus had good character. He was excellent, committed, dedicated, diligent, honest, truthful, good and kind to others. He displayed qualities the world is looking for today. If more people looked to Jesus, perhaps we would see more purpose and passion in our society today. I am sure the teenage suicide rate would drop drastically. Teenage suicide in the United States has tripled since prayer was taken out of schools in 1963.[7] Teenagers need someone to look up to, someone to respect and follow. Many teenagers today feel hopeless; they see no reason at all to continue a life they feel is always going to be filled with the emptiness they feel from being purposeless.

Jesus had purpose and He was passionate about His purpose. Young people today need to see that kind of example. In John 17:4, it is recorded Jesus said to His Father, 'I have glorified You down here on the earth by completing the work that You gave Me to do.' In essence, Jesus was saying, 'I went for it and I let nothing hold me back!' Every time I read that scripture, it grips my heart. I want to be able to say that to God myself. I believe we glorify God by pressing in and doing all He has given us to do. We cannot wait for others to cheer us on; we cannot follow the crowd; we cannot wait to feel like it; we have to just do it! Will you dare to live your life in such a way that someone else will say, 'I want to be like you!'

Jesus knew His purpose and He talked about it frequently. He said, 'For I have come down from heaven not to do My own will *and* purpose but to do the will *and* purpose of Him Who sent Me' (John 6:38). He said He sought only to do the will of the One who sent Him (see John 5:30). He knew He had been sent to destroy the works of the wicked one and did not turn from His purpose to the right or the left. He did not stray off His course at all, but He looked straight ahead with fixed purpose. In other words, Jesus had His mind made up. How solidly have you made up your mind? Without a right mind-set you will never succeed at fulfilling God's purpose. God's will does not just fall on us, but we must be determined to have it.

Do You Change Your Mind When
You Get Uncomfortable?

Now My Soul is troubled *and* distressed, and what shall I say?
Father, save Me from this hour [of trial and agony]? But it
was for this very purpose that I have come to this hour [that I
might undergo it].
   – JOHN 12:27

Jesus suffered such agony of mind in the Garden of Gethsemane He
actually sweated blood. We cannot even imagine how He suffered and
yet He refused to miss fulfilling His purpose. Sometimes we have our
mind made up until we get uncomfortable, and then we change our
mind. I can tell you ahead of time that if you intend to pursue anything
in life worth doing, there will be times when you won't be comfortable.

Satan hates true success. He despises seeing people fulfil their
purpose and he will fight against those who set themselves to do so.
He has many tools in his bag of tricks and is more than happy to use
as many of them as he can. His weapons of choice include lies and
deceptions, rejection from family and friends, discouragement, fear,
being alone, illness, family problems – the list goes on and on.

It is amazing what God can do with people who simply
refuse to give up.

But we have weapons as well as armour God has given us. We
must lift up the shield of faith with which we can quench all the fiery
darts of the enemy. No matter what happens, I encourage you to keep
trusting God because He is faithful. Don't give up! It is amazing what
God can do with people who simply refuse to give up. Stay positive.
Look at the possibilities, not the problems. Glance at your problems
and stare at Jesus. Stay focused! All of these things will help you, but

nobody can completely remove all suffering. The bottom line is this: If you are going to fulfil God's purpose for your life, you will have times when it is going to hurt and you are going to want to run. I encourage you to STAND STILL AND SEE THE SALVATION OF THE LORD.

Your Efforts Are Never Wasted

One of the tricks Satan uses is to tell people what they are doing is a waste of time and no good will come from their efforts. That is when we have to remember Satan is a liar! God says if we remain firm, steadfast, immovable, always abounding in the work of the Lord (always being superior, excelling, doing more than enough in the service of the Lord), that our labour is never wasted or to no purpose (see 1 Corinthians 15:58).

Any time that you are doing your best to serve God you are never wasting your time. God is faithful and He always brings a reward to those who diligently seek Him (see Hebrews 11:6).

Keep your eyes on the prize. Jesus despised the cross, but He endured it for the joy of the prize on the other side. The cross we all must bear to some degree or another has two sides. The cross has the crucifixion side and the resurrection side. Let me remind you that Sunday morning at the tomb was exciting. There were no tears, only awe and wonder and rejoicing! It was Resurrection Sunday, Jesus rose from the dead, but He also had to go through Friday to get to Sunday. So will we.

> Remember your labour in the Lord will never be wasted.

No matter what you might be going through right now or years from now, always remember your labour in the Lord will never be wasted. And remember to do it wholeheartedly because purpose is only fulfilled when you put enthusiasm and love for what you're doing behind it.

CHAPTER 5

With Your Whole Heart

What does it mean to do something wholeheartedly?

Deuteronomy 6:5 (The Message) says we should 'Love God, your God, with your whole heart: love him with all that's in you, love him with all you've got!' Passionate purpose requires everything we've got. No holding back. Anyone who actually fulfils their destiny will probably pay a greater price than they thought would be required. It will take longer than they expected and be more difficult than they could have imagined, but it will be worth it. There is no greater feeling than knowing you have completed a goal, and the truth is that the more you put into it, the more satisfaction you get out of it.

When Jesus spoke of loving God with our passion, prayer and intelligence, He was talking about what it takes to be wholehearted, not half-hearted (see Matthew 22:37). He is speaking of being passionate about Him and the life He has given you. It is not God's will that we be passionless or that we have misplaced passion. He does not want us to live making a half-hearted, lukewarm effort toward our mission in life. Actually, the Bible has a lot to say about wholeheartedness. David, Isaiah and Jeremiah all talked about the importance of serving God with a whole heart. To me, that means serving Him with passion. Passion is a powerful emotion, and it fills us with boundless enthusiasm and zeal.

> He does not want us to live making a half-hearted, lukewarm effort towards our mission in life.

God Is Jealous

So why does God want us to be wholeheartedly His? One reason is He doesn't want to share us with anyone or anything else. The Bible says God's jealousy cannot endure a divided allegiance (see Psalm 79:5). Yes, God is jealous over His children. Please consider the weight of what the following two scriptures are saying:

> You [are like] unfaithful wives [having illicit love affairs with the world and breaking your marriage vow to God]! Do you not know that being the world's friend is being God's enemy? So whoever chooses to be a friend of the world takes his stand as an enemy of God.
>
> Or do you suppose that the Scripture is speaking to no purpose that says, The Spirit Whom He has caused to dwell in us yearns over us *and* He yearns for the Spirit [to be welcome] with a jealous love?
> – JAMES 4:4–5

There are other places in God's Word where we learn God is a jealous God. He desires our affection and wants us to love and serve Him wholeheartedly. That does not mean we cannot enjoy other things, but God demands to be first. St Augustine, in the sixteenth century, said, 'Love God, then do as you please.' If we truly love Him with our whole heart, we won't do things displeasing to Him, but we will be able to enjoy all of life knowing He also delights in our enjoyment.

Do you enjoy it when people do things for you, but you can tell their heart is not in it? Of course you don't. You know they are just going through the motions, pretending, and their attitude is one of fulfilling an obligation, not one of doing something with joy and honest enthusiasm. We can pretend to be excited and enthusiastic and some people will be fooled. They don't always realise we are pretending, but God quickly spots a phoney person. He knows if we are serving Him out of wholehearted love and commitment or mere obligation and duty. There may be times when we begin by simply doing our duty, but we should remember what God really desires is passion and that cannot be genuine without putting your whole heart into whatever you do. We can pray about anything and open the door for God to work. We can even ask Him to give us passion in what we do.

God quickly spots a phoney person.

We can also make a decision to have a better attitude in life so passion can arise. A bad attitude can kill passion. If a person does something with an attitude of self-pity they will never be passionate about it.

I was sexually abused for many years by my father and when he was in his late seventies, God asked me to move him close to my home and take care of him. I admit I did not want to. I did not think it was fair to be asked to do such a thing after the way he treated me while I was growing up. At first I flatly refused. As God put that gentle pressure on my spirit that only He can bring, I submitted my will to His. I did it for a while in obedience to God, but I did it with a bad attitude in my heart. Then, finally, I changed my attitude and did it with joy. As a result of what God led me to do, my father eventually repented of his sin and accepted Jesus as his Saviour. When he died a few years later, I had peace, knowing he was in heaven.

I believe people can always tell if our actions are done with a good attitude or a bad one and they are not blessed unless we are wholehearted in our efforts. I doubt my father would have been moved to accept the Jesus I said I represented if my attitude had remained bad. Is there anything you are doing, but with a bad attitude? You can change your attitude by changing your mind. The Bible says we should renew our minds and attitudes daily (see Ephesians 4:23). Perhaps this is an area we should examine more often. It is easy to have a bad attitude and think it is not a problem. After all, we do what we are supposed to, so who cares if we are happy about it or not? God cares! He wants us to put our whole heart into what we do; no half-hearted effort is acceptable.

Sincere Worship

We are to worship and praise God with our whole heart. That means you don't go through the motions of clapping, singing or lifting your hands while your mind is at the restaurant eating lunch or while you worry about a problem or wonder what people in church think of your new outfit.

> I did certain things to impress God, not to love Him, and He always knows the difference.

If we do worship God that way, it means nothing to Him. Anything we do half-heartedly we might as well not do at all, as far as God is concerned. He may let us make a half-hearted effort for a while, but eventually He will deal with us about our attitude. I well remember when the Lord spoke to my heart and said, 'Joyce, I don't want you to do anything else for me unless you truly want to.' You may remember I said a lot of my motives were wrong in the early days of my ministry. I did certain things to impress God, not to love Him, and He always knows the difference. For example, I might pray and the first fifteen minutes were wonderful, but I wanted to impress God and my friends by praying an hour, so I forced myself to go on even though the Holy Spirit had finished in fifteen minutes. After the Holy Spirit was no longer energising my prayer, I didn't really want to be there. My mind wandered, I wasn't praying sincerely, but I was merely jabbering, waiting for the minutes to tick by on the clock.

I was trapped in what the Bible calls 'works of the flesh' (see

Galatians 5:19 KJV), which means, *I had a lot of plans on how I could get things done.* I wasn't being led by the Holy Spirit, so I wasn't doing many of the things I did with passion. It is the Spirit of God who gives us zeal and who is the reason that we should always strive to be filled with the Spirit as the Bible teaches.

I prayed a long time but got no reward because my motives were not pure. I was not praying with my whole heart. I was just putting my time in. God wanted me to pray for the fifteen minutes that were led by the Holy Spirit and drop the forty-five minutes I was putting in to be impressive. As I obeyed Him, He actually increased my desire to pray more. I refused to give Him lip service with no heart behind it and He honoured my decision.

> I prayed a long time but got no reward because my motives were not pure.

I believe if we refuse to do things with a *wrong* motive, then God will help us find what we can do with a *right* motive.

Do You Want a Deeper Walk with God?

Why do some people seem to be so close to God while others are not? There is a reason because everything has a reason. It is the principle of cause and effect. Whatever effects we have in our life are because of something done or not done either by us or those in authority over us.

David said we would find God when we sought Him with our whole heart. In Psalm 119, He said we should seek, inquire of and crave Him with our whole heart. How does a person behave who is craving something? They usually do whatever they need to do to get their craving satisfied. Pregnant women tell stories of sending their husbands out in the dead of night to get them a tub of ice cream or a full-course chicken dinner. I have been known to drive an hour, round-trip, to get a cup of Starbucks coffee. Does that sound ridiculous? Well, before you judge me, ask yourself how ridiculous you are when you are craving something.

God wants to be wanted.

If we would crave God and go after Him like we do other things, we would have a much more intimate relationship with Him. God wants to be wanted. He will not push Himself on us, we must pursue Him. Ask God to fill you with passion for Him. Perhaps you have never thought about praying to have a passionate desire for what God desires, but it is time to begin. One minister prayed for God to break his heart with what broke the heart of God, and he became a world-famous missionary who changed the lives of multiplied thousands. Instead of feeling guilty because you don't want to pray, ask God to give you a deep revelation on the power of prayer and the desire to do it.

A half-hearted effort will always be detected by God and ignored, so please don't just keep going through the motions hoping nobody will notice. We must put our whole being into seeking and serving God. If you really are not willing to do so, but wish you were, then ask God to make you willing to be willing. I believe God appreciates sincere, honest, straightforward communication. He will meet you where you are and help you get where you need to be if you're honest with Him.

You can be as close to God as you want to be.

You can be as close to God as you want to be; it is determined by how much time you are willing to put into getting to know Him. Remember, Paul said his determined purpose was to know Christ more intimately (see Philippians 3:10). He made a decision and was ready to pay a price to get the result he desired.

Rome wasn't built in a day, and you won't have the discipline needed in one day to have a great, intimate relationship with God. Start with small disciplines that are not overwhelming. If you are not reading your Bible at all, then start with one chapter per day. Read it slowly, digest it, and be sure you get at least one thing out of what you read that will have meaning for you. Practise reading your Bible for quality, not quantity. Don't approach Bible reading or Bible study just to get information. Approach it expectantly because it is filled with life. Jesus said, My words, they are spirit and they are life (John 6:63).

When you feel ready, you can increase to two chapters a day. Sometimes I like to read one chapter of Proverbs, because it gives such practical wisdom and insight for everyday living. I also like to read a chapter in the Psalms, because they bring encouragement and comfort. I switch between reading the Old and New Testament.

> Don't just try to 'conquer' a book – read it!

Read books that will help you understand biblical principles. And remember a book is read one page at a time. Don't just try to 'conquer a book' – read it! You don't need to try to impress God or yourself with huge amounts of anything. Just begin and keep making progress.

'The Tortoise and the Hare'
One of Aesop's Fables

Once there was a hare who, boasting how he could run faster than anyone else, was forever teasing the tortoise for its slowness. Then one day, the irate tortoise answered back: 'Who do you think you are? There's no denying you're swift, but even you can be beaten!' The hare squealed with laughter.

'Beaten in a race? By whom? Not you, surely! I bet there's nobody in the world that can win against me, I'm so speedy. Now, why don't you try?'

Annoyed by such bragging, the tortoise accepted the challenge. A course was planned, and the next day at dawn they stood at the starting line. The hare yawned sleepily as the meek tortoise trudged slowly off. When the hare saw how painfully slow his rival was, he decided, half asleep on his feet, to have a quick nap. 'Take your time!' he said. 'I'll have forty winks and catch up with you in a minute.'

The hare woke with a start from a fitful sleep and gazed around, looking for the tortoise. But the creature was only a short distance away, having barely covered a third of the course. Breathing a sigh of relief, the hare decided he might as well have breakfast too, and off he went to munch some cabbages he noticed in a nearby field. But the heavy meal and the hot sun made his eyelids droop. With a careless glance at the tortoise, now halfway along the course, he decided to have another snooze before flashing past the winning post. And smiling at the thought of the look on the tortoise's face when it would see the hare speed by, he fell fast asleep and was soon snoring happily. The sun started to sink below the horizon, and the tortoise, who had been plodding towards the winning post since morning, was scarcely a yard from the finish. At that very point, the hare woke with a jolt. He could see the tortoise, a speck in the distance, and away he dashed. He leaped and bounded at a great rate, his tongue lolling, gasping for breath. Just a little more and he'd be first at the finish. But the hare's last leap was just too late, for the tortoise had beaten him to the winning post. Poor hare! Tired and in disgrace, he slumped down beside the tortoise who was silently smiling at him.

'Slowly does it every time!' he said.

> You cannot get anywhere if you don't start in the direction you want to go.

If you don't feel you have time to spend with God, begin disciplining yourself by giving up half an hour of television or another entertainment you enjoy. Go to bed half an hour early, so you can get up earlier and spend time with God. You may eventually work up to enjoying spending entire days or evenings reading, praying, listening to music and worshipping God. You cannot get anywhere if you don't start in the direction you want to go. Just get going and keep going and you'll win the race because you will finish the race well. As the Lord once showed me, 'Just keep on keeping on!'

> God is pleased with your smallest effort if it is offered with a wholehearted attitude.

Any discipline you desire must be built up gradually. Not understanding this is the cause of a great deal of failure. Be patient with yourself and realise God is pleased with your smallest effort if it is offered with a wholehearted attitude. If you have never walked for exercise and your desire is to walk three miles a day, you will have to work up to that distance or you will probably strain muscles and be so discouraged you will give up. I used to complain that every time I tried to exercise I hurt myself and finally began using it as an excuse not to exercise. The truth was, I wasn't patient enough to begin gradually. I wanted to have the discipline in one day that others had developed over many months or even years.

Being impatient will cause you a lot of heartache in life. It is actually one of the root causes of failure, but very few realise it. You might say, 'Well, I thought you told me to be enthusiastic and filled with zeal.' I do want you to be enthusiastic, zealous and passionate. I want you to be fully committed, but wisdom must be the cornerstone of every venture. Zeal without wisdom works against us, not for us.

i dare you

Be Wholehearted

When you hear the word 'wholehearted', does it excite you or does it scare you? Does it make you want to run right out and serve God, or does it make you tired just thinking about one more commitment? Let me encourage you not to be hesitant in loving God with ALL of your heart. Here are some tips to get started using your whole heart for God.

1 *Be intentional.*

Ask yourself when faced with a choice or a question if this is going to add or subtract from what God has called you to do. Don't try to do so many things that you cannot do any of them wholeheartedly. Stay focused on the goal.

2 *Exchange your fear for faith.*

If fear of something is holding you back from giving your all, ask God to exchange your fears for faith – and be confident He is holding you up and walking right in front of you all the way. Courage is doing a thing while you feel fear, so don't wait for all the feelings of fear to go away – do it afraid!

3 *Be dedicated.*

Living out your life with a wholehearted attitude requires commitment and dedication. Choose something small you will dedicate yourself to doing every day or every week. Maybe it's collecting your infirm neighbour's post or writing a note to someone just to put a smile on his or her face. Maybe it's taking some coffee or a bottle of water to the lollipop lady near the local school. Pick something small, but commit yourself to do it. You'll be amazed at how your discipline in the small things can grow to much larger things God wants to use you for.

Wholehearted Obedience

King David said he would keep the commandments of God with his whole heart (see Psalm 119:10). That is easy to say, but do we mean it? How many people who call themselves Christians are genuinely keeping God's commands with their whole heart? If most Christians were keeping God's commands wholeheartedly and serving Him passionately we would see the Church, which is comprised of all Christians everywhere affecting society in a much more positive way than we do.

> How many people who call themselves Christians are genuinely keeping God's commands with their whole heart?

The truth is, the world is not very impressed with the Church in general and it is because of all the phoniness it sees. Certainly the world is judgmental and it is quick to yell 'hypocrite', but we need to make sure we are not giving people a good reason not to respect us.

> Obeying God is the purpose of every person on earth.

Make obeying God daily a priority in your life. When the Holy Spirit convicts you of the need to do something or not do something, be willing to change. Obeying God is the purpose of every person on earth. Solomon wasted his life pursuing wrong goals. He had passion, but it was misplaced. As we see in his writings in Ecclesiastes, he ultimately realised what was really important:

All has been heard; the end of the matter is: Fear God [revere and worship Him, knowing that He is] and keep His commandments, for this is the whole of man [the full, original purpose of his creation, the object of God's providence, the root of character, the foundation of all happiness, the adjustment to all inharmonious circumstances *and* conditions under the sun] and the whole [duty] for every man.

– ECCLESIASTES 12:13

> Many people don't pay any attention to small things, and it is a big mistake.

Begin by obeying God in small things. It is the training you will need to obey God in bigger things later on. Many people don't pay any attention to small things, and that's a big mistake. A lot of small things add up to big things. The Bible states if we are faithful in small things, we will also be faithful in larger things (see Luke 16:10).

I often tell a story of how God taught me to put my shopping trolley back into the space marked for shopping trolleys at the supermarket. It was difficult to do if the weather was bad or I was in a hurry, and actually it took me almost two years to get to the place where I did it every time. God was training me in small things so I could rule over greater things later in life. I had small children at the time and was not able to get professional training for the ministry, so God trained me exactly where I was. He used a lot of practical things like the shopping trolley example to prepare me for the things I am doing now.

> God was training me in small things so I could rule over greater things later in life.

God wants to teach us principles and build character into us. He can do that in a variety of ways if we will submit to Him wherever we may be.

As Christians, we should wake up every morning excited about the relationship we have with our Creator.

Are You Excited About Being a Christian?

As Christians, we should wake up every morning excited about the relationship we have with our Creator and what He's going to show us and teach us today. Instead, though, we often treat our salvation the same way we treat our breathing – we're glad it's there, but we don't really think about it unless something goes wrong. It's like the story I heard of a man who served as an interim pastor for a small church in a tiny town deep in the heart of Texas. He arrived early one Sunday and stopped at the local café with his Bible to review his notes for that morning's sermon. A man was sitting nearby and noticed the Bible.

'You a preacher or something?' he asked.

The pastor nodded his head and told him the name of the church where he was preaching.

The man got excited and said, 'Hey, I'm a member of that church!'

The preacher, looking a bit confused, said, 'Really? I've been preaching there for over three months and I don't think I've ever seen you there.'

Now it was the man's turn to have a strange look on his face. He told the pastor, 'Hey, I said I was a member of that church. I never said that I was fanatical about it!'

If you are a Christian, are you excited about it? Do you enjoy being with other Christians, worshipping with other believers, and talking about what God is doing in your life and in the lives of others? Or have you become accustomed to the idea you will live eternally and God is watching over you? God once spoke to my heart that

I should always live amazed and not get blasé about things that once thrilled me. I remember how excited I was when God revealed His love to me. WOW! God loves me and for no reason at all except He wants to. His love is unconditional and everlasting. I was so excited and enthusiastic I felt I was going to burst if I didn't get to tell somebody. But after a while, I got used to the fact that God loves me and I didn't feel the same passion. I am sure you have experienced the same thing, but is there anything we can do about it? I believe there is.

> I should always live amazed and not get blasé about things that once thrilled me.

Paul told Timothy to stir himself up (see 2 Timothy 1:6). To fan the flame and rekindle the embers of the fire he once had. Paul was talking about Timothy's faith passed on to him by his grandmother and mother. Timothy let himself become afraid and the message from Paul was 'Stir yourself up.' Apparently it was Timothy's responsibility, not someone else's.

What can we do to keep ourselves passionate about God and His purpose for our lives? We can be careful how we live. Be careful how we think. Be careful how we talk. And, be careful who we spend time with.

All of these things affect our attitude and emotions. We can think about something in the right way and it will fill us with enthusiasm. Likewise, if we think the wrong way, we can dread doing what we should be excited about.

> If you are serving to be thanked, then your motives are wrong.

Stop thinking this way: 'I'm so tired of doing the same old thing all the time. I go to church, but nobody appreciates the effort I make. I have helped in the Sunday School for three years, and nobody has even thanked me.' That kind of thinking will depress you and make you feel resentful. If you are serving to be thanked, then your motives are wrong. Serve God, not people, and your reward will come from Him.

Instead, think like this: 'I am looking forward to going to church today. I remember when I was miserable and didn't even know if I would go to heaven when I died. I am so glad to have an opportunity to serve God by helping in the Sunday School. God sees everything I do and none of my labours go unrewarded by Him.'

> You can choose to be with people who will always challenge you to rise to new levels.

If we spend a lot of time with people who have no vision for their lives, no purpose, no passion and no enthusiasm, we will probably start to be like them. However, if we spend time with people who challenge us to be better, we are making a wise choice. The Bible says unholiness is infectious, but holiness is not (see Haggai 2:12–13). For example, we can catch a cold from someone else, but we cannot catch good health, that must be chosen. If you aimlessly wander through life spending time with others who are aimless and vague, you will just get deeper and deeper in the trap of purposelessness. But you can choose to be with people who will always challenge you to rise to new levels. Don't hang out with someone just because they are available. Choose your friends wisely!

When we have our whole hearts committed and invested in something about which we're passionate and purposely seeking, we don't just drift along and go with whatever comes along. We pray, we think things over, and make purposeful choices. We should make choices that will help us fulfil our purpose. John Maxwell said we should put 80 per cent of our time into our top two or three main goals. In other words, stay focused! It is easy in society today to get sidetracked and begin drifting in a direction that will be detrimental to your future. Be determined to serve God whole-heartedly. I imagine someone is thinking about now, 'Joyce, I wish I felt that passion you're talking about, but I just don't.' Let me remind you: passion is a decision about how we will approach life before it becomes a feeling. A person with a purpose who pursues it passionately is a person who will glorify God and be remembered long after they have departed this life.

> A person with a purpose who pursues it passionately is a person who will glorify God and be remembered.

CHAPTER 6

Misplaced Passion

It is possible to be very passionate about the wrong thing. The Apostle Paul at one time was zealous about persecuting Christians. He pursued them vehemently and did everything in his power to see them imprisoned or destroyed. He said later in his life that he was full of zeal, but it was without knowledge. In other words, he was passionate, but he was passionate about the wrong things.

Many people spend their lives trying to climb the ladder of success only to find when they reach the top, their ladder was leaned against the wrong building all the time.

Are You Busy or Fruitful?

Everyone today seems to be busy. Ask just about anyone how they are and they will respond, 'Busy.' And it's no wonder. Roughly 78 per cent of women with children aged between six and seventeen in the United States work outside the home.[1] Though my children are now grown up I know what it's like juggling job, family, church, and everything in between – and not necessarily in that order. In fact, in 2003, Gallup reported, slightly more than a quarter (28 per cent) of adults with children under the age of eighteen in the States said that their families ate dinner together at home seven nights a week – down from 37 per cent in 1997.[2] Add to those facts the extra activities and sports our children are now involved in at an ever-increasing rate, and you're right – we're busy! But God never once told us in His Word to be busy. He told us to be fruitful.

We are making a mistake if we equate being busy with being

successful. I can remember when, as a young minister, I frequently heard other ministers talk about how they had not taken a day off in years. At the time, I was impressionable and inexperienced and I remember thinking how dedicated and committed they were. I now realise they were very unwise and in opposition to God's laws of rest. Their lives were seriously out of balance and, when that is the case it always opens a door for Satan to bring destruction.

Many marriages are destroyed because one or both partners are too busy to spend time nurturing their relationship. Many people lose their health because they are addicted to life in the fast lane. They don't rest properly and eventually their bodies break down under the strain of non-stop activity.

For many years I followed the examples I saw around me. I thought the busier I was, the more God would be pleased with me. The truth was, the busier I was, the less I had time to even hear from God concerning what His will was for me. I had a plan and I was working my plan. I was passionate, but my passion was often misplaced. I said yes to things God would have instructed me to say no to had I taken the time to ask Him. I eventually became ill and it took a long time to recover. Thankfully, I finally realised God has not called us to be busy, but to bear good fruit.

> Just being busy does not mean you are a success.

Once upon a time a very strong woodcutter asked for a job with a timber merchant and got it. The pay was really good and so were the work conditions. For that reason the woodcutter was determined to do his best. He wanted to be a success on his new job.

His boss gave him an axe and showed him the forest area where he was supposed to work.

The first day the woodcutter brought back eighteen trees.

'Congratulations,' the boss said. 'Go on that way!'

Very motivated by the boss's words, the woodcutter tried harder the next day, but he could only bring back fifteen trees. The third day he tried even harder, but he only brought back ten trees. Day after day, no matter how hard he tried, he was bringing fewer trees.

I must be losing my strength, the woodcutter thought. He went to the boss and apologised, saying he could not understand what was going on.

'When was the last time you sharpened your axe?' the boss asked.

'Sharpen? I had no time to sharpen my axe. I have been very busy trying to cut trees.'[3]

> Don't make the mistake of being too busy to do the things you need to do in order to be a genuine success.

Is Your Time Being Stolen?

This is a good place to think about our motives again. As I mentioned earlier in the book, God is not impressed with what we do or how much of it we do. He is only impressed with 'why' we have done it, and it must be for a good, godly reason. Doing things to impress people and to be admired are not good motives. Doing things just to please people is not always the right thing to do either. We are told to strive to please others and not to live to please ourselves (see Romans 15:2–3). However, that doesn't mean we are to be people pleasers at the expense of not being God pleasers.

If God says 'no', then we must say 'no', no matter how much we are pressured by others to say 'yes'. Likewise, if God is saying 'yes', then we must say 'yes', even if the whole world is saying 'no'!

If you don't learn to follow your heart and the spirit of God, you will always live under pressure. The devil is a thief and one of the things he thoroughly enjoys stealing is our time. Time is a precious resource God has given us. Each of us has a certain amount allotted to us, and once we have used up any portion of it, we can never get it back. That is a sobering thought and should provoke us to choose to use it wisely.

> If you don't learn to follow your heart and the spirit of God, you will always live under pressure.

Are you frustrated with your schedule? Does this prayer ring true with you?

The clock is my dictator, I shall not rest.
It makes me lie down only when exhausted.
It leads me into deep depression.
It hounds my soul.
It leads me in circles of frenzy, for activities' sake.
Even though I run frantically from task to task, I will never get
   it all done,
For my ideal is with me.
Deadlines and my need for approval, they drive me.
They demand performance from me, beyond the limits of my
   schedule.
They anoint my head with migraines,
My in-basket overflows.
Surely fatigue and time pressures shall follow me
All the days of my life.
And I will dwell in the bonds of frustration
Forever.[4]
   – Source unknown

Do you find yourself complaining a lot about everything you have to do? If so, you should inspect the fruit of each thing you are putting your time into. I can guarantee you will find a lot of your activities are not helping you fulfil your purpose in life.

The devil can steal your time by making you feel guilty about not doing something you have been asked to do. The *should's* and *ought's* in life can be very oppressive. I encourage you to realise everyone wants you to do their thing. They have plans and want you to help them fulfil them, but they are probably not concerned about whether or not you are fulfilling your purpose. Make a decision today about whether you are going to live for people or for God. And while you're making it, remember you will stand before God on Judgment Day to give an account of your life. The people who placed demands on you won't be with you to help you explain why you never got around to doing what God called you to do.

> Make a decision today about whether you are going to live for people or for God.

We All Have Resources

God has made resources available to all of us, but we must be willing to put them to proper use. The resources He has given us are gifts from Him and should be respected. We are called to be good stewards of God's grace, His gift and talents, our time, treasure and many other things. Even our energy is a resource God gives us to help us fulfil His will. If we misuse our energy, we are still using it, and although it is replenished daily with proper rest, I believe everything we misuse is something lost.

> You make your schedule and you are the only one who can change it!

The next time you feel really tired, ask yourself what is the cause. If you're tired from putting forth effort that is helping you fulfil your God-ordained purpose, then rejoice. If you are tired from running around in circles being busy, but going nowhere, then repent and make some changes in your schedule so you don't keep repeating the same wasteful cycle. You make your schedule and you are the only one who can change it!

People are frustrated when they are not fulfilling their purpose. Misplaced passion does not energise us, it drains us. We can get caught up in mere emotional hype that has nothing to do with our life's purpose. Don't make the mistake of wasting your life and having nothing but regrets to look back on.

i dare you

To Be Fruitful and Not Just Busy

Ask yourself these questions:

1 Are you doing what you truly desire to do, or are you trying to live up to the expectations and demands others have placed on you?

2 Do you see tangible results from your time and effort, or are you just busy?

3 Do you feel fulfilled and satisfied, or do you dread a lot of your activities?

4 Are you frustrated a lot, or do you have peace? Are you enjoying your life?

5 Are you taking time to build good relationships with God, yourself and those around you?

6 Are you confident that what you spend your time doing is what you are really supposed to be doing?

7 Do you believe you should be doing something else with your time, but just don't have the courage to say no to the demands placed on you?

Answering these questions honestly will help you decide whether or not you are fruitful or just busy.

Hoping and wishing for things to change will not change them.

Change Requires Decisions

Do you feel your priorities are out of balance? Do you feel you are wasting your resources? If you need change, don't start making excuses or feeling sorry for yourself. Many times excuses or self-pity are our way of not dealing with issues we really need to address. Hoping and wishing for things to change will not change them. Change requires decision and often some pain to go along with it. For example, you might have to make a decision not to do something and it will make someone else angry because they want you to do it. You will need to stand your ground and go through the emotional pain of real-ising they are displeased with you. But keep this in mind – if people have a bad reaction to you obeying God, it is their problem, not yours.

If you are over-committed and undersatisfied and you want to change, you have to make some decisions that will help you put your time into your purpose. You will have to eliminate some things from your 'to do' list. Say 'no' to some who want to hear 'yes'. You must face the reality that some people will get angry with you. They won't understand because they are the type of people who never understand anything except what they want.

A good thing can often be an enemy of the best that God has for you.

When you choose to stay focused, you may have to cut some things out of your life that you enjoy, but are not bearing fruit. There are a lot of things in life that are good things, but they may not be 'God' things for you. Many people have been deceived by 'good things'.

A good thing can often be an enemy of the best that God has for you. If Satan cannot deceive us with bad things, his next trick to deceive us may be the use of 'good things'. Good works done in the flesh without God's approval are just as dangerous as bad things done in the flesh. The term 'in the flesh' simply means done by man's decision and effort without God's approval. There are even people who do so many 'good works' at church that their families and marriages are falling apart. Actually, one of the best places to hide from God can be in church! We get busy doing things that we think are good and suddenly we are too busy to hear from God or be sensitive to what our friends and family are trying to tell us.

It doesn't bother us to cut things out of our lives we dread and despise anyway, but what if the thing we need to cut off is something to which we are attached? That makes it a lot harder, because our emotions are involved. I remember when God showed me I needed to stay home more to study and prepare for the ministry that He had called me to. That meant I couldn't socialise with my friends as much. They were 'good' friends. We had a 'good' time. There was nothing 'bad' about what we were spending our time doing. We went to garage sales; we went to the farmers' market downtown for fresh vegetables and fruits; we had lunch; and we enjoyed being around one another. I liked being involved. I didn't like the idea of being left out and not knowing what was going on with my friends, but God was clearly showing me I needed to be more focused on what He was calling me to do. Sure enough, they did not understand, and even accused me of going overboard and becoming a 'religious fanatic'.

That season in my life was a very trying time for me. But looking back now, I can see I was making a transition that ultimately allowed God to bring me into a new level spiritually, and the devil was trying to use my emotions to hold me back. I don't mean to say God was requiring me to give up all my friends, but He was asking me to say no to a lot of 'activity' that wasn't productive for me. It kept me busy, but wasn't fruitful. Many years later God dealt with me regarding a need to spend more time developing good relationships. I became so focused it was not healthy for me emotionally. I needed some good, clean fun. I was by myself too much and needed to be around more people socially. If we truly listen to the Holy Spirit He will lead us into balanced lives. He will also help us to discern the seasons in our lives.

> The Bible says everything is beautiful in its time.

The Bible says everything is beautiful in its time (see Ecclesiastes 3:11). Something may not be bad in itself, but if it is out of timing for us, that makes it bad for that particular season in our lives. At another time it may be perfectly permissible and something we should do. I have found staying balanced in life and doing enough of a thing, but not too much of it, is one of the greatest challenges we face. The Bible says in 1 Peter 5:8 we are to stay well balanced for our adversary the devil roams about like a lion roaring in fierce hunger seeking whom he may devour. This portion of Scripture is telling us Satan can devour those who are out of balance. Living in extremes is an open door for our enemy.

> Living in extremes is an open door for our enemy.

Some people tend to do 'too much' of everything. They work too much, eat too much, spend too much money, or talk too much. We need to do all of those things, but if these things are done to excess they become big problems. Seek balance and be open to God's pruning process. Let Him keep your life well balanced by adding or deleting whatever might be helpful in your current season.

> Seek balance and be open to God's pruning process.

I am asking you to honestly evaluate your life and be willing to change. You may be passionate about things that are not helping you pursue your purpose. Your passion could be misplaced and that is sometimes more dangerous than being passionless.

You may be passionate about making money and being successful, but you need to ask the question of whether your passion is driven by God's Spirit or more by mere ambition. I encourage you not to give money priority over your family. You may be trying to make a lot of money to take good care of your family, but the truth is they want you more than money.

Just because a person has money does not mean they are rich. The Bible says that there are those who are rich, when in reality they are poor (see Revelation 3:17).

How Poor We Are

One day a father and his rich family took his son on a trip to the country with the firm purpose of showing him how poor people can be.

They spent a day and a night on the farm of a very poor family. When they returned home, the father asked his son what he thought of the trip.

'Very good, Dad!' the son said.

'Did you see how poor people can be?' the father wanted to know.

'Yeah!'

'And what did you learn?'

The son answered, 'I saw that we have a dog at home, and they have four. We have a pool that reaches to the middle of the garden, and they have a creek that has no end. We have imported lamps in the garden, they have the stars. Our patio reaches to the front yard, and they have a whole horizon.'

When the little boy had finished, his father was speechless.

His son added, 'Thanks, Dad, for showing me how poor we are!'[7]

This father probably wanted to impress on his son how terrible poverty was, so he would follow in his footsteps and spend his life trying to be rich. His plan backfired. His son saw what has real value and probably learned one of the most important lessons of his life. It's a lesson all of us should learn.

Does Your Activity Energise You or Does It Drain You?

I believe when we are passionate about the right things, the activity required to accomplish those things will energise us. That doesn't mean we don't get tired, but our tiredness is a satisfying, fulfilling type of tired. It is not a tired feeling that leaves us feeling drained and empty. On the other hand, I have discovered first-hand that if my passion is misplaced, I am operating on emotions rather than true passion; by the end of a day or a project, I am exhausted and have a frustrated, unfulfilled feeling. This is one of the ways I have learned to discern whether I am in works of the flesh or if I'm truly following the Holy Spirit. It stands to reason if God leads me to do something, He will give me the needed ability and strength for the task. Where God guides, He provides!

God gives us joy for the journey He has laid out for us.

God gives us joy for the journey He has laid out for us. Jesus said His yoke is light and easy to be borne (see Matthew 11:30). It amazes me to find so many people doing things they seem to think God is leading them to do and yet they are miserable and have no joy. That means they are either going about it the wrong way or they have deceived themselves. It is easy for us to want to do something so strongly we convince ourselves our will is also God's will. If you have no joy in your pursuits, I strongly suggest you get very honest with yourself and locate the problem.

Perhaps you are not in God's will or perhaps you are doing what

God has called you to do, but you're doing it in *dependence upon yourself* rather than God. That is a mistake that many well-meaning people make and it will leave you empty and frustrated, simply because God resists the proud, but gives grace to the humble (see 1 Peter 5:5). The prophet Zechariah said our tasks are completed not by might, nor by power, but by God's Spirit (see Zechariah 4:6). The prophet Isaiah said if we wait upon the Lord, our strength will be renewed and we will be able to run and not get weary (see Isaiah 40:31).

If you have lost joy in your journey, perhaps it is because you have allowed a bad attitude to creep into your soul. Have you stopped being thankful and started complaining? Are you harbouring ill feelings towards anyone? Do you feel you are not appreciated? Any ungodly attitude can block joy and peace.

I am not willing to be joyless any longer. I will change whatever I need to change in order to enjoy my life. I spent a lot of years not enjoying my journey for a variety of reasons, but I finally decided that I would not just exist, but I would enjoy my life and my work. Joy is a fruit of the Holy Spirit. Jesus said He came that we might have and enjoy our lives in abundance (see John 10:10). I encourage you to make the decision to enjoy every aspect of your life and that you will do whatever you need to do to see it happen. It is part of your destiny and definitely part of God's overall purpose for your life.

> Put your energy into something that is deeply fulfilling and bears a lot of good fruit.

Find something you love to do and do it. If you do, you will feel like you never work a day in your life. When you are fulfilling your purpose, your work just seems to fit into your life and your life fits into your work, and your entire mental attitude towards it is healthy. I never count up how many hours a week I work. I just do whatever I need to do in order to fulfil my destiny. Don't let your passion be misplaced.

Put your energy into something that is deeply fulfilling and bears a lot of good fruit.

Stay Devoted to Your Purpose

The twelve apostles were devoted to their purpose; yet in Acts 6 we read about a situation where they found themselves getting too busy with the details of ministry rather than the preaching of God's Word. As in the case of many ministries and organisations today, their problem was a good problem to have, because they were growing in their ministry. The church was adding new members every day, but more people meant more responsibility for taking care of those who needed help, like widows and the elderly. People started complaining that certain people were being overlooked. It might have been very tempting for a few of those disciples to have taken time off from preaching and ministering to get in there, roll their sleeves up, and start distributing food, waiting on tables, and overseeing the work of meeting physical needs. However, they recognised their purpose, their calling, was to preach the Word. But they still had a problem they needed to solve.

> I have learned there are things I am called to do and things I can do.

Whatever your assignment is in life you probably won't be able to do all the parts of it by yourself. People who don't know how to delegate will always end up frustrated and too busy. I have learned there are things I am called to do and things I can do. The apostles were called to preach God's Word. Certainly, they could distribute food and wait on tables, but it would have been a waste of their gifts. They confronted the situation and found a solution. They selected seven men with good character and assigned them the task of taking care of the business. Actually, they assigned them the task of taking care of the 'busyness', while they devoted themselves to prayer and the ministry of the Word.

I could handle a lot of the details of running our ministry, but when I let myself get involved in it too deeply I always experience frustration. I can do it, but it is not what I am called to do. It is not my purpose in life. God has brought others alongside of Dave and me and they are gifted at business, so why not let them do what they are good at and give myself to what I am good at. If I didn't let them help me, they would soon be frustrated because they would feel unfulfilled. Each person has a part and we should work together for God's glory. Find out what your part is and be devoted to it.

> Find out what your part is and be devoted to it.

Know Your Priorities

On one of His many travels, Jesus entered a small village and a woman named Martha received Him into her home (see Luke 10:38). She had a sister named Mary, who seated herself at the Lord's feet and listened intently to His teaching while Martha was overly occupied. She became distracted with the meal and waiting on the guests and making sure everything was just right. As a result, she missed hearing what Jesus was saying, even though that should have been her first priority.

Jesus didn't always stop in and have personal teaching sessions with a room full of people. This was an important event that should have taken precedence over everything at that particular time, but Martha was addicted to being busy. She even got angry at Mary because she wasn't helping her with her busyness. In Martha's mind, she was working hard and trying to keep everything going – and all Mary could do was sit. Martha thought the least her sister could do was get up and help her serve and wait on tables; she didn't realise

Mary was exactly where she needed to be, doing exactly what she needed to do. It was Martha who was in the wrong place doing the wrong things.

Jesus told Martha she was anxious and worried too much.

'Martha, dear Martha, you're fussing far too much and getting yourself worked up over nothing. One thing only is essential, and Mary has chosen it – it's the main course, and won't be taken from her.'
    – LUKE 10:41–42, The Message

Mary chose what would benefit her later. She took advantage of a rare opportunity and realised she could go back to ordinary work after Jesus left.

I wonder, how often does God try to say something to us, or show us something about a situation we are in, but has trouble getting through because we are 'too busy' to stop and listen?

How often in life is a father or mother busy and one of their children tries to communicate something very important to them? Instead of finding a listening ear, a child only hears, 'I'm too busy right now.' If a child hears that too often, they may stop trying to talk altogether, or they may find someone else to talk to who isn't too busy to listen. I realise we cannot let our children disturb us whenever they feel like it, but we probably should be more sensitive to the urgency in their voices at certain times.

> How often does God try to say something to us, or show us something about a situation we are in, but has trouble getting through because we are 'too busy' to stop and listen?

I had to learn not to be so intense about what *I* was doing that I failed to notice important needs around me. Jesus stopped to hear what people had to say. He comforted and helped them.

How busy do you find yourself these days? Did you know you can be addicted to being busy? It's true. Stay busy for long periods of time, like weeks or months, and you'll find it's very hard to take a break when you have a chance to do so. It's hard to relax and give yourself permission to catch your breath, to read a book for enjoyment or to sit down and watch a film on television. Have you ever had a holiday where you were still tired after coming back? Your body wasn't used to a more laid-back lifestyle. Are you so addicted to being busy you don't have time for God or for helping hurting people? If so, this is a good time to change. Thank God, it is never too late to make a fresh start. If we are too busy to spend time with God or to help people, then something needs to change. Our attitudes need to change and our priorities definitely need to adjust.

> God has not called us to 'in-reach', He has called us to 'out-reach'.

If God is our number one passion, then we will have *compassion* for hurting, needy people. Selfish people are passionate about making themselves happy, but their passion is misplaced. God has not called us to 'in-reach', He has called us to 'out-reach'. When we reach out to others to make their lives better and help them see a little more happiness, we are fulfilling a major part of our own purpose in life.

Where Are You Going in Such a Hurry?

Some years ago two Princeton University psychologists, John Darley and Daniel Batson, decided to conduct a study inspired by the biblical story of the Good Samaritan. They met with a group of students, individually, and asked each one to prepare a short, spur-of-the-moment talk on a given biblical theme, and then walk over to a nearby building to present it. Along the way to the presentation, each student ran into a man slumped in an alley, head down, eyes closed, coughing and groaning. The question was, who would stop and help?

Darley and Batson introduced three variables into the experiment, to make its results more meaningful. First, using a questionnaire, they asked each student why they chose to study theology. Did they do it to find a means of personal and spiritual fulfilment? Or were they looking for a practical tool for finding meaning in everyday life? Then they varied the subject of the theme the students were asked to talk about. Some were asked to speak on the relevance of the professional clergy to the religious vocation. Others were given the parable of the Good Samaritan. Finally, the instructions given by the experimenters to each student varied as well. In some of the cases, as he sent the students on their way, the experimenter would look at his watch and say, 'Oh, you're late. They were expecting you a few minutes ago. We'd better get moving.' In other cases he would say, 'It will be a few minutes before they're ready for you, but you might as well head over now.'

If you asked people to predict which students played the Good Samaritan, the answers were highly consistent. They almost all said the students who entered the ministry to help people, and those reminded of the importance of compassion by having just read the parable of the Good Samaritan would be the most likely to stop. The truth is, it did not significantly increase helping behaviour. The only thing that really mattered was whether the student was in a rush. Of the group that had time to spare, 63 per cent stopped. Of the group that was in a rush, only 10 per cent stopped to help.[5]

Everyone is in a rush to get somewhere, and yet few even know where they are going.

Look around you. Your busyness is nothing new. The whole world seems to be in a hurry. Everyone is busy. Like those students, everyone is in a rush to get somewhere, and yet few even know where they are going. I really believe it is very easy to fall into the trap of merely being busy without bearing any good, lasting fruit. We get so caught up with being busy we miss seeing others in need and we possibly can miss our purpose completely. Jesus told His disciples He chose them that they might bear fruit and that their fruit might be lasting and remain (see John 15:16). Are you putting your time into something that will outlive you? If you have children, they will probably outlive you, so be sure you put enough time into them to bring them up properly. Don't let the television or internet bring up your children for you.

> Are you putting your time into something that will outlive you?

Right now I am spending a lot of time writing this book, and I believe it will bear good fruit and outlive me. My hope is people will be reading it long after I am dead. It is exciting to me to think my life can go on and endure for ever through the work I am doing now. We have brought up four children whom we believe will continue our ministry long after we are gone, and hopefully their children after them. I am excited to think I am leaving a legacy. I encourage you to live your life in such a way so that you leave something wonderful behind when your time here is up. Be a person of purpose!

> 'Being busy' is not the answer to fulfilment.

There is an urgency in my spirit to help people understand that just "being busy" is not the answer to fulfilment. It seems to me the world is full of frustrated, unhappy, unfulfilled people. It is also filled with 'busy' people in a hurry. Sometimes I feel busyness is like a curse; we get on a treadmill called 'busy' and cannot seem to find a way to get off.

Be sure you know where you are heading. Is your daily activity helping you reach your goals? Do you even have any goals, or do you just get up every day and get caught in the busyness of everyday life? If you don't have goals, establish some, know precisely what they are, and examine how close you are to fulfilling them. Having purpose and direction will give you an enthusiasm about getting out of bed every day. Developing long-term and short-term goals will help you towards completing your purpose.

Your goals may vary in different seasons of your life, but it's so important you have some. Always have something in front of you to reach towards. Refuse to be the kind of person who is always in a hurry, but who has no idea where they are going. Be passionate but stay focused. Be committed and, most important, be fruitful.

CHAPTER 7

Eight Ways to Waste Your Time

There is a website you can visit called Bored.com. Its whole purpose is to offer 'fun stuff while you are bored'. There are links to all sorts of things – you can read comics online, watch music videos, even tap out a tune on your keyboard's space bar so the computer can work out what song you're 'playing'! You can actually read, of all things, other people's break-up letters. You can play 'Rock, Paper, Scissors' online, just like when you were a child. All of this is provided for people who are bored, and although there is nothing at all wrong with having fun, we must avoid things that just waste time.

A woman I know told me she actually got addicted to playing computer games in the evening. She started playing Solitaire, and before long she was so caught up in this online card game that she was rushing home from work, hurrying to finish dinner – wanting to be alone to play. If we allow it, anything can become addictive.

Have you ever spent an entire evening looking for something decent to watch on television? I have! I have flipped channels using the remote control for two hours or more, watching a little bit of one programme and then another – all the while thinking 'this stuff is stupid'. At the end of the evening, I felt very frustrated because I 'wasted' my time. It is much better to keep things on hand to do that you know you will enjoy on the offchance you have time to fill. Planning ahead will help us not to waste time.

God doesn't want us wasting any of our resources, especially not our time. We should strive to use our time wisely. Do you ever lie in bed at night and feel frustrated because even though you were busy the entire day, you felt you got nothing done? You just wasted time? I have and I don't like the feeling at all. We are created by God for progress, accomplishment and fruit bearing. It is built into our spiritual DNA and without it we feel incomplete.

> We are created by God for progress, accomplishment and fruit bearing.

If we want to be sure we are being fruitful and passionately pursuing our purpose, we might have to take a serious look at our lives and see if there are any ways we are wasting time. It is possible to give yourself to a whole list of things that are not doing you or anyone else any good at all. I have discovered some things that waste time which I will share with you, but you can probably add to my list.

Worry Is a Waste of Time

Sometimes I like to sit in a rocking chair and teach on worry. I do it to make the point that, like the rocking chair, worry keeps us busy, but it gets us nowhere. I frequently run into people when I am out who tell me how much the 'rocking chair' example helped them.

Jesus told us not to worry because it does no good (see Matthew 6:34). There are many things in life we cannot do anything about, but God can. Worrying does not move the hand of God, but faith does. Exchange worry for trusting God and you will see progress. The next time you are tempted to worry, just remind yourself it won't do you or anyone else any good. After all, it is hard to be passionate about your purpose and worry. Worry slows down your drive and puts roadblocks up in front of your determination. Worry is a total waste of time.

> Worry slows down your drive and puts roadblocks up in front of your determination.

Be committed to not wasting time. Use the time you would spend worrying and meditate on God's promise to help you. If you know how to worry, then you also know how to meditate. Worry is rolling the same thing over and over in your mind, and so is meditation. Take one of God's promises, like Joshua 1:9 (NIV), and mutter it over and over under your breath: *Be strong and courageous. Do not be terrified; do not be discouraged, for the Lord your God will be with you wherever you go.* Roll it over several times in your mind. You will find hope rising in your heart. Your joy will return, and peace will reign.

You might feel you are facing an impossible situation, so you keep worrying about what you should do to fix it. Well, the first thing to realise is that if it really is impossible, there is nothing you can do anyway, so why worry about it? The next thing to realise is that what is impossible with man is possible with God (see Luke 18:27). God made everything we see out of nothing, so taking care of our problems is no problem for Him.

> If it really is impossible, there is nothing you can do anyway, so why worry about it?

Do what you can do and let God do what you cannot do. The Bible says we are to do what the crisis demands and then stand firmly in our place (see Ephesians 6:13). Our place is 'in Christ' trusting Him to make a way where there seems to be no way.

I was always more inclined to worry while my husband was easily able to cast off his care and trust God. I watched Dave enjoy his life while I was miserable. I wasted my time and he used his wisely. Whatever you are going through right now will eventually pass. It will be taken care of, so you may as well enjoy your life in the meantime.

Mary Hemingway said, 'Worry a little bit every day and in a lifetime you will lose a couple of years. If something is wrong, fix it if you can. But train yourself not to worry. Worry never fixes anything.'[1]

What should we do when God seems to be sleeping and we are having a problem?

Jesus and His disciples were in a boat crossing over to the other side of the lake when a furious storm arose and the waves were crashing into the boat, threatening to capsize and drown them all. While Jesus slept soundly in the stern of the boat, the disciples were worrying frantically and unable to understand how Jesus could sleep when they were in such danger. What should we do when God seems to be sleeping and we are having a problem? After He woke up, Jesus rebuked His disciples for being so fearful, timid and having no faith. He did stop the storm, and they did arrive on the other side just as He said they would. However, while Jesus rested, the disciples wasted the trip worrying (see Mark 4:35–41).

Whatever goals you are trying to reach in life, you will encounter many storms threatening to stop you. You can make yourself miserable with worry or you can trust God. You are the only one who can make the choice, so I suggest you seriously consider which way you want to live.

One day in March 1976, I was listening to the first recorded sermon I ever heard. I was making my bed and listening to a message called 'Cross Over to the Other Side'. The message was about trusting God and enjoying the journey. That was something I had never done in life and I was amazed to learn it was even an option. I had spent my life trying to take care of myself and fix all of my own problems. I was tired, weary and worn out emotionally and mentally. I was ready for a change and the scriptures in Mark 4 gave me the hope I needed to be willing to try a new way of living.

I was a worrier. It was my first response to any problem. I would love to be able to say I was able to immediately stop worrying and trust God, but that didn't happen. It took discipline and dedication to learn new ways of approaching problems instead of worrying. However, little by little, I saw first-hand the faithfulness of God and realised if I stepped out on His promises, He would always do what needed to be done. He might not always do it the way I thought it should be done, but He would do it. If you want to get out of the rocking chair of worry, begin by looking up all the scriptures in the Bible on worry and anxiety. Read them over and over and let faith rise up in your heart. Faith comes by hearing the Word of God.

> Faith comes by hearing the Word of God.

Next I recommend you use your faith on something small to start. Maybe you worry when you're out driving in torrential rain. Say a prayer before you put the car in gear and tell God you're exchanging your fear of driving in the rain for faith that He will take care of you. Don't try to tackle something really major your first time around. As you start erasing the small worries from your life, you will also experience the faithfulness of God, and it will become easier for you to trust God in every area of life, including the major ones.

I recently heard the story of a minister who was enjoying a film while flying somewhere on his private plane. Suddenly, the windshield on the plane cracked. The minister put the film on pause, prayed a prayer of protection for the plane and all those on board, and then announced he was going to finish watching his film because there was nothing more he could do.

The most important thing to remember when a problem comes up is that worry is useless. Don't waste your time doing it.

Guilt Is a Waste of Time

We are going to make mistakes and, to be honest, if we wanted to, we could waste every day of our lives feeling guilty about yesterday. But we don't have to, because Jesus bore our sins on the cross. He paid for them so we might live free from the tyranny of them. The Bible states He bore our iniquities and the guilt (see Isaiah 53:11). Feeling guilty about past mistakes won't undo them. You cannot do anything about your past, but you can do a lot about your future – and a lot of that has to do with your attitude.

Here's what Charles Swindoll has to say about attitude:

> The longer I live, the more I realize the impact of attitude on life. Attitude, to me, is more important than facts. It is more important than the past, than education, than money, than circumstances, than failures, than successes, than what other people think, say, or do. It is more important than appearance, giftedness, or skill. It will make or break a company . . . a church . . . a home. The remarkable thing is we have a choice every day regarding the attitude we will embrace for that day.
>
> We cannot change our past . . . we cannot change the fact that people will act in a certain way. We cannot change the inevitable. The only thing we can do is play on the one string we have, and that is our attitude. I am convinced that life is 10% what happens to me, and 90% how I react to it. And so it is with you. We are in charge of our attitudes.[2]

Do you feel obligated to feel guilty when you make mistakes? If so, you need a new attitude.

Perhaps you need a new attitude towards guilt, and a new way of looking at it. There was a time in my life when I did. Do you feel obligated to feel guilty when you make mistakes? If so, you need a new attitude. Our attitude is what feeds our feelings. Many people say they cannot help feeling guilty. They testify that no matter how hard they try not to feel guilty, they still do. Perhaps they have never changed their attitude and thoughts about their mistakes.

I spent most of my life feeling guilty about something. As soon as one thing was over, something new came along. I actually felt guilty for so long that I didn't feel right if I didn't feel wrong. My cycle of guilt started early in my childhood as a result of sexual child abuse. I believed the devil's lie that it was my fault, and from that point on everything that went wrong was my fault, and I constantly lived in the agony of guilt. It might have been guilt from my childhood or guilt from the previous day, but I constantly lived my life under the cloud of guilt and condemnation.

> Human beings make mistakes; this is precisely why we need a Saviour.

I finally reached a place where I was not willing to live that way any longer and I declared war on living in the past, which is what guilt is. God's mercy is new every day and when we don't use it, it is wasted, as far as we are concerned. The Bible would not teach us through countless verses of Scripture about the mercy of God if we were not going to make mistakes. Human beings make mistakes; this is precisely why we need a Saviour. We cannot measure up to God's standard of holiness, so Jesus did it for us. As long as we look to Him for our salvation, God views us as holy and in right standing with Him (see 2 Corinthians 5:21).

If you are ready for a change in this area, why not make a decision to leave the city of regret? Here is a story by Larry Harp to help you understand you are not helpless when it comes to guilt; you can do something about it.

leaving the city of regret

I had not really planned on taking a trip this time of year, and yet I found myself packing rather hurriedly. This trip was going to be unpleasant and I knew in advance that no real good would come of it. I'm talking about my annual 'Guilt Trip'.

I got tickets to fly there on WISH I HAD airlines. It was an extremely short flight. I got my baggage, which I could not check. I chose to carry it myself all the way. It was weighted down with a thousand memories of what might have been. No one greeted me as I entered the terminal to the Regret City International Airport. I say international because people from all over the world come to this dismal town.

As I checked into the Last Resort Hotel, I noticed that they would be hosting the year's most important event, the Annual Pity Party. I wasn't going to miss that great social occasion. Many of the town's leading citizens would be there.

First, there would be the Done family – you know, Should Have Done, Would Have Done, and Could Have Done. Then came the I Had family. You probably know ole Wish I Had and his clan. Of course, the Opportunities would be present, Missed and Lost.

The biggest family would be the Yesterdays. There are far too many of them to count, but each one would have a very sad story to share.

Then Shattered Dreams would surely make an appearance. And It's Their Fault would regale us with stories (excuses) about how things had failed in his life. Each story would be loudly applauded by Don't Blame Me and I Couldn't Help It.

Well, to make a long story short, I went to this depressing party knowing that there would be no real benefit in doing so. And, as usual, I became very depressed. But as I thought about all of the stories of failures brought back from the past, it occurred to me that the remainder of this trip and subsequent 'pity parties' could be cancelled by ME! I started to truly realise that I did not have to be there. I didn't have to be depressed. One thing kept going through my mind, I CAN'T CHANGE YESTERDAY, BUT I DO HAVE THE POWER TO MAKE TODAY A WONDERFUL DAY. I can be happy, joyous, fulfilled, encouraged, as well as encouraging.

Knowing this, I left the City of Regret immediately and left no forwarding address. Am I sorry for mistakes I've made in the past? Yes! But there is no physical way to undo them.

So, if you're planning a trip back to the City of Regret, please cancel all your reservations now. Instead, take a trip to Starting Again. I liked it so much that I have now taken up permanent residence there. My neighbours, the I Forgive Myselfs and the New Starts, are very helpful. By the way, you don't have to carry around heavy baggage, because the load is lifted from your shoulders upon arrival. God bless you in finding this great town. If you can find it – it's in your own heart – please look me up. I live on I CAN DO IT street.[3]

I overcame guilt and you can also. There are many scriptures God used to help me overcome feelings of guilt, but one in particular is as follows:

My little children, I write you these things so that you may not violate God's law *and* sin. But if anyone should sin, we have an Advocate (One Who will intercede for us) with the Father – [it is] Jesus Christ [the all] righteous [upright, just, Who conforms to the Father's will in every purpose, thought, and action].
  – 1 JOHN 2:1

The entire Bible is written for our instruction that we might live holy lives and not sin. Every day, our goal and purpose should be to live righteous lives that glorify God. But if we do sin, we must realise Jesus came for us and has already paid for every mistake we would ever make. If we live in the guilt of the past, we will have no energy to live today for God's glory. Guilt zaps all of your strength and does no good at all.

Guilt zaps all of your strength and does no good at all.

Guilt is anger directed at you alone for something you did or did not do. Jesus bore the penalty for our sins and His sacrifice was complete and perfect. No other sacrifice is ever needed. His was one sacrifice good for all time. He made it once and for all (see Hebrews 10:10–12). We don't need to add our sacrifice of guilt to the sacrifice He already gave of His life. I promise you – He did a thorough job and does not need our help!

Our position should be one of admitting our sins and repenting of them, which means being willing to turn from them to God and righteousness. We should be sorry for our sins and there is even a time we can be remorseful and dwell on them. But the time of mourning should not last past true repentance. If it does, we are basically saying by our actions that even though we have repented, our sin still has power over us and we must continue feeling guilty about it.

The Bible says in Romans 6 we are dead to sin and the power of it has been removed. Being dead to sin simply means the renewed part of you (your born-again spirit) does not want to sin. The new creature part of you hates sin, even though your flesh still has the sin principle in it and frequently gets the best of you. *The flesh wars against the spirit* (see Galatians 5:17). *The Spirit is willing, but the flesh is weak* (see Matthew 26:41). *Who can set us free from this body of death,* the Apostle Paul asked. *Jesus Christ is the only one!* (See Romans 7:24–25.)

Realising Jesus is the only one who can set us free helps us a bit more in our understanding of the next way we can waste time without sometimes even being aware that we do it.

Trying to Change What Only God Can Change Is a Waste of Time

Trying to change something you cannot control is a total waste of time! There is an old saying that the definition of insanity is doing the same thing over and over, expecting different results. Isn't that how we approach life sometimes? We know that ultimately it is up to God to work something out; yet we continue struggling, trying to do something that only God can do. We let something we've mentioned already, works of the flesh, take priority. Instead, we should remember we are partners with God and as such we do have responsibilities, but if we get mixed up and spend our time trying to do what only God can do, we will be frustrated because none of our efforts will produce any good fruit.

For example, only God can change a person's heart. We can pray for people, but only God can change them. We can't even change ourselves. We can try to behave better and have some success. We can discipline ourselves and learn better ways to respond to people and situations, but when it comes to genuine heart change, only God can do that. He is the only one who can reach down inside a person to heal what needs to be healed and change what needs to change.

> When it comes to genuine heart change, only God can do that.

Are you struggling with yourself? If so, turn your efforts towards prayer and you will begin to see amazing results. God responds to faith-filled prayer, not works of the flesh.

We all have things wrong with us that need to change, and it's usually a fairly long list. God changes us into His own image as we consistently study His Word. God's Word has innate power and works amazing things in our hearts.

Go to God totally dependent upon Him and tell Him you realise you cannot change yourself or anyone else for that matter. Ask Him to change you. Be excited and enthusiastic about the changes you do see, not depressed and discouraged about the things still to be done. Celebrate each victory God gives you. Think about how far you have come, not just how far you have to go.

> Think about how far you have come, not just how far you
> have to go.

God has begun a good work in you and He will finish it (see Philippians 1:6). He is the Author and the Finisher of our faith (Hebrews 12:2). He has called us to be a wholly sanctified body, soul and spirit and He will do it. He will fulfil His call in your life as you lean and rely on Him (see 1 Thessalonians 5:22–24). He will complete you and make you what you ought to be (see 1 Peter 5:10). You cannot reach perfection by dependence upon the flesh (see Galatians 3:3).

> God will never help you be anyone other than yourself.

I wasted many years of my life struggling with my personality. I didn't like myself and wanted to be someone other than who I was. Notice I said I *wasted* many years. I am asking you to learn from my mistakes and do things God's way, not man's way. God will never help you be anyone other than yourself.

Those years were frustrating and discouraging because I always felt like a failure. I always told God how hard I was trying, but I really needed to trade my trying for trusting Him. Once I did that, He started changing me, and He has done so much in me that I hardly recognise myself from those early days.

Another big waste of time occurs when we try to change other people. Trying to fix someone who does not want to be fixed is useless. I have spent years trying to help different people, only to have them keep doing things that are destroying them. I finally realised Satan was using them to drain me of energy I needed to help people who really wanted help.

People won't change unless they want to and are willing to turn to God for His help. We can point out people's flaws all day and it will only make them angry or insecure. Once again we should put our energy into praying and let God work. When we pray, it opens the door for God to work and then He gets the glory when change does occur.

Our children can be taught the way God wants them to live, but they can't be forced by us. Just like with anyone, they must ultimately make the choice. Now the Bible says if we train them right that when they are old, they will not depart from it (see Proverbs 22:6). Hopefully, they will never depart from doing what is right, but we have God's promise that even if they do, that eventually they will return to their righteous roots.

I wasted a lot of time trying to make my children be what I thought they should be. One of them was messy and I wanted her to be neat and tidy. Another one wanted to control everything and I wanted him to calm down and be easier to get along with. Another one just wanted to have a good time. He turned everything into a party and was not very concerned about school and other responsibilities. The fourth one was such a perfectionist and so detailed that she just about drove me crazy. All of my efforts to change them only frustrated me and them. Thank God I finally learned God creates each of us with a special purpose in mind. We are His clay and He makes of us what He wants us to be.

> Form a habit of finding the good in people, not their flaws.

In our pride we want everyone to be like us or be as we think they should be. God wants us to pray His will be done. He wants us to enjoy the people He has put into our lives, not judge and criticise them. Form a habit of finding the good in people, not their flaws. We all have our own little load of oppressive faults and we are called to be long-suffering and to forbear with others. That literally means we will have to put up with some stuff we don't like in order to have relationships that last and edify.

However, we must also remember other people have to overlook some of our faults as well. That is the only way we can have peaceful relationships. We must all practise being adaptable.

I am happy to say all my children and I made it through the rough years and we have great relationships now. I made a lot of mistakes, but God is our healer. They all work for the ministry and are extremely valuable to us. Some of the things I once saw as weaknesses needing to be changed, actually turned out to be strengths Dave and I didn't have, but needed. They do things in the ministry we could not do and they have made it better.

Let God be God in your life.

Let God be God in your life. Don't spend the energy you need for passion in life on wasted time trying to do what only He can do.

i dare you

Spend Your Time Wisely

One of the best ways we can know how much time we're wasting, and how much of our time we're using wisely, is to track what we're doing. For one day, write down everything you do. Take a little notebook with you wherever you go, and from the time you wake up till you return to bed, keep a record. If you spend an hour in front of the computer 'browsing', write that down. If you spend five minutes praying, write that down too. Get a call from a friend? Write down how much time you spent and what you talked about.

The next day, take another sheet of paper out and divide it into two columns with one side marked 'wise investment' and the other 'wasted time'. Then pull out your day's record and start putting each use of time under the appropriate column. After you're all done, take a look at how you did. Are you wisely spending your time doing things to honour God and fulfil your purpose? Or are you wasting a lot of it on meaningless things? Keep in mind it's OK to relax if it does the job of restoring and recharging yourself. Be honest in your evaluation and think about how you can move more from the 'wasted time' pile to the 'wise investment' side.

Complaining Is a Waste of Time

Most of us have a tendency to complain each time something displeases or upsets us. Actually I think it would be a great miracle of God if we could get through one complete day without complaining about anything or murmuring in our hearts.

Complaining is a total waste of time and nothing positive ever comes from it. It does, however, create a negative atmosphere where the devil finds opportunity to work. I actually believe there is biblical proof that grumbling, fault-finding and complaining open a door for the devil to bring destruction into our lives.

> Grumbling, fault-finding and complaining open a door for the devil to bring destruction into our lives.

Perhaps a lot of our problems are a result of us complaining when we should have been praising or thanking God. Complaining is certainly not God's will or purpose for His people. The whole world seems to be complaining about something, but each of us can make the decision to set a different and more positive example.

If you cannot change something, then change the way you think about it, but don't complain about it.

Here are some suggestions you might find helpful:

- We can complain about what we cannot do, or we can do what we can do.
- We can complain about the conditions in society and wish someone would do something about them, or we can pray.
- We can complain about what we don't have, or we can be thankful for what we do have.
- We can find fault with our friends and family, or we can thank God we are not completely alone in life.
- We can complain about the job we have, or we can thank God we have one.
- We can complain about traffic, or we can thank God we have a car when most of the world still walks everywhere they go.
- We can complain about the weather, or we can thank God we are healthy enough to go outside.

The next time you are tempted to complain, please remember it does no good at all. It is a complete waste of time and says loud and clear to God you are not at all satisfied with the way He is taking care of you. If you begin to thank God from where you are, He will help you get where you want to be.

How thankful you are in the valleys of life helps to determine

> If you begin to thank God from where you are, He will help you get where you want to be.

how fast you will make it to the mountaintops. Don't make the mistake of thinking the grass is always greener on the other side. If you were on the other side, you would find the grass there must be mowed too.

When you are tempted to murmur and complain about your life, just remember there is someone in the world who would love to exchange their problems for yours. There is always someone worse off than you.

The Bible tells us to be thankful in all things because it is God's will for those of us who are in Christ Jesus (see 1 Thessalonians 5:18).

I recently read a story about a man who went from being healthy one day to disabled the next due to a brain tumour. He had the tumour surgically removed, but it left him unable to do many of the things he was previously able to do.

The first thing he was tempted to do was have a pity party, but then he noticed nobody was coming but him. He decided another approach would be better. He decided instead of complaining about his *dis*-ability he would celebrate his *differ*-ability. He learned to do things in a different way than he had before. Because of going to rehab regularly, he met new people he really enjoyed meeting. He wasn't able to move as fast as he once could, so he started noticing things like the sunshine, roses and stars.

> If you have something in your life you would consider to be a disability, why not call it your differ-ability and make it an opportunity to explore a whole new world.

He also learned humility. Where he once was very self-sufficient, refusing to ask for help or depend on anyone, now he had to let others help. He discovered their love gave him hope to press on. If you have something in your life you would consider to be a disability, why not call it your differ-ability and make it an opportunity to explore a whole new world. Remember – complaining won't change it anyway!

Anger Is a Waste of Time

In an article in *Healthy Living Magazine,* Joan Lunden said, 'Holding on to anger, resentment and hurt only gives you tense muscles, a headache and a sore jaw from clenching your teeth. Forgiveness gives you back the laughter and the lightness in your life.'[4]

I would actually go a little bit further from what she said and add that refusing to be angry gives you back your life. I teach people to 'forgive and live again'.

You see, being angry and bitter doesn't hurt your enemies but it does hurt you. They are probably out having a good time while you're sitting home upset.

The world is becoming filled with more and more angry people all the time. Most of mankind operates on a short fuse. Patience and long-suffering are character traits we don't see very often any more, but we need to.

Jesus gave us the perfect solution to anger. He said to forgive those who hurt, abuse or misuse you. He said not to take offence (see Luke 17:4). Offence will be offered frequently, but we don't have to take it. I would not take poison if someone offered it to me, and that is exactly what offence is. It is poison to our minds, emotions, personalities, attitudes and spiritual lives. I recently heard someone say that anger and unforgiveness are like acid that eats away the container it is in.

Anger is an emotion that will surface from time to time, but Jesus said not to let the sun go down on our anger. The longer we keep anger, the more opportunity it has to take root in our lives and choke the life out of us. You might be angry at God, yourself or someone else, but it is time to give it up. Anger is useless. It doesn't change anything except you, and not for the better. Anger is one letter short of danger.

Anger is one letter short of danger.

God has promised to be our Vindicator. He brings justice into our lives and makes wrong things right if we trust Him. I was a victim of incest and for many years I was very angry. I was so filled with anger it came out of me in situations and towards people who had absolutely nothing to do with the pain of my past. I felt I was owed something and I was trying to collect from the whole world.

I finally realised nobody could pay me back for what my abuser took from me. That is, nobody but God. He has promised to give us a double recompense for our former trouble, and I am a living testimony of the faithfulness of God.

> Instead of being angry, go and find people you can be good to.

Don't spend your life trying to collect past debts from people who have no ability to pay. Give up anger and start overcoming evil with good (see Romans 12:21). Instead of being angry, go and find people you can be good to. Find someone else who is hurting and help to replace their frowns or worries with smiles and hope.

A person who cannot control the emotion of anger is like a broken-down city without walls to protect itself from its enemies. Paul told the Corinthians they should forgive in order to keep Satan from getting an advantage over them. He told the Ephesians if they stayed angry, it would open a door for the devil and give him opportunity.

I encourage you to walk in wisdom. Don't let the negative emotion of anger control your life. Make a decision right now not to waste any more of your time being angry. If you do, I believe it will open a door for God's blessings to flow into your life in a new way.

Fear Is a Waste of Time

Fear can actually steal your destiny. Anyone who lives in fear will never fulfil God's purpose for their lives. Fear hinders progress and that is exactly why the devil uses it as his favourite weapon against people. The devil does not want you to go forward. If you do decide to go forward, you will have to confront fear, and fear will never evaporate or disappear. It must be confronted.

Courage is fear that has said its prayers and decided to go forward anyway.

Courage is fear that has said its prayers and decided to go forward anyway. Fear is a feeling and should never be allowed to control someone's life. From now on, when you feel fear, just make the decision you are going to keep pressing forward. Decide to do whatever you want or need to do even if you have to 'do it afraid'.

God has not given us a spirit of fear. He gives us faith and expects us to use it. Faith will overcome fear because it is more powerful than fear. I don't believe any great work has ever been accomplished without someone needing to face fear and do whatever needs to be done anyway. Fear robs the mind of its reason and ability to help us make decisions. When fear comes in, it seems that common sense and reason go out of the window. Our minds sort of go wild. We imagine all kinds of bad things, and the more we see those awful images on the picture screen of our minds, the more paralysed we become.

When trouble comes, the natural response is to be afraid. But after feeling fear, our next response should be to seek God. It's sad to say, but not nearly enough people have trained themselves to take that next step. They allow fear to paralyse them, and the devil steps in and steals God's purpose for their lives. If we would seek God when we are afraid, we would hear Him say what He said to the Israelites: *Fear not for I am with you. I will never leave you nor forsake you. This battle is not yours but God's. Fear not, there is nothing to fear.*

Don't make the mistake of listening to what the world, the devil, and circumstances have to say without also listening to what God has to say. Joseph found himself in dire circumstances, but God was with him! He found favour everywhere he went and prospered in everything he laid his hand to. He had trouble, but he also had God!

David had to face the giant Goliath because the rest of the soldiers were afraid to do it. He took one look at Goliath and ran quickly to the battle line. Sometimes we stare at our problems too much. The Bible says we should look away from all that will distract unto Jesus who is the Author and Finisher of our faith (see Hebrews 12:2).

Fear torments and does no good at all. It does block our ability to be passionate and enthusiastic about life. It holds us back and it prevents us from getting closer to achieving our purpose. There is not one positive thing about fear, so I encourage you to stop wasting your time being afraid of things that have not even happened yet. Believe that no matter what happens in your life, God is greater than any problem you will ever have. Fear is expecting something bad to happen, but God wants us to aggressively expect good things to take place in our lives every day.

> God is greater than any problem you will ever have.

Blame Is a Waste of Time

Are you trapped in playing the blame game? If so, perhaps you need to stop it and start taking responsibility. I am sure your first thought after reading that comment may have been, 'Joyce, it is not my fault.' When I said that to God, He told me what happened to me was not my fault, but I couldn't use it as an excuse to stay miserable and waste my life. I wasn't responsible for the abuse in my life, but I did have to take responsibility for how I responded to it.

I blamed a lot of people, and in reality most of them should have taken their responsibility and helped me, but they didn't. Each one of them had their reasons for not helping, and now some of them spend their days blaming themselves for not doing what they should have done. That does no good either.

As humans, we seem to be determined to waste our time on things that never fix the problem. We blame each other, we blame ourselves, and we even blame God. Instead of blaming, we need to let go of the past and press into the future. Actually, we need to learn from the past and let it tutor us for the future. God doesn't want us to spend our days feeling guilty; He wants us to be responsible.

> We need to learn from the past and let it tutor us for the future.

After thirty years, my abuser finally took responsibility and apologised to me. By then I didn't really need his apology, but he needed to apologise for his own sake. I moved on; now he was free to do the same thing. Facing hard issues like this one enables us to move past them, because anything we refuse to deal with has power over us. Blaming is unhealthy emotionally, mentally and spiritually. Certainly, we can try to evade issues, but deep down inside we feel the weight of them. Many people never experience peace or joy because of unresolved issues in their lives.

Don't be the kind of person who always has to find someone to blame for everything that goes wrong. If you're late for work, do you blame traffic, the kids, the telephone that rang as you were going out the door, or any number of other things? If you don't manage your money well, do you blame your employer by accusing him of not paying you enough? If your life is confusing and out of order, do you simply blame the busy schedule you have, forgetting you are the one who made it?

> Be responsible! Be bold!

The first step towards change is the decision to take responsibility to do what needs to be done and to stop blaming. It is a new day, and God wants us to approach life in a new way. Be responsible! Be bold!

Believe with God's help, you can do whatever you need to do in life. Realise blaming others, yourself or God is fruitless. It is vain and useless and it only traps you in all kinds of negative emotions and prevents you from making progress.

Comparisons Are a Waste of Time

Does this sound like you?

I am really content – until I start looking through the fifty mail-order catalogues that arrive at my home each month.

I liked my car – until I saw the new Lexus.

I am satisfied with my clothes – until I stroll through the stores in the high street.

I love our home – until I think of what it would be like to own a bigger home with a sea view.

I am satisfied with every area of my life – until I start comparing it with someone else's life.

I feel like I have enough of everything – until I see someone who has more.[5]

Isn't it always tempting to compare what you have to what someone else has? My advice is to stop looking to the side and worrying about others and start concentrating on what's in front of you – God's incredible individual plan for each of us! When Peter was in prison, God sent angels to shake the place until the doors flew open and Peter walked out. John the Baptist was in prison and he was beheaded. Why, God, why? Only God knows and He isn't telling. Trust always requires that we have some unanswered questions in our lives.

When John was in prison, he sent a message to ask Jesus if He was

> Start concentrating on what's in front of you – God's incredible individual plan.

the One to come, or if he should look for another. Jesus told him to examine the works He was doing, to notice the blind seeing, the deaf hearing, and the lame walking. Jesus also said something else that is extremely important. He said, 'Blessed (happy, fortunate and to be envied) is he who takes no offense at Me and finds no cause for stumbling in or through Me . . .' (Matthew 11:6).

It appears John was wondering why he was sitting in prison if Jesus was the real Messiah he was waiting for. After all, John had been faithful, and he gave up everything to serve God. I think John was wondering how Jesus could leave him in a bad situation. When John asked Jesus if He was really the Messiah, Jesus in essence told him not to be offended because of his circumstances.

We all have times when we wonder why God doesn't deliver us from a difficult situation or why He has not done something we have asked Him to do. We also have a tendency to look at someone else we know who definitely seems to have life easier than we do and the comparisons begin. Don't waste your time comparing, because it only leads to jealousy, envy, resentment and confusion and it's one more distraction Satan uses to keep you off course.

Embrace the unknown as well as you embrace the known.

Trust God that He has a good plan for you. Embrace the unknown as well as you embrace the known because you can be confident God is in control. He may take you on a route you would not choose, but He has a reason.

CHAPTER 8

Dream Big Dreams

When we talk about embracing our purpose passionately, it is natural to talk about our dreams, because dreams help to stir our passion just as passion helps to stir our dreams. It's important to think big when it comes to dreams for our future. Too many of us don't think big enough, but I believe little thinkers will live little lives. People who cannot conceive of anything beyond what they can see with their natural eyes miss out on the best God has planned for them. I recommend you think big thoughts, dream big dreams and make big plans. We serve a big God who is able to do exceedingly, abundantly, above and beyond all we could ever hope, ask or think (see Ephesians 3:20).

A hope, vision, dream or plan is like a seed. It is a small thing leading to something big. Everything starts with a seed. We can never have a harvest without a seed and it's the same way with our dreams. If you have no positive hopes or dreams for the future, you will either stay where you are or begin to slide backwards. Your current condition could get worse, unless you think creatively and aggressively. Don't wait for some great idea to fall into your mind; instead, search for one. Pray for creative ideas, think about what you would like to do, and then believe you can do it.

> Pray for creative ideas, think about what you would like to do, and then believe you can do it.

Some people believe everything in life is a matter of chance. There is nothing they can do about anything except to wait for what's going to happen to happen and then they accept it. It is true we will have to accept some things we cannot do anything about, but many things can be changed if we pray and do our part. Many dreams can be realised if we only apply the passion and the persistence to realise them.

Creating Opportunity

What does it mean to create opportunity for yourself? Take a lesson with the following from entrepreneur and motivational speaker Jim Rohn:

I used to say, 'I'm just not a very creative person', but I don't say

be enterprising

An enterprising person is one who comes across a pile of scrap metal and sees the making of a wonderful sculpture. An enterprising person is one who drives through an old decrepit part of town and sees a new housing development. An enterprising person is one who sees opportunity in all areas of life.

To be enterprising is to keep your eyes open and your mind active. It's to be skilled enough, confident enough, creative enough and disciplined enough to seize opportunities that present themselves . . . regardless of the economy.

A person with an enterprising attitude says, 'Find out what you can before action is taken.' Do your homework. Do the research. Be prepared. Be resourceful. Do all you can in preparation of what's to come.

Enterprising people always see the future in the present. Enterprising people always find a way to take advantage of a situation, not be burdened by it. And enterprising people aren't lazy. They don't wait for opportunities to come to them; they go after the

opportunities. Enterprise means always finding a way to keep yourself actively working towards your ambition.

Enterprise is two things. The first is creativity. You need creativity to see what's out there and to shape it to your advantage. You need creativity to look at the world a little differently. You need creativity to take a different approach, to be different.

What goes hand in hand with the creativity of enterprise is the second requirement: the courage to be creative. You need courage to see things differently, courage to go against the crowd, courage to take a different approach, courage to stand alone if you have to, courage to choose activity over inactivity.

And lastly, being enterprising doesn't just relate to the ability to make money. Being enterprising also means feeling good enough about yourself, having enough self-worth to want to seek advantages and opportunities that will make a difference in your future. And by doing so, you will increase your confidence, your courage, your creativity and your self-worth – your enterprising nature.[1]

that any more. Now I pray for God to give me creative ideas and I admit that I am creative. Have a positive attitude about yourself and your abilities. Just because you have never been a certain way in the past does not mean you can't be that way in the future.

On one of my trips to India, I went to a remote area to visit a slum. Some 200,000 people lived in this slum and 50,000 of them were children. As I drove through the area, I was appalled at the conditions the people lived in. Every day they sat passively in the midst of dirt, mud and rubbish. A typical house was four sticks in the ground with cardboard or other pieces of material, like rags and metal, propped together to make a roof. Children wandered about with no clothes or very dirty ones. Men sat in groups doing nothing, while women held their babies and stirred whatever was in their pots. It was a pitiful sight. I still shake my head in disbelief when I remember my visit.

It only takes one person with a dream and vision for improvement to light a spark for others and provoke great change. On the surface it appears they have nothing to work with, but an enterprising person would find something. I did see a few people who put together makeshift businesses. One woman had a sewing machine and a homemade sign advertising her sewing business. Another woman had an ironing board and an iron and was obviously offering her services to do laundry. I was proud of them – at least they were trying to do something.

I often think, when I go to those types of places, how much better

> It only takes one person with a dream and vision for improvement to light a spark for others.

things would be if the people would just band together and get rid of the rubbish. If there was nothing else they could do, with a minimum amount of effort they could keep their surroundings clean.

We had a small feeding programme that day for fifty of the children, and as I sat in the mud with them, scooping out their rice and lentil soup, I asked myself what I could do to help the other 49,950 children who were not there that day. That's when I had the thought I would like someday to feed 1 million children a day in various parts of the world. I spoke this new dream out loud to some of our team and their eyes filled with tears. Three of us immediately committed several hundred dollars a month to start feeding more children right away. What we gave didn't even make a small dent in the 1 million-child goal, but at least we were doing something. We were making a difference in the lives of at least some of those children, and to them it mattered a great deal and made a huge difference to them.

I will continue pressing towards the fulfilment of that vision as long as I am alive. I hope and pray to see it, but even if I don't, I am passionate about attempting to do something besides just shake my head and say, 'Isn't that a shame!'

I saw a mess and decided to create an opportunity for myself and other people who would join us over the years to make a difference. You can do the same. It simply starts with a dream.

Passivity

The people in villages like the one in India are people who have grown up in poverty of such magnitude they don't even know how to think about getting out of it. They need to be taught how to think aggressively and take aggressive action.

Passivity is the opposite of activity and it is very dangerous. A

> The devil can easily manipulate a passive person.

passive person would like to see something good happen and they commit to sitting where they are and waiting to see if it does. The devil can easily manipulate a passive person. He oppresses their will until they are unable to make any decisions or take any action without being moved by an outside force.

God, however, wants to motivate us from the inside. He gives creative ideas, big dreams and an aggressive, active attitude. God's only gear is forward. He wants us to be decisive, energised by His Spirit and enthusiastic about life. People who have allowed themselves to become passive have a type of deadness inside them that is frightening. Their get-up-and-go has got up and gone!

Passivity is not always, but can be accompanied by depression, discouragement, self-pity, blame, excuses and laziness. Once passivity has taken hold of a person, it takes a lot of determination to break free from it.

My husband, Dave, once had a problem with passivity. He was

not depressed or discouraged, but he wasn't taking care of his responsibilities.

Dave was in the army for three years and during those years his job was mainly to play baseball and basketball to entertain the troops. He did do technical training in air conditioning, heating, refrigeration, etc. for part of the time, but most of the time he played sports. After practising on the days they did not have regular games, he was free to spend the rest of the day on the beach or doing whatever he wanted to do. He has shared that during those three years of his life he didn't have to make many decisions. He was told when to eat, what to wear, and where to go. By the time he got out of the army, he had formed bad habits not easily broken.

Dave and I got married in 1967, and although he went to work every day and earned a living for us, he did not do much beyond that except to play sports and watch sports. I became very frustrated, and although he did make some effort to change, he recalls it was very difficult simply because he had no feelings to support those efforts. He had been dormant in so many areas, for so long, that his will to do things literally became passive.

Through reading a book by Watchman Nee, Dave learned about the dangers of passivity and recognised he had a problem. He has shared many times how difficult it was at first to begin doing things he knew he should do, but had no desire to do. However, with persistence and help from God, little by little he broke free.

Dave loves to share about the dangers of passivity with other people because he knows first-hand just how deceptive it is and how the devil uses it to steal people's passion and purpose, as well as their dreams.

Several months after my trip to India, I also travelled to Rwanda in Africa. Between April and June 1994, the country of Rwanda experienced a horrific genocide, where almost 1 million people were brutally slaughtered. This tragedy left them and their nation devastated. Their economy was destroyed, along with their homes, businesses and the countryside itself.

When I visited there in April 2006, I was pleasantly surprised to find the nation very clean and well kept. Although they have many problems to overcome, they have started in the right direction. Their president has passed a law demanding everyone clean their homes and the neighbourhood one Saturday per month. They also have neighbourhood meetings in which they discuss ways to improve their areas. I cannot tell you how excited I was about what I saw. They had terrible problems, but they were doing what they could. I firmly believe if we do what we can do, God will do what we cannot do.

> If we do what we can do, God will do what we cannot do.

If you have serious problems in your life, please understand the key to a breakthrough is to trust God and do what you can. Are you doing your part, or just passively sitting around with a bad attitude waiting for someone else to sort out your life? If this is you, you can change it right now. Declare out loud you will not just sit in the middle of a mess and waste your life. Declare you are an active, aggressive, creative, passionate person and you refuse to give up! Initially, you may not feel passionate or aggressive, but you have the ability to make decisions that override your feelings. Your will is the strongest part of your soul, and when you place your will in agreement with God's will, there is nothing in this world that can stop you from succeeding in life.

> Your will is the strongest part of your soul.

I saw a major difference between the slum in India and Rwanda. The interesting thing is that probably as far as circumstances are concerned, the Rwandans have endured more difficult times than the people we met in India, but their nation is in better shape, simply because someone was willing to stand up and say, 'We are going to do *something* just to keep us from doing *nothing*!'

The biggest mistake anyone can make is to have no dreams for the future and do nothing to make anything in their life better. It doesn't have to be this way for you. God has so much planned for your life – be ready to do something about it.

> Pregnancy is very similar to holding and living out a dream.

You Cannot Give Birth Until You Conceive

The process of pregnancy is very similiar to holding and living out a dream. When a baby is conceived by the seed of a man planted in the womb of a woman, it is much like a thought formed or imagined in the mind. The woman spends approximately nine months being pregnant, then goes into labour and gives birth to a child.

> You're never too young or too old to dream big dreams.

In the spiritual realm, the same thing happens – except it all happens in the mind, heart and spirit of a man or woman. A creative idea, a dream or vision is the seed. It is planted in the heart or spirit of an individual, who also goes through a season of pregnancy, labour, and finally gives birth. In the spiritual realm, both men and women can get pregnant. The Bible says old men shall dream dreams and young men shall see visions (see Acts 2:17). You're never too young or too old to dream big dreams. You're never the wrong sex or race. The amount of money or education you have doesn't matter. All that does matter is you are willing to dream big dreams, depend on a big God who loves you and wants to see you do great things in life, and you are willing to press beyond all opposition.

Many of the ideas and dreams we have in our hearts are revealing the purpose of God for our lives. We sense or feel things, we desire to do things, and it is God's way of showing us our purpose. It is possible to have carnal desires, which are not godly, but if that is the case, God will show you the truth if you're willing to be corrected. Be the kind of person who only wants what God wants and you won't get into much trouble. I have made mistakes in my life by thinking something I wanted was God's will for my life only to discover my motives were all wrong. God gently corrected me and got me back on the right path, and He will do the same thing for you. It is impossible to find God's purpose if you live frozen in fear, unwilling to ever take chances. I repeat – don't live in fear!

i dare you

Dream Big!

1 Think about how great God is and then remind yourself that He is on your side.

2 Make a list of your dreams and don't limit yourself to a certain number. Keep adding to the list as ideas come to you. You'll be amazed at how many of them will indeed come true.

3 Make a plan to pursue at least one of your dreams. Ask yourself what it will take to succeed: Money? Work ethic? More education? A team of people? Once you have a good idea, work hard to make it happen.

4 Dream big, but celebrate the small steps of success along the way. Realise that each effort you make is one step closer to the discipline and dedication required in order to focus your passion for what God's calling you to do.

5 Keep your passion large and in charge of your dreams. Give it your all and refuse to give up.

Fear of Failure

Fear is what you pass on the way to success. I always say that most people fail their way to success. In other words, it is impossible to ever find out what God has for your life without making a few mistakes along the way. Don't be so addicted to your own perfection that you live a little life with no passion for much of anything because you've chosen to play it safe.

> Most people fail their way to success.

The history books are filled with stories of great men and women who did great things, but prior to their success they encountered failure after failure. Thomas Edison tried 2,000 experiments before he successfully invented the lightbulb. Abraham Lincoln lost several elections and had a nervous breakdown before he became president of the United States. The first time I tried to go on television, it was a total failure.

Why are we so afraid of failure anyway? I believe it is one of the devil's greatest tactics to prevent people from trying. He tells us to stay safe and that sounds good, but safe can also be boring. Safe usually means sameness, but God has created us for diversity and growth. He wants us to face new challenges, try new things, experiment and be creative.

> Safe usually means sameness, but God has created us for diversity and growth.

The fear of failure is actually one of the biggest fears people have to confront if they intend to fulfil their purpose in life.

Here are three women who dreamed a dream, persevered and knew what it meant to conquer fear:

Queen Elizabeth I

Elizabeth's father cursed her at birth because she was a girl. The pope declared her illegitimate, and her half-sister imprisoned her in the Tower of London. Later in life Elizabeth reigned as queen for forty-five years, during which time England grew in prosperity, peace and power. She instituted the right to a fair trial and pioneered social welfare programmes for the elderly, the infirm and the poor.[2]

Elizabeth Blackwell

Twenty-nine medical colleges rejected Elizabeth Blackwell before she became America's first female doctor of the modern era. Can you imagine being rejected twenty-nine times and still having the courage to try again? After Elizabeth did become a doctor, several hospitals refused to employ her. She eventually opened the New York Infirmary for Indigent Women and Children, among several other medical dispensaries. She later founded the Women's Medical College.[3]

Mary McLeod Bethune

Mary McLeod Bethune was the youngest of seventeen children. When she was turned down for missionary service, she started a school instead. Her students used boxes for desks and elderberries for ink. To raise money, she and her students hauled thousands of pounds of rubbish for a local dump owner. President Franklin Roosevelt distinguished Mary as the first African-American woman ever to be a presidential adviser.[4]

I am greatly encouraged by people who refuse to give up in the face of opposition. We can offer God no greater worship than to pursue His purpose aggressively, pressing beyond all opposition and leaving apathy and passivity behind.

> We can offer God no greater worship than to pursue His purpose aggressively.

These three women are examples of people who conceive and are determined to give birth to their dreams. They lived passionately!

I was watching a biography of a famous actress recently and was surprised to find her life had been very challenging. She was married and divorced three times. One husband committed adultery with her best friend, who was also a well-known actress. Another was a gambler who gambled away millions of dollars and left her broke. The third invested all of her money in a hotel, restaurant, and theatre he horribly mismanaged, and once again left her broke. If you saw her on screen or in magazines, you would never know the tragedies she encountered. When she was asked how she was able to go on and be successful after having so many devastating things happen to her, she said, 'You simply put your trust in God, and you begin again.'

You begin again. Starting all over seems like a huge job, doesn't it? It especially can feel that way if you have already put a great deal of your life into something, only to see it fail. However, we only have two choices: to go on or go under. We must choose to go on.

Don't Abort Your Dreams

There is one simple rule to success and that is 'Don't give up!' As we know, many women today get pregnant and have abortions. (More than 848,000 abortions were performed in 2003 alone, according to the Centers for Disease Control and Prevention.) It is tragic because a life that God had plans for was snuffed out before it was ever given a chance to blossom and thrive. I encourage you not to abort your dreams for your life and for your future. Satan will try everything to get you to give up. At times you may feel so weary you think you just cannot go on. During those times you need to be encouraged by spending time with God and godly people who also have dreams of their own and can serve to motivate and inspire you. If you are already discouraged, you certainly don't want to spend the day with someone else who is discouraged.

People are not always going to be available for you, but God has promised never to leave you or forsake you.

People are not always going to be available for you, but God has promised never to leave you or forsake you. He is always with you! There will be times on your journey when you will have to press forward, with just you and God. Those are trying times and it is often during those times that people abort their dreams. If you can push through the bleakness and despair, you will come out on the other side more rooted and grounded in God. You will develop a deep walk with Him that will be amazing. David of the Bible spent a lot of time alone in the fields worshipping God and being left out of things going on at home, but David also became king. Don't give up during those times when you have to go it alone. God will bring the right people into your life at the right time, but if you are in one of those 'alone seasons' right now, just trust God that He knows what He is doing and that everything will work out for good if you love God and are called according to His purpose (see Romans 8:28).

If you give up, though, there is nothing God or anyone else can do to help you. The Bible tells us many afflictions come against the righteous, but God delivers him out of them all (see Psalm 34:19). When you are going through trying times, just remember they will not last for ever. They come in seasons, and seasons will pass.

Pregnancy and Patience

Pregnancy is an interesting time in a woman's life. If having a baby has been her desire, the news that she is pregnant brings her great joy. She shares her good news with everyone and they are excited, but after a while she is just pregnant. And to be honest, before she finally gives birth, she usually feels like she will be pregnant for ever, and she gets really tired of being pregnant. There are actually a few spiritual lessons we can learn from looking at pregnancy.

When a woman conceives, at first there are no signs anyone can see that she is pregnant. Someone might look at her and say, 'You certainly don't look pregnant.' Starting to 'show', as we call it, takes time. Likewise, when you have a dream or vision for your life, you might tell someone else what you believe will happen and they may look at you and not see anything that makes them agree with you. I remember how excited I was when I initially realised what the purpose of God was for my life. God not only called me, but also gave me passion, motivating me to pursue His will. I told many people about what I thought I was going to do in the future and most of them were very critical. They told me it was not possible and gave me a variety of reasons why. I didn't have the education, I didn't have the right personality, nobody knew who I was, I had no open doors, I was a woman, and on and on they went. Their reaction was, of course, discouraging to me, which is exactly what the devil wanted – and I must admit I was tempted to abort my dream. Thankfully, I did not give up.

When a woman gets pregnant, things begin to change inside her body and it affects her physically and emotionally. She may be tired or more emotional. She can sense things are changing, but may not even understand it well enough to know how to talk about it. God is getting her body ready to give birth. He is changing some of her desires. For instance, she wants to take care of her baby and she feels more of a nesting instinct; she wants to read material on motherhood and raising children, and she's drawn more to people with children than she once was. Things she used to spend her time doing no longer interest her as much as thinking about her baby.

When we realise what our purpose is or we get pregnant with a dream for our lives, we also sense changes we may not understand. When my dream took hold in my heart, I became more serious and wanted to invest my time in things that would help me prepare for my future. Some of my friends didn't understand and were critical. My thoughts were changing, my desires were changing, and even the type of people I wanted to spend time with changed. Any time we are in a season of change, we must be patient. Change does not come easily, but we must be prepared for the transition coming in our lives.

When a woman is pregnant she gets uncomfortable. Her clothes don't fit, and she may feel very impatient, waiting for her dream to become a reality. When I was pregnant with my dream to teach God's Word and help people, I can remember feeling I did not fit anywhere. I was not what I used to be and I wasn't yet what I was going to be. I was uncomfortable and very impatient to see things take shape. I felt ready, but day after day I just stayed pregnant with my dream. My desire was getting bigger and bigger, and I felt as if I would burst if God did not give me an open door to minister soon.

When I was pregnant with my children, I actually went three weeks over my due date with one, four weeks with another, five with another, and five and a half weeks with my last child. My doctor told me I stayed pregnant as long as an elephant, and we often feel that way when we are trying to birth our dreams and visions for the future. I tried extra walking and taking castor oil, hoping to move things along, but nothing worked. I went to the hospital where they tried to start my labour, but that did not work either. I was sent home and I just stayed pregnant! I was very frustrated, but God had a right time – and nothing was going to happen until then.

But sure enough, in due season, at just the right time, I finally went into labour and, after some intense pain, gave birth to a beautiful child.

Those of you who have dreams for your lives, those of you who feel you know your purpose and you're ready to pursue it, you must be patient. It won't happen overnight. You will be pregnant longer than you would like to be. There will be a lot of changes. You will

> If you don't give up too soon, you will eventually see the
> fulfilment of your purpose in life and experience all the
> joy that comes with it.

experience the pain of labour and delivery, but if you don't give up too soon, you will eventually see the fulfilment of your purpose in life and experience all the joy that comes with it.

Pregnancy is not just a time of patience and monotony, but it is also a time of expectancy! We look forward to the good things to come. Actually, when we can look forward with joy, we help ourselves endure the things we need to go through. David said, 'I would have despaired unless I believed that I would see the Lord's goodness in the land of the living' (Psalm 27:13).

When a young woman does not look pregnant, she puts her hope in the doctor's word. When there are no visible signs our dreams will ever come to pass we must put our hope in God's Word. 'I wait for the Lord, I expectantly wait, and in His word do I hope' (Psalm 130:5).

> Be adventurous and do something you've never done
> before.

It's Worth the Wait

So, do you think it's worth it to dream big dreams? Perhaps after some of the things I have told you, you're saying, *I'm not sure I want to go through all of that.* Let me encourage you to take the chance. Don't live a safe, little life. Get out of the boat and try to walk on water, like the Apostle Peter did. Don't be afraid of change. Be adventurous and do something you've never done before. Make a decision right now that at the end of your life you won't look back and have nothing but regret, wishing you had done the things in your heart, and knowing it is too late. If you make the decision right now to just be comfortable, you could be allowing comfort to steal your passion, and your purpose from you.

I have gone through a lot to get from where I was to where I am, and thousands of times I thought of giving up. I thought, *This is just too hard,* or, *The price is too high.* Now, I am so glad I went all the way through with God. Believe me, being in God's will, and passionately fulfilling His purpose for your life, is worth the wait.

CHAPTER 9

Take Responsibility

I hope by now you have embraced a dream for your life or have a sense of one, if you did not have one when you started reading this book. I hope you are beginning to sense the purpose of God for your life, or you are at least determined to pursue what it may be, and to pursue it passionately.

If this is the case, I want you to go and stand in front of a mirror, look at yourself, and say out loud, 'I will do my part and I will finish what I start.'

We always have to remember that just because God shows you your purpose, this does not mean it is absolutely going to happen. Dreams and visions operate in the spiritual realm. They are possibilities, but they are not guaranteed to take place unless we are willing to do our part.

> Just because God shows you your purpose, this does not mean it is absolutely going to happen.

Being responsible is something a lot of people don't know much about. God's definition of a dreamer is not someone who sits around with his head in the clouds, wishing upon a star. It is someone who sees the possibilities of great things, but understands it will take a lot of hard work and determination to see it through to the finish. Dreamers are people who are willing to sacrifice and pay the price up front in order to cross the finishing line with self-respect and honour.

Don't Be Lazy

Lazy people are always unhappy and they don't understand why. The reason they're unhappy is because God did not create them in such a marvellous and magnificent way just so they could sit around and do nothing – bearing no good fruit. Do you know anyone like that? Maybe someone who spends way too much time talking about all the television programmes he's keeping up with? Or, someone who seems to know everyone else's business, yet she isn't taking care of her own? That's not action! That's not being engaged with life! We were created for movement; that's why God has given us so many joints all over our bodies. We're supposed to move with them and get things done!

The lazy man never sees anything good happen. Everything around him is in shambles and everyone else is at fault; because he never takes responsibility, nothing ever changes, including his spiritual life. A survey of *Discipleship Journal* readers ranked the areas of greatest spiritual challenge to them and 'laziness' was fourth, just under materialism, pride and self-centredness.[1]

If you want to see change in your life, then start asking yourself what you can do to make things different. Don't just sit idly by wishing something good would happen to you. A lazy man sees the problem and talks about it, but he offers no solution.

There are those who wait for something to happen and those who make something happen. It is true we need to wait on God and not get into works of the flesh. But on the other hand, as I have mentioned previously, God cannot drive a parked car. Even if you are in a waiting season of your life, keep your motor running and be ready to go forward as soon as you get a green light from God. It is not wise to do the wrong thing, but neither is it wise to do nothing.

> It is not wise to do the wrong thing, but neither is it wise to do nothing.

The best-selling armchair sitting in most living rooms in the United States is a brand called La-Z-Boy. It's true, we enjoy the idea of comfort and we hate inconvenience. There is nothing wrong with a comfortable chair, but laziness destroys the plan of God for your life. The Bible says, 'He who is loose and slack in his work is brother to him who is a destroyer . . .' (Proverbs 18:9). We usually don't see doing 'nothing' as action, but it is. It is a negative action, a non-action that produces nothing, and it is the biggest waste of God's abilities and power we will ever see. I wish someone would produce and sell a chair called 'Work-R-Boy'. I honestly don't know how many people would even be willing to have that brand in their homes.

God gives us everything we need to live fruitful, successful, prosperous and joyful lives. All we need to do is turn the motor on and get going in the right direction. Too many of us, however, feel like we are entitled to live a good life, like somehow we have the right and privilege of success without doing anything. We don't realise God has endowed us with certain rights and the ability to succeed, meaning He's supplied us with what we need, and if we do our part we will get a good result. There is a big difference between endowment and entitlement. We aren't entitled to anything we have not earned through obedience to God.

> We aren't entitled to anything we have not earned through obedience to God.

Believing Is Our First Responsibility

Our first responsibility when it comes to following our purpose with passion is to believe God's Word, and to believe in Jesus Christ. Through believing, we become joint heirs with Jesus. Everything He earned, we inherit. But God's Word also says those who do (genuinely) believe will also obey what God says. I hear a lot of people say they are believers, but I do not see them obeying God.

The Apostle James said faith without works is dead, and if we are hearers of the Word and not doers, we are deceiving ourselves (see James 1:22, 2:17).

The main thing we should be passionate about is obeying God. We should focus on obeying God or we probably won't remain obedient. The guidelines in God's Word are for our benefit and obeying them is the wisest thing we can do. The flesh is basically lazy and not very interested in moral excellence; therefore, we should always follow God and His Word. The flesh will lead us into destruction, but God leads us into the good life He pre-arranged and made ready for us to live (see Ephesians 2:10).

Stay Active

Being responsible means being intentional, and that means being active in what you're passionate about. Jesus always encouraged people to stay active and the apostles taught people to stay active – not just busy doing anything, but active in things that would help them be prepared for their future. Being active in studying God's Word will help us be prepared for obedience. We cannot do what is right if we do not know what is right. If you have been doing nothing much to help yourself or other people, then get up and get going because the longer you do nothing the less you are going to want to do.

The apostles gave the people a lot of instructions to follow. Among them were things like praying, being attentive to God's Word, being a blessing to one another, working with their hands, minding their own business, not gossiping, judging or criticising. They were encouraged to forgive, not be offended, and reject resentment or bitterness. They were certainly taught to be responsible, active, and to do their part in every way they could. The more active we are in obeying God, the more our joy and peace increase.

Paul actually said that if a man didn't work, then he should not eat (see 2 Thessalonians 3:10). That does not sound to me as if Paul condoned laziness. Anyone who is physically able needs to work and stay active. If you are currently out of work, stay active volunteering while you are looking for a steady job. Do whatever you can do, and refuse to sit and do nothing. Remember, do what you can do, and God will do what you cannot do. Doing nothing is not God's purpose for you.

> Do whatever you can do, and refuse to sit and do nothing.

Throughout the years I waited for God to open doors for me to teach His Word, I stayed active studying, praying and laying my hand to what was in front of me. I taught small Bible studies, counselled people, visited a nursing home weekly, passed out Gospel tracts on the street corners, and anything else I could do that I felt might even remotely help someone. God gave me a desire to help people and I was aggressive in trying to do so.

I'm reminded of the story we can read in the Bible about ten virgins who were waiting for the bridegroom to arrive. Five were wise; they prepared ahead of time and brought extra oil with them in case they had to wait. The other five virgins were foolish; they did not want to do anything extra, and instead did the minimum. They weren't prepared.

The bridegroom was slow in coming and they all fell asleep. Suddenly, a shout was heard – the bridegroom was coming. Because they didn't make proper preparations for his delayed arrival, the foolish virgins ran out of oil. They asked the wise to give them some of theirs and were told they didn't have enough to share. The result was the lazy, foolish virgins were left out because they had not done what they should have done (see Matthew 25:1–13).

This is the way it is with lazy people. They don't do what they should do or rise to the occasion and be responsible. But they also wonder why they never have enough and always want someone else to be responsible to do for them what they should have done for themselves. Success in life is often fleeting for them, and often they feel sorry for themselves and resent those who are enjoying success.

I must admit people like this aggravate me. I have a short fuse with lazy people because they have the same opportunities as everyone else, but they sit and do nothing while life passes them by. Their excuses never seem to end.

Be intentional about actively pursuing your dreams. Don't convince yourself you deserve to do nothing for a while.

I Have Attended My Last Pity Party

Are you willing to take responsibility for what you do and acknowledge that your life's outcome depends on those actions? If so, you will need to turn down every invitation the devil gives you to a pity party. I spent a lot of years feeling sorry for myself, but it was just a way of avoiding responsibility. It is easy to follow our feelings, but it takes spiritual maturity to do what Jesus would do in every situation. He certainly would not waste His time feeling sorry for Himself.

> It takes spiritual maturity to do what Jesus would do in every situation.

He didn't feel sorry for Himself when Peter denied Him or when Judas betrayed Him. He did not feel sorry for Himself when His brothers were ashamed of Him or when His disciples disappointed Him in His most difficult time. Jesus continued being responsible for what God called Him to do, and He kept His eye on that, even when others walked away. We must realise when life or people disappoint us, we have one responsibility – and that is to remain stable and continue with the purpose of God for our lives. We will not be held responsible for what other people do, but we will be held responsible for ourselves. I certainly don't want to stand before God and be asked why I wasted my time in self-pity.

> I certainly don't want to stand before God and be asked
> why I wasted my time in self-pity.

Take responsibility for your emotional responses to life. Even if your emotions want to sink, you can call on God to lift you up. He will give you the strength to remain stable in the storms of life.

> Blessed (happy, fortunate, to be envied) is the man whom You discipline and instruct, O Lord, and teach out of Your law,
>
>   That you may give him power to keep himself calm in the days of adversity, until the [inevitable] pit of corruption is dug for the wicked.
>   – PSALM 94:12–13

This scripture does not say God keeps us calm. It says He gives us power to keep ourselves calm. As I have said before, we are partners with God. His part is to give us ability and our part is to be responsible. Responsibility means to respond to the ability you have. A lazy person wants God to do everything, while he does nothing except follow his feelings.

You should declare out loud right now, 'I have attended my last pity party.' I can promise you in the end you will feel much better about yourself if you take responsibility than if you avoid it.

I Choose to Be Responsible

When we put the blame for why things aren't going the way we want them on to other people or circumstances, we aren't taking responsibility. We've already talked about how blaming is a waste of time, but it's a game that began in the Garden of Eden and has never ceased.

We often blame people, life, the devil and ourselves, but none of that changes anything. If you truly want to change something, you must begin by taking responsibility for yourself and your life. We must choose to be responsible, even if it seems unfair. You may have been hurt or mistreated and there is nothing you can do about what has already been done – but you *can* do something about how you respond. If you're discouraged, depressed or in self-pity you can take responsibility for that and say, 'I'm not going to sit here blaming any more. I am going to take a stand and take control of my emotions.' I feel blaming others for our problems is one of the biggest ways we avoid taking responsibility. It may not be intentional; nonetheless we are trying to avoid what we should really be dealing with, and it is the devil's way of keeping us trapped in a lifestyle we hate.

> There is nothing you can do about what has already been done – but you *can* do something about how you respond.

Even blaming yourself is not the way to freedom. When we make mistakes, we often think it is spiritual to wallow in blame and condemnation, but it isn't. I spent a lot of years thinking, *everything is my fault,* but that is still not a *responsible* attitude. Someone who wants to be responsible will freely admit their failure, be willing to turn from it, pray and ask God to help them in the future and then press on. They go forward. They refocus on their passion and what they're supposed to be doing to get back on track.

There are people in psychiatric hospitals simply because they blamed themselves for something for so long it finally destroyed their mental health. If you have a season in your life where you made a huge mistake, stop looking back and realise there is only one thing you can do: let go, and go on!

> Life isn't always fair, but God is.

Life isn't always fair, but God is – and you can be assured He will bring justice in your situation if you will give up the blame game and be responsible in pursuit of His purpose for you. We can also get stuck in blaming the devil and never make any progress. My point is that no matter whose fault your problems were, you have to realise blaming is non-productive and then make a decision to move on. Even if the responsibility for the mess is not yours, the solution to getting out of the mess is. I dare you to stand firm, take responsibility, and start working with God to have the best life you can have.

i dare you

Be Responsible

1 Remember no one cares more about your passion or purpose than you.
2 Avoid blaming others for your problems and do what you can to make things better.
3 Believe first and foremost that God has given you the desires of your heart; now get ready to do something about it.

Nobody Cares Like You Do

The reason you must take responsibility for the outcome of your life is that nobody cares about your life like you do. Just like no one will take care of your children the exact way you do, or care for your pets, or care for your house, no one will care about you the way you will. You have a vested interest! Of course God cares, but He won't do the part for which you are responsible. He enables you to do it, but I want to emphasize *He won't do it for you!* Other people may care about you and the purpose God has for your life. But believe me, nobody cares like you do. Nobody is willing to put the time and effort into you being all you can be because they are, and should be, concerned with becoming all they should be. If you don't care about your life, then there is nothing anyone else can do that will make that much difference.

Throughout the years I have been pursuing God's purpose for my life, He has sent me many wonderful people to help. I thought some of them would be with me for ever, but quickly learned that people come and go. No matter who has left, Dave and I have stayed because the final responsibility is ours.

Other people can give up, but if you're on fire with God's passion for your life, you cannot give up. It is not an option for you! No matter how you feel, you must go on because you are the only one who can run your race. Nobody can cross the finishing line of your race but you.

> Nobody can cross the finishing line of your race but you.

I recently heard a fable about a dog that loved to chase other animals. He bragged about his great running skill and said he could catch anything. Well, it wasn't long until his boastful claims were put to the test by a certain rabbit. With ease, the little creature outran his barking pursuer. The other animals, watching with glee, began to laugh. The dog excused himself, however, by saying, 'You forget, I was only running for fun. He was running for his life!' We need to run for our lives, to find our motivation and our passion and our drive to keep going, even when the rest of the world tells us to stop.

> We need to run for our lives, to find our motivation and our passion and our drive to keep going.

Sometimes we get frustrated with people because they don't seem to have the same commitment that we do, but in reality that isn't fair to them. God did not put into their hearts what He put into yours about your dream.

For instance, if a woman is pregnant, she is the one who has to give birth. Nobody can do it for her. She can have a good doctor, good nurses and a good midwife, but it comes down to her and the baby to do the work.

Instead of thinking, 'Well, it's not fair for me to have all this responsibility', just remember you will be the one to reap the reward of fulfilment. Jesus endured the cross for the joy of obtaining the prize, and we must all take up our own cross and carry it to the finishing line for the joy of the prize.

I have tried on occasions to let others take responsibility for what I should have been responsible for, and it has always ended in disaster. Dave watches over the ministry money with a magnifying glass. In other words, he *diligently* watches over it. Our sons have a lot of authority, but Dave and I know in the end we are the ones with the final responsibility. We are directly involved in everything at this point in our lives, but we will never allow ourselves to sit idly by while someone else makes all of our decisions. We will get older as the years go by, but we will never get too old to be responsible for what God has given us.

> Never get too old to be responsible for what God has given you.

Watch Over What Belongs to You

I know a minister who once had a very large ministry. Although he had many fruitful years and made an amazing contribution to God's Kingdom, he eventually had terrible financial struggles and had to downsize his ministry. He told me the reason for it was he turned too many things over to other people he should have watched over.

We know another man who had a lucrative business. He also had a partner he trusted to run everything while he chose to play a lot of golf. Years went by and suddenly everything fell apart when it was discovered that the so-called responsible partner was embezzling money from the firm. The active partner went to jail and the non-active one ended up with a very mediocre job and a lot of embarrassment. He realized too late that he had been irresponsible.

Christian parents often make the mistake of thinking the children's ministry at church or the youth group leaders or the Christian school their children attend, will make sure their child has proper spiritual training, but that is not always true.

> Your children are *your* children and you have the responsibility for their spiritual training.

Your children are *your* children and you have the responsibility for their spiritual training. I know one family who thought their child would certainly be spiritually strong because they had a so-called 'awesome' youth leader. They later discovered that the 'awesome' youth leader was not teaching the children much of anything and was sexually involved with one of the girls in the youth group. Don't be impressed with someone just because they are a big talker or put on a slick performance. Don't mistake hype for the anointing (God's presence) on a person's life.

Ask questions. If you have final responsibility, you have the right to ask questions, and I know at my office I ask a lot of questions. Insecure people can be offended by questions, but it is my responsibility to know what is going on. Ask questions about what kind of education your children are getting. Don't assume everything is fine if you really don't know. Don't assume your children have friends who are good kids. Ask them what their friends are like and get to know them yourself. Don't assume anything; know where they are, what kind of films they go to, what they do on the internet, what kind of television they watch – remember, it is your responsibility.

Set a Good Example

When we talk about taking action and taking responsibility, part of the reason it's so important is that people believe a lot more of what they see you do than what they hear you say. So take the responsibility to set a good example. How I live my life in front of people and even behind closed doors at home is very important to me.

Don't just tell others what to do, but let them see you set the example. If a parent tells a child to have good manners, and then the child sees Mum and Dad being rude to one another, they have wasted their words.

Living responsibly in society is a big job. The Bible says we should 'watch and pray' (Mark 14:38). I think we need to watch ourselves a little more and pray we will not be hypocrites. Doing what I say I am going to do is very important to me. I am not perfect in this area, but I believe I have to set a good example. If you want those under your authority to be dependable, then you set the example.

Author and speaker John Maxwell says everything rises and falls on leadership, and I believe that. If you want authority, then you have to take the responsibility that goes with it.

PART II

The Pursuit of Passion with Purpose

CHAPTER 10

Keep Yourself Stirred Up

I have a burning desire to see people live passionately. I am weary of lukewarm, ho-hum, I'm-bored-with-life people. To live passionately, we must avoid becoming stagnant and inactive. Water that is not moving becomes stagnant. If you've ever seen a puddle of stagnant water, you know it's murky and smelly and there may even be some mould or bacteria forming. Who can become stagnant? Absolutely anybody! No matter how enthusiastic you once were, you can become stagnant if you don't do your part to keep yourself stirred up. Water that's constantly stirred doesn't grow mould, it stays fresh longer. It breathes and it flows because of the impact the action of stirring has on it. Leaders have an additional responsibility when it comes to this, because they not only have to keep themselves stirred up, but they have to help others stay stirred up as well.

> Who can become stagnant? Absolutely anybody!

Stagnation can occur in marriage, in a job, at church, school, in your personal life, your spiritual life, and many other areas. When does stagnation occur? When we stop investing in something, it stops growing. Anything not moving is on its way to becoming stagnant and dull, which is definitely what we want to avoid if we're talking about truly embracing our lives with passion and purpose.

Marriage, Friendship and Work Colleagues

Most people who get divorced blame the other party, but if both parties were investing in the relationship, there is a good possibility the divorce could have been avoided. Nobody just automatically has a good marriage; we all have to work at it. Dave and I were married in 1967 and that means we have been married a long, long time, but I can assure you we still have times when we have purposely to invest in our relationship.

> Pray for all the people you have relationships with and ask God to help you find ways to make them feel valuable.

If you live with or know someone a long time, it is easy to take him or her for granted. It's like the eight-year-old who wisely once said, 'Don't forget your wife's name. That will mess up the love.' If you start viewing your spouse like a favourite piece of furniture that is always there, there's a good chance that will 'mess up the love'! I encourage you to pray for all the people you have relationships with and ask God to help you find ways to make them feel valuable. Don't just expect them to do something for you, but ask what you can do for them. If you invest in your relationships, you will reap from them. I realise some situations just won't work out, but if yours is one of them, I encourage you to make sure it isn't because you did not do your part.

> Don't get into a relationship thinking it is the other person's job to keep you happy.

Don't get into a relationship thinking it is the other person's job to keep you happy. You must be responsible for your own joy – it is not someone else's job. Be willing to adapt and adjust to the people around you. I am not suggesting that you let people control you, but be willing to change if it will help bring peace into your relationships. We often argue over petty things that really don't make much difference at all when we consider all of life.

Good relationships require an investment of time. If you have so many people in your life you cannot pay attention to any of them, perhaps you need to know the difference between acquaintances and good friends. I know a lot of people, and I love everybody, but I have learned I can only have a few really good friends. Decide which of your relationships are vital and make sure you put adequate time into them.

My husband is my friend and that means we have to be intentional when it comes to spending time together. I don't want to merely live in the same house with Dave, I want to be close to him, so I have to do my part not to let our relationship stagnate. Recently, I was praying for Dave, and God told me to pay him more compliments. Dave does not even seem like the kind of man who cares about compliments. He is very secure and doesn't seem to get excited or have much reaction at all when he is complimented. But in obedience to God, I started complimenting him several times a day. It wasn't very long until I realised I felt closer to him than I had in a while and he seemed to be paying more attention to me and we were having more fun. Wow! I invested and I reaped!

I also have to take responsibility to invest in the lives of the people who help me keep mine together. I have people who help me do what God has called me to do and I need to make an effort to show them how important they are. I don't want them to stagnate because if they do, they may not want to do their jobs any more. When people get stagnant, quite often they think they need a change, but the truth is they just need to be stirred up again. They need a new and fresh breeze to blow around them and motivate them to keep going.

I pray about being sensitive to the needs of people around me and mostly try to follow my heart. When I was working on this book, the thought came to me to send my secretary flowers with a note that I appreciated her. So I did it! I could have said, *I'll do it after I finish what I'm working on,* or I could have just forgotten about it entirely, but I didn't, because it's very important to show people you care.

Watching television one Valentine's Day evening, I thought about a woman I knew whose husband had passed away a few months previously. I felt I should phone her and wish her 'Happy Valentine's Day'. When I did, she responded by saying, 'You must have known that I needed this phone call. This is my first Valentine's Day without my husband.' God knew what she was feeling and He allowed me to be His agent in encouraging her. I believe God wants to use all of us a great deal more in these areas than we realise.

> Learn to listen to people and to your heart.

Learn to listen to people and to your heart. They often tell you in general conversation what they want or need, and as we take action to meet those needs, the people we care about are encouraged. If we train ourselves to pay attention, we can often see by people's countenance or body language that they need to be encouraged and edified. God may put something special in your heart, or you could just use common sense. Common sense tells us people need to be encouraged and stirred up from time to time. We definitely reap what we sow in the lives of other people. The more we try to make others happy, the happier we will be ourselves.

> Common sense tells us people need to be encouraged and stirred up from time to time.

If you think you can have good relationships but never take the time to invest and put effort into them, you are not using common sense and wisdom. Everyone likes compliments and gifts. Everyone wants to be appreciated for the work they do. Everyone needs to feel loved and valued.

Try New Things

In 1901 the following ad is said to have appeared in a London newspaper: 'Men wanted for hazardous journey. Small wages, bitter cold, long months of complete darkness, constant danger, safe return doubtful.' The ad was signed by Ernest Shackleton, Antarctic explorer. Amazingly, the ad drew thousands of respondents, eager to sacrifice everything for the prospect of meaningful adventure.[1]

> Don't give in to fear of the unknown or of being adventurous – move past it and follow your heart.

I believe we should live our lives with an enormous spirit of adventure and risk. We only get one trip through life and I don't want to be old and have nothing but regrets. We always face the struggle between faith and fear, and we need to fight the temptation to build up our bank accounts and our retirement savings and then plan on living the lives we have always dreamed of later. Don't give in to fear of the unknown or of being adventurous – move beyond it and follow your heart. There will always be critics and those who warn us of impending failure, but they are not really that important in the end. Theodore Roosevelt said, 'It's not the critic who counts; not the man who points out how the strong man stumbles, or where the doer of deeds could have done better. The credit belongs to the man who is actually in the arena . . . who, at the best, knows in the end the triumph of high achievement, and who, at the worst, if he fails, at least he fails while daring greatly, so that his place shall never be with those cold and timid souls who neither know victory nor defeat.'

> It's their home runs baseball players remember, not their strikeouts.

If you step up to the plate in baseball, you might strike out, but if you don't try, you will never know the joy of hitting a home run. Even the best players strike out. However, it's their home runs baseball players remember, not their strikeouts. They become heroes and icons simply because they were brave enough to try, and keep trying, until they found their 'sweet spot' in life. This is a term familiar to golfers and tennis players who know it's the sweet spot on a ball about to be hit that can determine the distance it will soar or the abrupt end of flight. These baseball players found the place that was just right for them and realised that along the way to success they would experience some failed experiments.

Stagnation can occur when we are afraid of trying new things, or when doing too much of the same thing all the time. It's getting so comfortable you become almost comatose. You might be feeling stagnant in your job, and just driving a different route to work could help. Perhaps you never go out to lunch, and going out in the middle of the day for a while might help you gain some fresh perspective and a new spring in your step. It is so easy to get into a rut; but to keep doing what we are familiar with and not wanting to venture out into the unknown isn't emotionally healthy.

Be courageous and try new things. If you're bored with yourself or the way you look, try a different haircut or hair colour. Go and eat at a new restaurant, go to an amusement park, or do something out of the ordinary for you. Take a risk! You might not like it, but then again it may be just the thing you need.

Refuse to risk and you'll never really experience life as it could be.

John Ortberg said in his book *If You Want to Walk on Water (You've Got to Get Out of the Boat)*: there is a danger in getting out of the boat, but there is a danger in staying in it as well. If you live in the boat (whatever your boat might be), you will eventually die of boredom and stagnation. *Everything is risky!* Take a risk and embrace life – refuse to risk and you'll never really experience life as it could be.

Even though I feel I am in the centre of God's will for my life and I have definitely found God's purpose for me, I still have to do things to keep myself from feeling stagnant and dull. You can have the best job in the world and still find yourself feeling inactive and stale from time to time. God has created us to enjoy variety, so therefore we need adventure! We need a change of pace, a new experience, or something out of the ordinary that will wake us up, stand us on our toes, and push us out into the open.

Everybody always seems to think it would be so exciting to travel all the time, as I do, but when you do it all the time you get tired of it. I have to do things to make sure I don't get an attitude that says, 'I'm bored with this.' One of the things I do is remind myself regularly of how blessed I am and that God could have chosen someone else. I remind myself of how bored I was when I was a bookkeeper and spent days looking for three cents so the books would balance. Some people are created by God to work with numbers all day, but I was not one of them.

I also take risks, try new things, and I am determined to be a 'water walker'. I hope you will share that determination with me.

> You will get bored if you don't stir yourself up and do some daring, out-of-the-box things to keep life exciting.

No matter what your station is in life, you will get bored if you don't stir yourself up and do some daring, out-of-the-box things to keep life exciting. You can look at someone else's life and think that if you had his life, you would feel excited all the time, but you wouldn't. I recently watched a film about Jackie Kennedy's life and heard her remark how tired she got of having Secret Service with her all the time, and being expected to be at so many functions. She had the privilege of being the First Lady of the United States and there were times she didn't like it; even something as grand as serving as First Lady can get boring.

If you feel stagnant, a major life change may be in order for you, but before you jump ship and run off to start another new thing, make sure you do your part to stir yourself up right where you are. There are times when we should move on, but I get concerned about people who are constantly starting new things and never finishing anything. When I'm feeling stuck in one place, not moving and quickly going stale, I don't leave my ministry and open J's Clothing Boutique, though I must admit I have thought about it on occasions! I know I would not be satisfied, nor would God be glorified if I were pursuing anything other than my purpose.

> Make sure you do your part to stir yourself up right where you are.

In the Bible, Jesus encountered a man who was ill for thirty-eight years (see John 5: 1–9). He had been lying by a pool of water all that

i dare you

Keep Yourself Stirred Up!

Too many of us are bored with life. It is time to get moving and passionately get on with the life and purpose God wants us to have! Here is a list to get you started:

1 Think about a need in your community you care about. It could be related to children, women, families or senior citizens – anything you feel passionate about. Now volunteer either to help with that need yourself or encourage other people to volunteer with you and do it as a group.

2 One of the surest ways of getting refreshing, flowing movement in your life again is doing something for someone else. Collect a few addresses from either your workplace, Sunday school class, or perhaps a local old people's home. Take a few minutes to write an encouraging note to someone you may not even know. Let him know how much you care and that you're praying for him this week.

3 Need a boost in energy? Then get moving, literally! Just thirty minutes a day of light to brisk walking can do wonders for your circulation, your oxygen levels, and even your thinking!

4 Have a serious talk with yourself. Remind yourself of all the ways you are blessed. Make a list of the people in your life and how they benefit you. Refuse to complain or be negative. A thankful person is a happy person!

time waiting for a miracle. Jesus' answer to this man's stagnant life was: 'Get up and get going.' As simple as that sounds, I do believe it is the answer for many people. Stir yourself up!

Discerning Life from Death

On the first day of the week, the women went to the tomb of Jesus, taking with them prepared spices. They found the stone rolled away, and when they went inside, Jesus' body wasn't there. While they were perplexed and wondered what happened, two men in dazzling white (angels) suddenly stood beside them. The men said, 'Why do you look for the living among [those who are] dead?' (Luke 24:5). I think this is a statement from which we can learn a lot.

If we complain ourselves, we can minister death to ourselves.

Some people don't understand why their lives are so boring and dull, and yet they spend all their time around dead things rather than living ones. For example, if you spend your time with critical people, they minister death to you, not life. You may not even realise it, but you are not edified or encouraged when you are with them. If we complain ourselves, we can minister death to ourselves. The power of life and death is in the tongue and we eat the fruit of it (see Proverbs 18:21).

The Bible tells us not to sit inactive in the path of the ungodly and not to take their advice. Do you sit at a lunch table daily with people who are ungodly and listen to them tell dirty jokes and gossip? If you do, you are making a big mistake. You are fellowshipping with dead things that won't produce any good thing in your life. We have to be intentional with our time, as well as the relationships we keep.

Why would you keep inviting someone over who brings only criticism and ill will?

We need to learn how to discern death from life. The minute we come in contact with something dead, we should get away from it. You wouldn't keep the dead carcass of a squirrel in your house, so why would you keep inviting someone over who brings only criticism and ill will? If we start to feel dead inside, we need to take action and do something about it. If you're feeling discouraged, don't sit at home by yourself all day and think of every depressing thing you can. Get up and get out of the house and take a walk in the sunshine and fresh air. Go for a walk, make a cup of coffee, talk to somebody, or have a good talk with yourself. Sometimes I have to have a talk with myself if I feel a bad attitude coming on. I say, 'Joyce, stop it right now. You are very blessed and have nothing to be crabby about.'

There are times when I wish someone was around to encourage

me, but if no one is and I need encouragement, I talk to myself so I can be reminded of the blessings in my life and all the good going on. The Bible says King David encouraged himself in the Lord. You do have the ability to either encourage or discourage yourself depending on how you think, which is self-talk. When David was facing Goliath, nobody was encouraging him, so he started talking about how great God is and how he knew he would be victorious. Sure enough, he won the battle. We can win our battles as well, with God's help and sometimes a pep talk or two from ourselves.

The Power of Laughter

Chuck Swindoll, in his book *Laugh Again,* writes that he knows 'of no greater need today than the need for joy. Unexplainable, contagious joy. Outrageous joy . . . Unfortunately, our country seems to have lost its spirit of fun and laughter. Recently, a Brazilian student studying at a nearby university told me that what amazes him most about Americans is their lack of laughter. I found myself unable to refute his criticism.'[2]

Laughter is a surefire solution to becoming stagnant. I encourage you to laugh a lot in life because laughter is one source we can always depend on to stir things up. It is like internal jogging and is actually very healthy for us. One study on laughter showed several benefits:

- The effect of laughter on the body is immediate. Laughing actually lowers blood pressure, reduces stress hormones and increases muscle flexion.
- Laughter increases your resistance to infections.
- Laughter also triggers the release of endorphins, the body's natural painkillers, and produces a general sense of well-being.
- In the United States, laughter is used as a pain management technique for terminally ill cancer patients. Patients who regularly employ laughter therapy are found to be more tolerant of pain than those who don't.[3]

Maybe you're saying, 'Joyce, there is nothing funny about my life.' If that is the case, then do something amusing yourself. Rent a funny film or get together with someone you know who usually makes you laugh. I recently spent some time with someone I didn't normally spend time with and ended up laughing all night. I remember thinking, *I didn't know he was that funny, but I am going to make it a habit to be around him more.* I need people in my life who make me laugh and so do you. I work hard and laughter helps balance things out. If you are a workaholic who never takes time for fun, you will definitely stagnate and probably get resentful. God has created us for work and play, not just work, work, work, and more work! Fun and laughter bring restoration and rest to your soul.

God has created us for work and play.

For many years I was a workaholic and it was killing me in a variety of ways. I had no joy, I was tired all the time, I resented people who did have fun, I felt sorry for myself, and I complained. All I had to do was get some balance in my life. But it was up to me to do it! I learned I must be responsible to do whatever it takes to help me enjoy this journey, and that included knowing how to laugh – at life, with others, and even at myself.

Don't Look Behind You

When you're passionate and stirred up about life, you don't have time to look backwards. Maybe you've experienced hurts and disappointments or you've done things you wish you could do again in a different way. We all have those buried regrets, but those are

You are alive and it's time to look ahead and focus on living.

finished and over with. Those things are dead, but you are alive and it's time to look ahead and focus on living.

The answer to our problems is not always a deep, hidden thing that takes months of counselling to reveal. Sometimes it is very simple and a minor adjustment can bring tremendous change. It could be as simple as making a decision to let go of the past, or getting more balance in life, laughing more, doing more for others, or choosing some more positive and uplifting friends. One thing is for sure: nothing ever changes unless we make a decision and take some action. So I encourage you to get moving!

Stop looking behind you and start looking in front of you! And don't ever say, 'I have nothing to look forward to.' You have the rest of your life, and if you expect God to do something wonderful, He will. He wants you to live expecting something good to happen to you every day of your life. Pray for good news because the Bible says it nourishes the bones (see Proverbs 15:30).

Don't Do Foolish Things in Desperation

Some people are very desperate for answers to the lifeless state they find themselves in. Many are so desperate to know what their futures have for them, they turn to psychics for answers, either in person or through a psychic telephone hotline, which seems to be so popular today. These things may give people temporary, false hope, but they don't minister life. One psychic in the US took $360 million before the state she lived in finally shut her down. She was as phoney as a three-dollar bill, but desperate people may believe just about anything. I encourage you to be discerning when it comes to your life and thinking about your future. Get a relationship with God through Jesus Christ and learn how to hear from Him.

God is life, and when you touch Him, you always touch life.

A word from God will minister life to you. Sometimes when I am weary and feel a little stagnant, I just spend some extra time with God and ask Him to speak a fresh word to me. He reassures my heart that I am on the right path and He has His hand on me. God is life, and when you touch him, you always touch life.

God's Word strictly forbids going to mediums, witches and psychics for direction (see Leviticus 19:31, 20:6–7). Some people may think they are just playing cute little games when they read their horoscopes every day, visit a fortune-teller, or get their palms read. But they are actually offending God and opening a door in their lives for the devil. The Bible says if you seek these things out, you will be defiled by them (see Leviticus 19:31). These things poison your life and minister death to you.

> God has your future planned and He will lead and guide you.

If you have done something like this in your past, ask God to forgive you, and don't ever do it again. God has your future planned and He will lead and guide you as you look to Him for direction.

Don't seek answers for the living among the dead.

And when the people [instead of putting their trust in God] shall say to you, consult for direction mediums and wizards who chirp and mutter, should not a people seek and consult their God? Should they consult the dead on behalf of the living?

And they [who consult mediums and wizards] shall pass through [the land] sorely distressed and hungry; and when they are hungry, they will fret, and will curse by their king and their God; and whether they look upward or look to the earth, they will behold only distress and darkness, the gloom of anguish, and into thick darkness and widespread, obscure night they shall be driven away.

– ISAIAH 8:19, 21–22

Some people are so desperate to ensure their future with a spouse that they get married to the wrong person, knowing deep down inside they are making a mistake. Don't be desperate, be patient! Trust the plan God has and understand He may not be in a hurry, but He also promises us He won't be late.

Desperation often leads to things that don't minister life to us. People who are desperate to make more money can get caught in the trap of compromising their consciences. I wonder how many young girls have got into pornography because they had a dream to be a model, but would not wait for God to open right doors of opportunity.

Don't make decisions when you feel desperate; instead, just go somewhere and calm down. If you are emotionally distraught, wait at least twenty-four hours before you decide anything important.

I once heard a story about a desert nomad who awoke in his tent one night feeling extremely hungry. He sat up, turned on the light, looked around his tent, and saw a bag of dates in the corner. He reached into the bag, took one, and bit into it, only to discover there was a worm in it. He spat it out and took a second one, but he found another worm. He tried one more time and all he had in his mouth was a worm. Because his hunger was so intense, he pondered for a moment what he should do. He turned off the light, reached into the bag, and proceeded to eat all the dates.

> God's will is not that we have a moment, but, rather, a lifetime of happiness, adventure, romance and fulfilment.

At times people turn out the lights of their consciences and do things in desperation, trying to fill the longing in their hearts. They are willing to bear the consequences of their sin in exchange for a moment of happiness. God's will is not that we have a moment, but rather, a lifetime of happiness, adventure, romance and fulfilment. If we discipline ourselves in those times of feeling desperate and wait on God, He will surprise us with something far better than we could have grabbed for ourselves.

The Law of the Spirit of Life in Christ Jesus

The Bible tells us the law ministers death, but the Spirit ministers life. The Spirit stirs us up! Are you living under the bondage of a lot of religious laws (rules and regulations)? If you are, then you may be a stagnant Christian. It is God's Spirit who gives life and we are to be led by the Holy Spirit, not man-made rules and regulations. Some religions only tell people what they can't do, and they fail to tell them what Jesus has done. Are you enjoying freedom, or do you feel condemned most of the time because you can't keep all the rules? A man recently told me that in the religion he grew up in, all the people had one extra gene: *guilt!* Sadly, that is often true. People go to church looking for God, help and comfort, and they get weighed down with rules they cannot keep and guilt because of their failure. Where the true Spirit of the Lord is, there is liberty and freedom from bondage (see 2 Corinthians 3:17).

If you are going to a dead church and wondering why you have no passion and enthusiasm about being there, perhaps you need to find a place to go that is ministering real life. But how do you know?

You Just Might Be at a Dead Church

Do you feel worse after going to church or better? If you're more miserable than before you went, you just might be at a dead church.

Are the same people who sang in the church choir twenty years ago the same ones singing in the choir today, sitting in the exact same spots they've always sat in, and singing to the same music they've always sung to? You just might be at a dead church, because living things must change and grow.

Is your church the kind where everyone has reserved seating and guests are welcome – so long as they don't sit in someone's pew? You just might be at a dead church.

Is the most exciting topic of conversation on a Sunday morning the new colour and carpet choices for the church renovation? You just might be at a dead church.

Does the pastor frequently talk about dead churches in his sermons, yet never addresses his own church's lack of attendance or participation? Chances are, you're at a dead church.

Do you hear a lot of gossip at your church about the pastor, his staff and members of the congregation? Chances are, you're at a dead church.

Going to church is supposed to encourage you and give you energy and excitement and an opportunity for the Holy Spirit to stir you up for the week. Jesus is your glory and the lifter of your head. When you are in His presence, He gives fullness of joy. Ask yourself some tough questions: Do you go to church just to fulfil an obligation, or are you glad when it is time to go and sorry when it is over? The psalmist David said he was very glad when it was time to go to the house of the Lord.

> Going to church is supposed to encourage you and give you energy and excitement.

Do you go to church just to get your blessing for the week, or do you go to give to and help other people? Are you a channel or a reservoir? A channel has something flowing in and something flowing out, but a reservoir just sits there and collects whatever is offered. There is no movement, but great potential to become stagnant.

The Bible says the law of the Spirit of life in Christ Jesus has set us free from the law of sin and death (see Romans 8:2). That simply means we are incapable of following all the religious laws (rules and regulations) and they, in fact, cause us to sin. However, if we are committed to following the Holy Spirit, we will be touched by life. The Spirit of God not only shows us what to do, He gives us the ability to do it. The law tells you what you should do and then condemns you because you cannot do it.

The new covenant of salvation through Jesus Christ is a new way of living. Perhaps you are looking for a new way of living. Perhaps you want a life that is truly filled with energy, passion and enthusiasm. If that is the case, you must learn to recognise and follow the Holy Spirit, not people, not man-made rules, and not your own ideas. Jesus said, 'Follow Me.'

Only God's Spirit can energise your spiritual life and keep it from stagnating. If you learn to listen to Him, God will lead you in what to do to stay stirred up and ready for passion and insight into the life He has planned for you.

We must learn how to avoid stagnation in every area of life. Being stagnated and lifeless is no way to live, and it does not give glory to God. Whatever you put into something is what you will get out of it. So, if you are merely going through the motions and not really investing anything in your marriage, job, church, home and friendships, it's time to make a change. The choice is yours: God said, 'I have set before you life and death . . . Choose life, so that you and your children may live' (Deuteronomy 30:19 NIV).

Learn to Love Your Life

When you feel good about yourself, it is easier to feel good about other people.

The life you have is the only one you have right now, so you might as well learn to love it. When you feel good about yourself, it is easier to feel good about other people and other things. If you start having a good attitude right where you are, in your present circumstances, God will help you get to where you want to be. If you really cannot stand your life, then do something about it. Don't just sit and complain – do something to make it better. What do you want out of life? Are you doing anything to make it happen, or are you just wishing things were different?

> Are you doing anything to make it happen, or are you just wishing things were different?

If you don't like your job, you hate the atmosphere at work and dread going every day, ask yourself if you're doing anything to change it. Do you smile at everyone when you get there, or do you frown like everyone else? Have you said anything encouraging to your colleagues or your boss?

Why not change the way you talk about your life and all its aspects? I heard a song the other night, 'I Love My Life', and I thought, *That is a great song I wish everyone was singing.*

One of the fastest ways to stagnate is to find something wrong with everything and everybody, including yourself. On the other hand, thankful people are usually happy people. The Bible tells us to be ever filled with God's Spirit, and one of the ways it lists to do it is to be thankful in everything (see Ephesians 5). Thank God for your life and your job. Thank God you are breathing and that all things are possible with Him. God never changes, but everything else is subject to change. You are not at a dead end; you're not stuck in a place you cannot escape. Today is the beginning of the rest of your wonderful life, and you should make a decision that you are going to love your life and enjoy it. Remember: it's the only one you've got.

> Today is the beginning of the rest of your wonderful life.

Familiarity

One of the reasons we lose our joy and the freshness and newness of things is familiarity. That simply means we get so accustomed to something that we no longer see how special it is. It's like the mother who started reading the Bible to her young son. A few weeks later they were reading from the Gospel of John. When she read John 3:16, her son commented, 'Oh, I know this. This is an old one.' Being familiar with a scripture can do that to us. We can know it so well, we feel we know all there is to know about it. It's the same with the blessings and the joys we experience in life. We need to make an effort not to take those things for granted. Being continually thankful is one of the ways to do that. Bless the Lord at all times and let His praise continually be in your mouth (see Psalm 34:1).

Be thankful and say so (see Psalm 100:1). Make a list of all the things you are grateful for, including the people in your life. Think about the big things, but think about the small things too. I frequently thank God for hot water, especially when I am tired and am taking a nice, hot bath. I also thank God for quiet. I really enjoy quiet times, because they seem to restore my entire being. Not one of us will just automatically be thankful on a regular basis; we have to be intentional about it. It's important that we dedicate and exercise ourselves not to become familiar with things that should amaze us, for it is the little things in life we appreciate that will keep our souls stirred up with joy.

It is the little things in life we appreciate that will keep our souls stirred up with joy.

Little Things Make a Big Difference

Don't forget to do little things that potentially have big power. So often, when we think of passion and drive, we think of big undertakings and wonder how in the world we'll accomplish them. But little things can be just as effective, if not more powerful. A hug or a smile can change someone's day. Showing appreciation can save a marriage. An extra five minutes at work every night could mean you are the one who doesn't get laid off. Saying little prayers throughout the day can bring you closer to God. Letting someone else with fewer groceries go in front of you in the supermarket queue could cause her to pay more attention to your 'Jesus loves you' bumper sticker the next time she sees you.

> Little things in life can change the course of someone's life completely.

Little things in life can change the course of someone's life completely. A group of men were carrying on a friendly conversation. One of them remarked that he had learned to be especially careful about small things. 'Would you believe,' he said, 'that a little thing like a pair of socks changed the entire course of my life?' 'I can hardly believe that,' replied another man. 'Well, it's true! Once I planned to take a trip with some of my friends on a canal boat, but two days before we intended to leave, I injured my foot while chopping wood. It was only a small cut, but the blue dye in the homemade socks I wore poisoned the wound, and I was compelled to stay home. While my friends were on their journey, a powerful preacher came to our town to hold revival meetings. Since I didn't have anything else to do, I decided to attend. The message touched me deeply, and as a result I surrendered my heart to the Lord. Afterwards, I saw I needed to change my life in many ways. New desires and purposes took hold of me. I determined also to seek an education, for I trusted this would enable me to live more usefully for my Lord.' The man who made these comments was none other than the former president of the United States – James A. Garfield![4]

I am a strong advocate of paying big attention to the little things in life. I pick up pennies everywhere I go. People usually don't pick them up because they're not worth much, but I believe there is a principle involved we need to see. If I feel a penny is not worth bending down for, then I am probably the type of person who lets a lot of other little things slide.

> Refuse to be lazy, avoid stagnation, love your life, and look for opportunities to tend to the little things.

Make a commitment right now to be the kind of person who always does his or her part in every situation. Refuse to be lazy, avoid stagnation, love your life, and look for opportunities to tend to the little things in life others are ignoring. Your passion will grow and your purpose will be surer and it won't be long before your reward will come!

CHAPTER 11

Passion for Your Spirit

When we think about being stirred up with passion, it's crucial we understand the purposes God has for us in every area of our lives. Without that understanding, we would be like the occasional group of kids you see on a playground running around all excited and screaming for joy at the top of their lungs, but when they're asked by someone watching them what they're so excited about, they just shrug their shoulders and say, 'We don't know.' Passion must be applied with purpose, and one of the greatest purposes God gives us is for our spirits.

Your spirit is the deepest part of you. It is not the part people see, but it is the most important part. Just as the engine of your car contributes greatly to how your car performs, the condition of your spirit determines the quality of life you will have.

Our spirit and soul is the eternal part of us, and as such we should

> The condition of your spirit determines the quality of life you will have.

pay more attention to it than to the outer areas of life. God is concerned with all areas of our lives, but He is especially concerned with the 'hidden person of the heart' (1 Peter 3:4).

For example, the Bible says a man is blessed, fortunate and happy if there is no deceit in his spirit (see Psalm 32:2). Some people deceive themselves into believing wrong is right and right is wrong. When they do this, they are not facing truth and are sowing seeds for a miserable life. However, if a man faces truth, acknowledges his sin and prays for forgiveness, he will be so strong in spirit that even when great trials come into his life, they will not reach his spirit. He will experience the protecting power of God (see Psalm 32:6). We are told to have a right spirit, one that is persevering and steadfast, not one that is weak and gives up easily (see Psalm 51:10).

We can learn a great deal about God's will for our spirit by reading His Word. We learn, for example, the strong spirit of a man will sustain him in bodily pain or trouble (see Proverbs 18:14). A broken spirit dries the bones (see Proverbs 17:22). King David prayed that he would have a willing spirit (see Psalm 51:12). A man is to have a trustworthy and faithful spirit (see Proverbs 11:13). Proverbs speaks of long forbearance and calmness of spirit.

The Bible also mentions several conditions a man can allow his spirit to be in that are not God's will and not good for the man. King David wrote at one time his spirit was overwhelmed and fainted within him (see Psalm 143:4). Proverbs speaks of a hasty spirit that is foolish, a spirit that has wilful contrariness in it, a proud and haughty spirit that goes before destruction, and a greedy spirit that stirs up strife.

> We should lean on the Holy Spirit for strength and use the God-given fruit of self-control to keep our spirits in the right condition.

We should lean on the Holy Spirit for strength and use the God-given fruit of self-control to keep our spirits in the right condition. The Bible says a man who has no rule over his own spirit is like a city broken down without walls (see Proverbs 25:28). In other words, by not keeping his spirit in the right condition, he has removed the protection from his life that God desires him to have.

Yes, a man's spiritual condition is very important. What do you have going on inside you? Whether you know it or not, it affects your daily life in an amazing way.

Spiritual Boredom

In his book *Enjoying God*, S. J. Hill wrote:

> Why does entertainment fascinate the human spirit? Why do certain movies capture the imaginations? It's because there is something in our human fabric that longs to be transported beyond our mundane living. Hollywood tries to grab our dreams and passions through films – drama, adventure, romance – and does a fairly good job. But these are just counterfeits of the real drama, adventure, and romance that are a part of God's design.
>
> One of the biggest problems the Church faces right now is spiritual boredom. Why? Because believers were never made for a program, an institution, or a weekly pew-warming ceremony. Christians were never made to be satisfied by a three-point outline that contains just enough advice to get over the 'hump' of the week. The human heart was made for passion. It was created for relationship. It was designed to experience the fullness of God.[1]

God desires a deep, intimate, passionate relationship with His people, but in order to have it, the spirit of man must be in the right condition. Our spirit is the place where we commune with God; it is His dwelling place. God is righteous and holy, and in order for Him to dwell in our spirits, He must make them righteous and holy.

Our spirit is the place where we commune with God.

A Righteous Spirit

> How you feel about yourself in your spirit (heart) is a
> determining factor in your life.

How you feel about yourself in your spirit (heart) is a determining factor in your life. It sets the stage for all of your relationships, including your relationship with God. It affects your job performance and your level of peace and joy. It affects your confidence and courage and how you respond to failure. You can go backwards or keep going forwards – it depends on how you feel about yourself.

Do you feel deep inside something is wrong with you? Do you compare yourself with others and assume you should be like them? God wants your spirit to be covered with righteousness – not guilt, condemnation and insecurity. Do you have any understanding of the righteousness of God available to you through faith in Jesus Christ? We should always see ourselves as righteous before God. It is a gift He gives to those who accept Jesus as their Saviour, and it is the condition our spirits must be in if we are to properly fellowship with God. God's own righteousness is credited or transmitted to those who accept Jesus as their Saviour. Jesus died so we might stand boldly before God and not shrink back in fear and shame.

> Jesus died so we might stand boldly before God and not
> shrink back in fear and shame.

Dare to Come Boldly

When I believe I am in a right relationship with someone and he loves me, it enables me to approach him boldly when I need him to help me with something. It also frees me to express my love and affection for him because I don't fear rejection.

How do you approach God? His Word says we are to come boldly. It actually says we should 'dare' to come boldly before Him.

> In Whom, because of our faith in Him, we *dare* [emphasis mine] to have the boldness (courage and confidence) of free access (an unreserved approach to God with freedom and without fear).
> – EPHESIANS 3:12

> Jesus did not die for us so we could have a religion. He died so we could have our sins forgiven.

Jesus did not die for us so we could have a religion. He died so we could have our sins forgiven, be made right with God, and enjoy fellowship with Him. Religion is man's attempt to get to a place where God will accept Him. It is man's idea of God's expectations, but Christianity is God taking on humanity in the person of Jesus Christ and coming down to man.

Righteousness is described in the Bible as a breastplate that covers the heart or spirit of man (see Ephesians 6:14). Our spirits must be covered with righteousness if we are to have rich fellowship with God and walk in victory. God gives it to us by His grace, but we must receive it by faith and walk in it.

The God Kind of Righteousness

There are two kinds of righteousness: the kind we try to earn by right behaviour, and the kind given as a gift through faith in Jesus Christ. There is self-righteousness and the God kind of righteousness. The latter is not only much better than the former, but it is the only type God will accept.

One of the most wonderful things about accepting Jesus Christ is that our relationship with Him gives us right standing with God. God views us as righteous. It has nothing to do with our behaviour; He simply views us that way because it is the only way He can have an intimate relationship with us. God is holy and completely righteous and cannot abide in the presence of sin. Since we are imperfect and unable to manifest perfection, God chooses to see us through the blood of Jesus that was poured out on the cross as payment for our sins. He sees us the way He sees Jesus!

> God views us as righteous.

If we feel bad about ourselves all the time and feel guilty and condemned, we are not able to enjoy the life Jesus died to give us. Our witness to others is also very poor because we cannot be a light to those living in darkness if we are living in a dark place ourselves. Any person filled with self-loathing, shame, reproach and guilt is filled with darkness.

> We cannot be a light to those living in darkness if we are living in a dark place ourselves.

God's Purpose Is Multifaceted

God's purpose for our lives has many, many parts to it, so don't make the mistake of thinking that finding God's purpose means only that you are to discover your vocation or the type of job you are supposed to be doing. Before we ever get around to doing, we need to be good at 'being'. *We must be what God wants us to be before we can truly do what He wants us to do.* True success is based on who we are, not what we do.

> Before we ever get around to doing, we need to be good at 'being'.

God gives us right standing with Him as a gift to be received through faith. It would not be right for Him to expect us to do something unless He gave us the ability to do it. *He expects us to behave right, so He gives us righteousness.* If you asked your child to sweep the floor, you would give him a broom. If you asked your child to mow the lawn, you would provide a lawn mower.

We are justified (made as if we never sinned) through our faith in Jesus Christ. We are viewed as being in Christ and, as such, God sees us the same way He sees Jesus. Wow! Accepting that truth can cause rejoicing, and that's exactly what it does for those who accept being in Christ before they try to 'do' in Christ.

Are you missing joy in your life? If so, you may have a poor self-image; you don't value yourself or you've believed negative things people have said to you. You will never experience true joy as long as you feel wrong about yourself. God wants to give you the gift of righteousness. Your righteousness is not based on *your* doing everything right, but it is based on faith in Jesus Christ and what He has done right.

Do You Need Some New Clothes?

Many of you may remember the Hans Christian Andersen story, 'The Emperor's New Clothes'. It's the tale of an emperor who was so fond of new clothing he spent all of his money and time and attention on it, and did very little else in the way of running his kingdom. When he wasn't showing off a new outfit, he was in his dressing room, trying on new outfits.

When two con men came to town passing themselves off as master weavers, they convinced the king they knew how to make the most exquisite outfit that not only looked beautiful, but actually appeared invisible to someone who was exceptionally stupid. The king, who was so full of his own greed and selfish desires, allowed himself to be duped, and marched down the street in front of his subjects basking in the glory of the new threads. Then a child cried out, 'But he's not wearing anything!'

It wasn't the master weavers who tricked the emperor into believing those invisible garments were real. It was the emperor's own self-righteousness; his pride, conceit and vanity brought him down. Often we find ourselves in the same position, unwilling to look outside our own egos; yet our purpose isn't to please ourselves, it's to please God.

> Are you able by faith to see yourself as royalty, a child of God's Kingdom?

According to the Bible, we are all kings and priests unto our God (see Revelation 1:6, 5:10). Now, we know that there are people called into the priesthood or those who are actually kings of nations. Being a king or a priest may never be our job, but it is our position before God, as far as He is concerned. That gives some insight into how valuable God believes we are. Can you begin to think of yourself as a king and a priest? Are you able by faith to see yourself as royalty, a child of God's Kingdom? I hope so, because as a child of God that is exactly who you are: Let Your priests be clothed with righteousness (right living and right standing with God); and let Your saints shout for joy!' (Psalm 132:9).

Unlike the emperor who wanted new clothes made of deception and self-centredness, God wants His priests to be clothed with righteousness, which includes right doing and right being. The question, of course, is which one comes first. Do we have right standing with God because we have done what is right, or do we have right standing with God as a gift from God – and because of that, we are motivated to do right things? Does the cart come before the horse, or the horse before the cart? Do we love God first and He loves us because we have first loved Him? Absolutely not! The Bible says plainly, 'We love Him because He first loved us' (1 John 4:19 NKJV). What do we have that God did not first give us? Nothing!

> The Bible teaches us we must believe and God will be pleased.

Many religions teach people they must do something or perform a certain way and then God will be pleased. The Bible teaches us we must believe and God will be pleased. Without faith it is impossible to please God (see Hebrews 11:6).

What About Good Works?

Do our good works count for anything? Should we strive to do right? Well, of course God is pleased when we do right, but, as I said earlier in the book, our motive for doing what we do is very important. If we do right, hoping to be made righteous through our good works, God is not pleased at all. Our righteousness cannot come from our own efforts, but it must be the result of believing and leaning entirely on Him. Everything is from Him and through Him and to Him, including our righteousness (see Romans 11:36).

The Apostle James said faith without works is dead (useless, lifeless), and that is true. Works are necessary, but faith must come first. Otherwise, we have the cart before the horse again. Just imagine for a moment you are going on a carriage ride. There are two beautiful horses and a lovely carriage for you to sit in. If the carriage was hooked up in front of the horses and they tried to push the carriage around the city, you would have a very rough ride. It would not be pleasant at all and could be downright frightening.

Believe first and then do good works for the right reason.

Believe first and then do good works for the right reason. Do them because you love God, not to get Him to love and accept you. You are accepted through faith in Jesus. You can come just as you are and God will help you become what He wants you to be. And this includes you, called of Jesus Christ and invited (*as you are*) to belong to Him. (Romans 1:6 (emphasis mine)).

If we could be perfect in our behaviour, then we would not need a Saviour at all.

You come as you are, and while God is working His purpose and will in you and your life, you can enjoy the journey. You don't have to be angry at yourself if you don't manifest perfect behaviour all the time. If we could be perfect in our behaviour, then we would not need a Saviour at all. The next time you sin, just admit it – ask God to forgive you and help you not to do it again. Thank Him that even though you made a mistake, you still have right standing with Him through faith.

Can You Believe What Seems Too Good to Believe?

A personal relationship with God through Jesus offers a new way of living. We are invited to receive Christ by faith, and when we do, righteousness, as well as many other wonderful blessings, is imputed (put on our account) (see Romans 4:11, 10:6). However, it matters very little what is legally ours unless we believe we have it. Without faith, we will never make use of what God provides.

When I am cold, if I don't believe I have a coat in my wardrobe, I will remain cold. When I am hungry, if I don't believe I have food in the cupboard, I will remain hungry. If a poor person is told he has inherited millions and it has been deposited in the bank, he will remain poor unless he believes what he has been told and actually goes to the bank to cash a cheque.

A great many Christians are like the poor man. When Jesus died, they inherited righteousness, justification and freedom from the power of sin, as well as many other amazing things described in God's promises to His people. However, the inheritance does them no good at all, and even though a new covenant (agreement) has been signed and sealed in the blood of Jesus, they continue to live under the old covenant (agreement), which brings sin and death (misery of every kind) (see 2 Corinthians 3:6).

> You should see yourself as God sees you, not as the world sees you.

Take a step of faith and see yourself as one chosen by God, who has obtained an inheritance. *God's Word gives you permission to have a good attitude towards yourself.* You should see yourself as God sees you, not as the world sees you.

> In Him we also were made [God's] heritage (portion) *and* we obtained an inheritance; for we had been foreordained (chosen and appointed beforehand) in accordance with His purpose, Who works out everything in agreement with the counsel *and* design of His [own] will.
>   – EPHESIANS 1:11

> It takes a daring step of faith to live in God's Kingdom and enjoy His Kingdom benefits.

I must admit some of these Bible truths seem almost too good to be true. It takes a daring step of faith to live in God's Kingdom and enjoy His Kingdom benefits. Receiving total forgiveness for all of our sins as a gift from God – through faith in Jesus – is so good, many people just cannot believe it. Believing God views them as righteous – even when they make mistakes – is hard to fathom. They are looking for something hard, something they can spend their lives struggling with. The intellectuals cannot work out salvation through Christ and they refuse to believe what their minds cannot comprehend. However, God promises that if anyone comes to Him as a little child and simply believes what He says, he or she will be saved (delivered from sin and given a new life).

I have been criticised for teaching people they are the righteousness of God in Christ, even though the Bible clearly states it in 2 Corinthians 5:21. I have also been criticised for saying, 'I am the righteousness of God in Christ.' When I say it, I do not mean I am righteous in myself or due to any right acts I might perform. I am simply agreeing with God's Word. I know all of our own righteousness is like filthy rags, according to Isaiah 64:6. I have decided to believe God's Word and take it for myself, and it has changed my life from one of defeat and misery to victory and joy. We all sin and make mistakes, but thank God we can be forgiven and stand before Him clothed in righteousness.

> Thank God we can be forgiven and stand before Him
> clothed in righteousness.

For ten years of my life, I was a Christian who went to church every Sunday and even did various kinds of good deeds through my church. I believed, like many of my other Christian friends, that I was a wretched, miserable sinner, and as a result my behaviour changed very little. I went to church, but I remained wretched and miserable. I could not rise above what I believed I was, and neither can you or anyone else. I finally became unwilling to continue living in defeat, began a serious study of God's Word, and I decided I would believe the Word of God rather than man-made doctrines that had no power. Like multitudes of other seekers throughout history, I discovered wonderful truths that promised me eternal life, victory, peace, joy, righteousness, justification, freedom from guilt and condemnation, hope, prosperity, healing, power and authority. And I discovered these things were for my life here on earth, and not just for when I die and go to heaven, as so many people believe. We can't just think about some day, we have to think about now. It's hard to be passionate about some day, which seems way off in the distance. It's imperative to be passionate about today.

> We can't just think about some day, we have to think about now.

At church we need to learn about sin and forgiveness, but we also need to learn about our right standing with God. If we don't, we are in danger of spending our lives rejecting ourselves, even though God has accepted us. A great many people do not like themselves, and in fact some even hate themselves and find various ways to punish themselves for their perceived wretchedness. I believe God wants us to receive His love, love ourselves in a balanced way, and let His love flow through us to others.

> God wants us to receive His love, love ourselves in a balanced way, and let His love flow through us to others.

I watched a film recently about a young girl who hated herself so much she starting cutting and burning herself as a form of punishment.

I punished myself by not allowing myself to enjoy life. Some people isolate themselves and live lonely lives; some are so insecure they never dare take a risk or have an adventure. I am encouraging you to value and respect yourself, to have a good relationship with yourself! If you are against yourself, then you are defeated before you ever begin. You are God's creation and He paid a high price to purchase you from a life of sin and oppression; so act as if your believe you are valuable and start enjoying yourself and the life Jesus died to give you.

> Act as if you believe you are valuable and start enjoying yourself and the life Jesus died to give you.

> You were bought with a price [purchased with a preciousness *and* paid for, made His own]. So then, honor God and bring glory to Him in your body.
>   – 1 CORINTHIANS 6:20

The Bible says you are a chosen race, God's own special purchased person, and you are called to set forth the wonderful deeds and display the virtues of God, who called you out of darkness to live in His marvellous light (see 1 Peter 2:9). Believe in the work God is calling you to do, and commit yourself to just 'be' in Jesus. He will see you through any difficulties you encounter and help you do all He wants you to do.

> You are called to set forth the wonderful deeds and display the virtues of God.

A New Identity

In the 1950s, Sao Kya Seng, the prince of thirty-four independent Shan states in northeastern Burma, also known as Hsipaw, came to Denver,

i dare you

Believe

When you try to understand God's purpose for your spirit so you can have the passion He desires for you, it requires a certain amount of trust and belief. Trust that God is in control, and believe that He will give you what you need to achieve and succeed! If you struggle in this area, here are some verses to look up and some of God's promises to think about.

1 God will never abandon you (see Hebrews 13:5).
2 God wants the best for you (see Jeremiah 29:11).
3 God wants the best *from* you and He will do everything He can to help (see John 14:26).

Colorado, to study engineering. Since he wanted to experience what it was like to be a student in the United States, he kept his identity secret. Not even his professors knew who he really was. One of his fellow students was Inge Sargent, from Austria. Both of them being exchange students, Inge and the Burmese prince quickly found they had a lot in common and started to spend more and more time together.

Soon their friendship grew into love, but the Burmese prince decided he would not reveal his true identity, even though they were seriously dating. He did not want Inge's decision to go out with him to be coloured by the fact she could marry into royalty. So when he finally proposed, with an engagement ring of ruby and diamond, Inge still did not know who he really was. Loving him very much, however, Inge said yes and they got married, like any other couple, in the United States. For their honeymoon, Sao Kya Seng took Inge to his home country, so she could meet his family and see where he was from. When their ship reached the shores of Burma, hundreds of people were waiting at the harbour and many of them had gone out in small boats, holding up welcome signs. A band was playing and some people were tossing flowers at the ship. Surprised at all this excitement, Inge turned to her husband and asked whose arrival the people were celebrating.

'Inge,' the young man said to his new bride, 'I am the prince of Hsipaw. These people are celebrating our arrival. You are now the princess.'[2]

> Jesus also gives us a new identity.

Just as this young woman received a new identity, Jesus also gives us a new identity. He says, 'You are My child and I love you unconditionally.' He also says we have right standing with God through Him; that we are justified, sanctified and glorified. Old things pass away and all things become new. He offers us a new way of living.

> And those whom He thus foreordained, He also called; and
> those whom He called, He also justified (acquitted, made
> righteous, putting them into right standing with Himself).
> And those whom He justified, He also glorified [raising them
> to a heavenly dignity and condition or state of being].
> – ROMANS 8:30

> We may not be where we need to be, but thank God we are
> on our way!

Although these things are being worked out continually in the life of a believer, they are spiritually his and he should not be afraid to say so. We may not be where we need to be, but thank God we are on our way! We are becoming what God made us to be!

Stop feeling bad about yourself and know you are the righteousness of God in Christ. It will motivate you to produce right behaviour.

It will motivate you to embrace with passion what has been given to you by God. As you continue to study God's Word, you are continually being transformed into His image from one degree of glory to another (see 2 Corinthians 3:18). You don't have to be stuck in sinful behaviour. You can overcome it through God's power, but you must believe the right things. Jesus said it would be done unto us as we believed (see Matthew 8:13).

> If you continue believing what God's Word says, your feelings will eventually catch up with your faith.

All the changes you desire will not take place overnight. However, if you are willing to make an investment of time, little by little you will unwrap and begin to use every gift God has given you through Jesus Christ. You may not feel righteous at first, but if you continue believing what God's Word says, your feelings will eventually catch up with your faith. Faith reaches into the spiritual realm and believes what it cannot see and feel, and waits for it to be manifested in the natural realm.

> You can spend your life as a labourer or an inheritor; the choice is yours.

Put on righteousness by faith and see yourself clothed in it, because when you do, your joy will increase. Isaiah said that because he was clothed with the garments of salvation and covered with the robe of righteousness, he would rejoice (see Isaiah 61:10). You can do the same thing, but it takes a step of faith. You can continue believing if you try hard enough and can manage to be really good that God will accept you – or you can decide to believe the Bible, which says we are made acceptable to God through faith in Jesus Christ, and not by our works.

You can spend your life as a labourer or an inheritor; the choice is yours. You can work yourself practically to death trying to earn God's approval, or you can inherit righteousness through faith – the decision is one only you can make. God provides for us, but we must receive it!

> You can work yourself practically to death trying to earn God's approval, or you can inherit righteousness through faith.

What if someone sent you a gift, but you never opened it? Would it do you any good if it stayed in the box? Of course not! Then why not start finding out what God has given you by unwrapping His gifts now? Begin with the gift of salvation and then move on to the gift of righteousness through faith in Christ. The Holy Spirit will continue revealing truth to you and you can open, one by one, the wonderful gifts of God that will truly usher you into a brand-new way of living.

> Why not start finding out what God has given you by unwrapping His gifts now?

CHAPTER 12

Passion for Your Mind

Man's mind is a most noble organ indeed. It is not merely his brain; it is much, much more. It is spoken of as being synonymous with the heart. Man's thoughts proceed out of his mind, but so does his entire attitude towards life. How we position our minds towards a certain thing makes the difference between success and failure, joy or misery, peace or turmoil, passion or apathy.

The Bible speaks of 'mind-sets' or how we set our minds towards things. It says, for example, we are to set our minds and keep them set on things above, not on things on the earth (see Colossians 3:2). The thoughts of man are given a place of prominence in God's Word – in fact, it actually says as a man thinks, so shall his life be (see Proverbs 23:7). I always liked the saying 'Where the mind goes, the man follows.' That is one reason why our thoughts about ourselves are so important. You simply cannot rise above your own thoughts. They become a lid on your life!

Our minds must come into agreement with God, and that won't happen by accident. It is something that must be done purposefully and relentlessly. God has a very good plan for each of our lives, but He says our minds and attitudes must be transformed (changed) by an entire renewal (see Romans 12:2). In other words, we must learn to think thoughts that will assist God in bringing His plan to pass in our lives.

Our minds must come into agreement with God.

> We are partners with God, and as such we must co-operate with Him.

Far too many people make the serious mistake of thinking good things will simply fall on them, but that is just not true. We are partners with God, and as such we must co-operate with Him. There are many things we will have to do on purpose. If we set our minds or, as we often say, 'make up our minds' to do a thing, then we are more likely to follow through with corresponding actions.

On What Is Your Mind Set?

The Bible teaches us in Romans 8:5–6 if we set our minds on the flesh, we will be controlled by the flesh and its lusts and desires. However, if we set our minds on the Spirit, we will be controlled by the Spirit. Many people don't realise whatever we set our minds on is what we are seeking in life. What has your mind been on lately?

Have you set your mind to pursue the purpose of God passionately, or are you pursuing your own plan and expecting God to bless it? Sometimes the best thing we can do is throw away all of our own plans and say, 'God, Your will be done in my life.' When we do this, we discover a fresh passion, one that's free and full and not held back by our own desires.

> Have you set your mind to pursue the purpose of God passionately?

The Apostle Paul said when he was a child, he thought, talked and reasoned like a child, but after becoming a man, he laid aside childish ways (see 1 Corinthians 13:11). What do children think about? Mostly, they think about themselves, what they want and how to get it, like the seven-year-old girl who was given a prize of some coins for her memory work in Sunday school and proudly announced to the pastor's wife that she had put it all in the offering plate that morning in church.

'My, how wonderful!' the pastor's wife exclaimed. 'I'm sure God will be pleased.'

'Yes,' the child replied, 'and now maybe God will let me do some of the things I want to do!'

When I was forty years old, I was still doing that and I can tell you, God was not pleased. I wasn't enjoying the good plan He had for me either.

> Thinking about oneself first and foremost is immature.

Paul told the Corinthian church members not to be immature in their thinking. Thinking about oneself first and foremost is immature. Thinking negative, critical, judgmental, jealous, envious and greedy thoughts is immature. It is not the type of thinking God expects from His family. Have you ever found out someone in your family was thinking some awful thing and you said, 'How could you think that?'

> It is truly amazing what our own thoughts can do to us.

Not long ago I found out a trusted and valued employee was thinking I was thinking all kinds of things about her, and I was not thinking that way at all. I recall saying to her, 'How could you even think that I would think that?' Her thoughts about my thoughts were stealing her peace and joy, and they were not based on anything but her imagination. In reality, my thoughts towards her were very appreciative, good and positive. It is truly amazing what our own thoughts can do to us. They become the house in which we live. My employee was thinking things that were totally untrue, but those things were making her miserable. Her thoughts had become her reality.

Are You Ready to Take Control of Your Thoughts?

Do you just think whatever comes into your mind? We should always choose our thoughts with care, since they are what we become and can determine the courses of our lives. We aren't without opposition. Our enemy is the devil, a liar and deceiver who constantly tries to inject wrong thoughts into our minds, hoping we will accept them as truth. If we accept his deceit as truth, we let him win and hand him the keys to our futures. Many people live their lives in a deceptive fantasy the devil planted in their minds. Until we learn God's Word, which is the Truth, we have no hope of being able to recognise the devil's lies. If he goes undetected, he can destroy our lives and we can totally miss the purpose of God.

> Many people live their lives in a deceptive fantasy.

Here's a scenario to help you better understand what I'm talking about.

Sarah had always been a bit shy and timid. Like most children, she encountered other children who were cruel to her and said lots of things that made her feel bad about herself. In addition, Sarah's parents seemed to favour her sister, Julie, over her and had a bad habit of comparing the two. Julie was bold and confident and her parents said things to Sarah like 'Why can't you be like your sister?'

Taking advantage of the situation already set in motion, the devil planted wrong thoughts and imaginations in Sarah's mind. He told her she was not worth anything and that something must be wrong with her, since she could not seem to do what people expected of her. He told her no one liked her, which only increased her timidity and shyness. She withdrew even more and isolated herself, mingling with people only when she had to.

Sarah experienced a very lonely and unhappy childhood and adolescence. As she entered her teenage and young adult years, her fears about herself only deepened. She had a teacher who delighted in correcting her in front of the other students, which embarrassed her and made her feel terribly ashamed. She was about twenty pounds overweight and that also made her feel bad about herself. Her mother frequently dropped hints that she needed to lose weight so she could be slim like her sister.

Even people who might have wanted to be friends with Sarah didn't venture to try, because they misunderstood her personality and thought she didn't like them. It is amazing how often people who don't like themselves experience rejection from others. I have learned if we don't like ourselves, we behave in a way that makes other people think we don't like them.

Sarah got through school, got a job, and continued her lonely life. She was not happy. She was single, with no prospects, and felt stuck in a job she hated, but didn't have the courage to leave. At the age of thirty-seven, Sarah was invited by a colleague from work to attend a Bible study fellowship. By then, she was so miserable that she was ready to try anything. The Bible study was being done around my book *Battlefield of the Mind*. The participants were studying the book together and going through the study guide, answering questions and discussing the mind.

Sarah began to realise she was a prisoner of her own thoughts, and even if some people rejected her throughout her life, that did not mean she had no worth and value. She was hearing God's Word for the first time in her life and was amazed at the things she was learning.

She accepted Jesus Christ as her Saviour and continued to study. Gradually, she started noticing changes in her life and her attitude, simply because the Word of God was helping her to renew her mind. She was learning she had options about the way she thought. She began to recognise the devil's lies and resisted them, and when wrong thoughts came into her mind about herself, she refused them and replaced them with something uplifting she had learned from the Bible.

By the time Sarah was thirty-nine years old, she was engaged to be married to a wonderful man. She forgave her mother for being critical of her and they began developing a healthy relationship, the kind where Sarah was able to confront her mum in a loving way whenever her mother criticised her unjustly. Sarah also found the courage to leave the job she hated and pursue her real dream of becoming a nurse.

Had Sarah not learned how to think right, she would have continued her miserable lifestyle, even though God loved her very much and had a good plan for her. It grieves me terribly to realise how many precious people there are in the world who have been deceived by the devil and miss out on fulfilling their true purposes in life.

Aggressively make the choice of what you're going to think about.

I believe it is time for you to take control of your thoughts. You need to think what you want to think, not just whatever falls into your mind. Don't passively receive lies from the devil, but aggresively make the choice of what you're going to think about.

Peace of Mind

God's will for you is peace of mind, because it is part of Kingdom living. I was a middle-aged woman before I ever even knew what peace of mind felt like. I grew up in an atmosphere of turmoil. Everyone in our household was upset about something most of the time, so worry was my normal state. Since that was all I ever knew, I did not realise there was any other way to live.

After Dave and I married in 1967, I saw a big difference in how we handled everyday life or the challenging situations that came our way. Dave stayed calm; he didn't worry or become anxious; he continued to be positive and enjoy his life. Meanwhile, I worried and was miserable enough for both of us! I always wanted him to '*do something*' about our problems, but he told me he had already done what God required him to do. He shared that he prayed and did what he could do, but felt no responsibility to try to do what only God could do. He was trusting God to take care of the situation, but to me that sounded completely irresponsible because I was accustomed to taking care of myself and everyone else. I never had anyone truly take care of me, and even though I was a Christian and went to church regularly, I knew nothing about trusting God or Dave. I prayed and then worried! I prayed and then searched for my own solutions! I could not settle down until I thought I had worked out how to take care of the need.

> Even though I was a Christian and went to church
> regularly, I knew nothing about trusting God.

After many years of living the roller-coaster life, being up when my circumstances were good and down when they were not, I finally was ready for a change. I think sometimes we would like a change, but we don't want one badly enough to do what we need to do to get it. So we keep going around and around the same mountains, and there is really nothing God can do to help us until we are ready to receive His solutions and obey His commands about how to do things.

> There is really nothing God can do to help us until we are
> ready to receive His solutions and obey His commands.

He tells us not to be anxious or worried about anything, but to continue to make our wants known to Him in everything by prayer and petition with thanksgiving, and the peace that passes understanding will be ours (see Philippians 4:6–7). I wanted the peace, but wasn't willing to give up the worry. The truth was, I trusted myself more than I trusted God, and until I came to the end of myself, God couldn't help me. He can only help those who are totally leaning on Him and obeying His commands. I thought worry was an option, but now I realise it is a sin. God tells us not to worry or be upset, and anything He tells us to do or not to do is sin if we don't obey Him. Whatever is not of faith is sin (see Romans 14:23).

> God tells us not to worry or be upset.

Jesus left us with some parting words that certainly convey His purpose for us. Just prior to entering His time of suffering in Gethsemane and going to the cross to die for our sins, He said:

> Peace I leave with you; My [own] peace I now give *and* bequeath to you. Not as the world gives do I give to you. Do not let your hearts be troubled, neither let them be afraid. [Stop allowing yourselves to be agitated and disturbed; and do not permit yourselves to be fearful and intimidated and cowardly and unsettled.]
> – JOHN 14:27

I read this scripture many times and thought, *Well, if You left me peace, then why don't I have it?* I still had the wrong mind-set that whatever God's will is will just happen, but that is not true. We must do our part and God will do His part. You can have the easiest one-step casserole recipe in the world, but if you don't stick it in the oven, it's never going to cook. It's the same with our relationship with God: He won't do our part and we can't do His part. When we understand this and decide to be responsible believers, things begin to change rapidly.

God made peace available to us through Jesus Christ. He did His part. Now our part is to stop letting ourselves be upset, afraid, worried, anxious and troubled. You may be thinking what I thought initially: *I can't help it . . . I just get upset!* But the truth is, we can learn a different way to respond to life's challenges. The truth is, we can control our emotions, if we choose to. True, it is a new way of living, but it is what God wants for us.

> Now our part is to stop letting ourselves be upset, afraid, worried, anxious and troubled.

The Ability to Concentrate

We live in an age of information, where literally thousands upon thousands of images come at us every day. We are bombarded with information overload. Did you know that a single edition of today's *New York Times* contains more information than a British citizen of the seventeenth century would encounter in a lifetime? And the technology we now have at our fingertips isn't really saving us time – it's actually costing us more! The amount of leisure time enjoyed by the average American has decreased 37 per cent since 1973. All these gadgets, like cellphones, laptops, personal digital assistants, and the Blackberry, that we are so proud to own take time to learn and maintain. It's estimated the average person must learn to operate 20,000 pieces of equipment.[1] This morning I spent about one hour on my computer answering e-mails, which is a nice convenience, but about forty minutes of that hour was spent trying to get the equipment to work right. My e-mails were not downloading properly, so I had to shut everything down and restart the computer. Then I had a virus warning to deal with and one e-mail that I could not open because of some special block.

> God wants us to keep our minds on what we are doing.

It's sad to say, but it's no wonder that most people have lost the ability to concentrate on any one thing for a very long period of time.

We're juggling so many things that when we do have a moment to focus, it's often lost because we're still trying to catch up from the frenetic pace we've been keeping. God wants us to keep our minds on what we are doing, because as we concentrate our powers in one area, we are more creative and the job gets done better.

> Our lives are fragmented because our minds stay fragmented.

Our lives are fragmented because our minds stay fragmented. We pick up bits and pieces of things and end up feeling confused because we have difficulty concentrating. Over the years God has challenged me repeatedly to practise doing one thing at a time and actually be intentional about keeping my mind on it. When we have overcrowded schedules – which most people do these days – it's a challenge not to think about all the things we need to do *while* we are doing the thing we are presently doing.

For instance, I found that if I eat a meal while my mind's on business matters, half the time I can only vaguely remember eating. I know I ate, but I didn't really enjoy it because I had my mind on so many other things.

I believe this could be one of the reasons why so many people over-eat. If we didn't enjoy eating when we ate, or if we barely remember it, perhaps we are still looking for an emotional satisfaction we missed because of multitasking. I am convinced it is not really possible to thoroughly enjoy life unless we learn to slow down and concentrate on

i dare you

Slow Down and Use Your Mind Properly

1 Be determined to pay attention to the things around you, like flowers, trees, a child playing, or your family who love you.

2 Commit to reading something that is not work-related for at least thirty minutes a day.

3 Get up twenty minutes earlier than you do right now and spend that time with God. Ask Him to show you how He wants you to use your time that day.

what we are doing. Otherwise, life goes by in a blur. We know we are busy, but we seem to get very little satisfaction out of our activities.

Your Imagination

The Bible says in Genesis that God confused the language of the people because they came to the point where nothing they imagined would be impossible for them. The power of concentration and imagination is greater than we realise.

When you are asking God to do something in your life, do you see in your heart what you are asking Him for, or do you allow fearful thoughts and images to dominate your mind? We cannot control our lives with our thoughts, but we do need to co-operate with God by having minds full of faith and seeing what we hope to have, not merely what we have always had. As the Bible says:

> Now faith is the assurance (the confirmation, the title deed) of the things [we] hope for, being the proof of things [we] do not see *and* the conviction of their reality [faith perceiving as real fact what is not revealed to the senses].
> — HEBREWS 11:1

You can close your eyes and see a disaster or you can choose to see victory.

You can close your eyes and see a disaster or you can choose to see victory. The imagination is a wonderful thing God gave us and we should not turn it over to the devil to use as his rubbish dump.

I heard an interesting story about a man who enjoyed golf, but he was an average golfer with a dream to improve his game. A war broke out and he joined the army. During a battle he was captured and spent seven years in a prison camp. His cell was more like a cage and was so small he could not even stand up straight in it. For most of the seven years, he had no physical activity and talked to no one. Of course his mind wandered in every direction, and I imagine many of his thoughts were fearful and negative. One could probably come up with very gruesome mental images if he pondered all the things that could take place in a prison camp.

He realised he had to find something to do with his mind to keep himself from going crazy, so he began to play golf in his mind. He saw the course, he saw himself make each shot, and, of course, everything he saw himself doing was being done very well. Day after day he played eighteen holes of golf. He invested about four hours a day, and when he was released from prison, although he had not touched a golf club in seven years and his physical condition had deteriorated, he went around the course in 74, which was twenty strokes fewer than he ever scored previously. Amazing! His golf game improved because he saw himself doing it well, over and over.

> God wants us to see good things happening to us.

The devil loves for us to imagine disaster, failure, rejection, illness, financial struggles, loneliness, and all kinds of other negative things. However, God wants us to see good things happening to us. Be daring! Start seeing what you believe God wants you to do and have. It is one way you can release your faith instead of your fears.

Be Positive

God wants us to be positive. There is nothing negative about God, and if we want to walk with Him and have His plan manifest in our lives, we also have to refuse to be negative.

In his book titled *Failing Forward,* John C. Maxwell shows the vicious cycle that is set up in our lives when we yield to a fear of failure, which includes fear, inactivity, inexperience and inability. To break that cycle of defeat, we must commit ourselves to positive action. We must be willing to risk failure in order to succeed.[2]

There are two ways you can look at life, and your decision determines the quality of it. You can be the type of person whose glass is always half empty or you can see it as being half full and enthusiastically look for ways to fill it up completely. If you feel your life stinks, perhaps it is because of 'stinking thinking'.

The Whole World Stinks

Wise men and philosophers throughout the ages have disagreed on many things, but many are in unanimous agreement on one point: we become what we think about. Ralph Waldo Emerson said, 'A man is what he thinks about all day long.' The Roman emperor Marcus Aurelius put it this way: 'A man's life is what his thoughts make of it.' In the Bible we find: 'As a man thinks in his mind, so is he.'

One Sunday afternoon a cranky grandfather was visiting his family. As he lay down to take a nap, his grandson decided to have a little fun by putting some strong-smelling cheese on his grandfather's moustache. Soon, Grandpa awoke with a snort and charged out of the bedroom saying, 'This room stinks.' Through the house he went, finding every room smelling the same. Desperately he made his way outside only to find that 'the whole world stinks!'

So it is when we fill our minds with negativism. Everything we experience and everybody we encounter will carry the scent we hold in our minds.[3]

> When we are intentionally thinking and living in a positive manner, our lives can change for the better.

When we are intentionally thinking and living in a positive manner, our lives can change for the better. Our physical energy increases and our overall attitude remains more positive.

Do You Wish Your Circumstances Would Change?

Are you waiting for your circumstances to change, believing then you will be able to enjoy peace? Do you get frustrated because it seems that life offers one challenging thing after another? If your answer to these two questions is yes, then you are like most people. It took me years to realise God wanted *me* to change more than He wanted to change my circumstances.

> If God makes our lives perfect and we never have to face life's challenges, we have no need for faith.

If God makes our lives perfect and we never have to face life's challenges, we have no need for faith. He desires that we rise above the storms of life and learn to soar with eagles who learn to use storms to lift them to new levels. Jesus had trials, but He remained stable and peaceful. When He and His disciples were in the boat crossing to the other side of the lake and a terrible storm of hurricane proportions arose, Jesus slept and His disciples became frantic, worried and anxious. The Apostle Paul encountered many trials that were extremely severe yet he remained stable and said we should rejoice in the Lord, and rejoice again and again.

Jesus said that during tribulations we should cheer up (see John 16:33). It all sounds backward to anything we have learned to do in the world – at least that was the way it seemed to me. Not worry when I have a problem – what kind of nonsense is that? Cast my care? Well, if I do that, then who is going to solve the problem?

I just wanted peace and I wanted my circumstances to change so I could have it, but, as I said, God wanted to change me more than my circumstances. I finally took staying calm as a challenge. I am the type of person who likes a challenge, so I decided it would be my goal to remain calm in every situation. Since that did not come naturally to me the way it did to my husband, I knew I was in for quite a battle, but gradually I began forming new habits.

Form a Habit of Peace

I formed a very bad habit of responding to trials by becoming upset. That was my first and only response. I had a problem, I got upset! If I had a need I couldn't meet, I got worried! That was me, that was what I did, and everyone in a relationship with me knew it. Dave always knew exactly how I would respond before I even responded. If he had to tell me we needed new tyres for the car, he knew I would get upset as soon as he told me. Why? Because I had other plans for the money and now I had to work out where we would get the money for the tyres, plus the other things. Now I had another problem I had to solve. My husband was a peaceful man who learned early in life to trust God, and he became very weary of my negative reactions and emotional upset. He knew my response was not changing anything for the better, but my negativity and upset reactions were stealing joy from our family, robbing my health, and preventing God from bringing answers.

We had a small bank account (very small) and every time we had to take any money out of it, I got upset. I wanted that money in the bank to lean on! I remember Dave telling me God could not move in my life until that money was gone because I was depending on it instead of God. Some of us are so stubborn we won't trust God until we have no other choice at all. The bank account finally dwindled away and, sure enough, I learned to trust God. As I watched Him being faithful over and over again, trusting got easier.

> Some of us are so stubborn we won't trust God until we have no other choice at all.

Soon I started forming new habits, especially in the area of how I responded to trials, tribulations and disappointments. I exercised myself to remain calm and sometimes I had to actually walk out of a room into another, take a few deep breaths, pray a little, and then return to deal with the situation, but I was determined I would not live my life in turmoil. I started pursuing peace and not expecting it to merely fall on me.

The Apostle Paul said that we have to habitually put to death the evil deeds prompted by the body.

> For if you live according to [the dictates of] the flesh, you will surely die. But if through the power of the [Holy] Spirit you are [habitually] putting to death (making extinct, deadening) the [evil] deeds prompted by the body, you shall [really and genuinely] live forever.
> – ROMANS 8:13

Putting to death the evil deeds prompted by the body simply means embracing and maintaining self-control. It means we say yes to God and no to the flesh. My flesh (emotions) wanted to get upset when things did not go my way, but I said no and eventually my emotional feelings had to calm down. I was no longer willing to let my mind and emotions control me.

Today I have a habit of peace. It has developed over years, but I encourage you not to dread making an investment of time in making your life better. Wouldn't you rather be moving in a positive direction than continuing to move in a negative one? If you are going to put your time into anything, make sure it is something that renders progress, and not something that always leaves you at the same place that you have always been.

> I encourage you not to dread making an investment of time in making your life better.

Do I ever get upset? Of course I do. We all have emotions and there are times when mine get the best of me, like everyone else. Recently, I had a rather frustrating week. I had been working very hard and just returned from a weekend conference where I did a lot of speaking. The day after I got back, things just did not go the way I planned. I wanted to enjoy my day and rest, but the devil had other plans and I guess God thought I needed a test. I did not pass my test, so I suppose I will get to take it again some day.

For three days in a row, I encountered various individuals who were not satisfied with anything I was giving them. They were all family members I support and take care of, or employees who chose that time to grumble. In all of the situations I felt I had bent over backwards to make their lives good and I could not believe the way they were acting. I got mad, and when I say I got mad, I mean I got really mad! I have to be honest and admit I got angrier than I had been in a long time. Just that weekend, I spoke on the words of our mouths, and I think during those three days of being upset, I broke every guideline I'd established through my teaching.

Once I let myself get upset, I just could not seem to calm down and I got worse instead of better. By the fourth day I finally calmed down and managed to forgive everyone, and peace was restored.

But suddenly, at a very early hour, another totally unexpected thing happened along the same lines as the other situations and I started to blow my top – but then I chose to stop, and right there I made a decision. *I am not going to get upset! I have had enough of this! I am going to stay calm and take away the devil's power!*

Remaining peaceful in hard times completely disarms the devil.

Our remaining peaceful in hard times completely disarms the devil. He does not know what to do with someone who refuses to get upset. Well, the bad news is, I didn't pass the first three tests, but the good news is I did finally see what was going on and I passed the fourth test! *Peace is power!*

When we remain calm, God moves to help us. Keeping our peace shows we trust God, and then He defeats the devil and we are set free. God told the Israelites the battle was not theirs but His, and I believe that promise is also for us today. Let God fight your battles while you remain at rest, trusting Him.

Let God fight your battles while you remain at rest, trusting Him.

Form a habit of peace. It will be one of the best things you have ever done for yourself!

Creating an Atmosphere in Which God Can Work

As Jesus was on His way to heal a sick girl, He received word that she had died. Jesus told the father not to be seized with alarm but simply to believe and she would be made well. When Jesus arrived at the home of the dead girl, He permitted no one to enter with Him except Peter, James, John and the girl's parents. When He told the others not to weep because she was not dead, but sleeping, they laughed scornfully at Him. Despite their disbelief, Jesus did follow through with His promise to heal the girl, but the lesson we want to learn is why He would allow only certain people in the room with Him. I believe it was because He needed to be surrounded by faith, not by doubt, unbelief, fear and mourners. He wanted an atmosphere that He could work in.

Our thoughts, words and attitudes create an atmosphere. It can be hectic and stressful, or it can be calm and positive and even enjoyable. Think positive thoughts! I can remember when I thought my thoughts didn't make much difference. After all, they were in my head and certainly weren't affecting anyone but me. I was wrong – and so are you if this is your attitude.

Thoughts operate in the spiritual realm. You cannot see thoughts just as you cannot see angels, but they are real; they merely function in a realm not visible to the eye. Thoughts become words, attitudes, body language, facial expressions and moods – and all of these affect the atmosphere we dwell in.

> You cannot see thoughts just as you cannot see angels, but they are real.

The people we allow into our inner circle also affect our atmosphere. People we encounter occasionally don't affect us that much, but those we spend a lot of time with do. We should make sure we surround ourselves, as much as possible, with people who are positive and full of faith. Some of you might be able to change your life for the better just by choosing some different friends.

Lucinda Norman, in an article for *Lookout* magazine, described a Christmas shopping experience she once had at a busy shopping mall. People pushed, elbowed, and cut in front of her all day. After having a woman literally try to grab a lace tablecloth from her hands during a ten-minute 35 per cent-off special, Lucinda had to yank it back and actually won. However, she became belligerent and grumpy for the rest of the afternoon.

At a restaurant in the shopping mall, she met some friends and flagged down a waitress and said, 'I need hot tea, now!' The lady snapped at her and said, 'I'm not your waitress. Wait your turn.'

Angrily, Lucinda replied, 'Look, I've been waiting my turn all day, bring me some tea!' But the waitress ignored her.

A few moments later, a smiling young man came to their table and said, 'I'm Rob, your waiter.' After he took their order, she noticed that Rob stopped to help the rude waitress with her tray. He greeted the other customers and staff.

In the midst of dozens of hurried shoppers and restaurant staff, he conducted himself in a polite, unhurried atmosphere of calm. When he refilled her teacup, Lucinda noticed a silver ring on his right hand made of connected letters. After he walked away, she said to the other ladies at the table, 'Did you notice that our waiter is wearing a ring that spells Jesus?'

From that moment her attitude changed. This one young man's example reminded her of the peace Christ came to bring. For the rest of the day, she enjoyed shopping, opened the door for others, and let people go in front of her at the queues at the tills in an atmosphere of calm.[4]

God works in a positive atmosphere, not a negative one. If we have a negative situation, but a positive attitude, it is a good example to others and it opens the door for God to work and change our negative situation into a positive one. But if we have a negative situation and a negative attitude to go along with it, we usually keep both, because God works through faith, not doubt and unbelief.

God's purpose for us and our minds is that we learn to live with a positive attitude. No matter what our circumstances, our minds belong to us and no one can do our thinking for us if we don't let them. I encourage you to be passionate about being positive. A positive attitude lifts us above our circumstances and enables us to have peace in the midst of the storm and to have joy when there is no visible reason to rejoice.

> Our minds belong to us and no one can do our thinking for us.

You have probably heard the saying 'Attitude determines altitude', and it really is true. A person with a good attitude and almost no physical advantages will go further in life than someone with a lot of advantages and a bad attitude. No matter how qualified someone may be for a job, I refuse to work with negative people. They kill creativity and put a damper on enthusiasm and passion.

> We flourish in a positive atmosphere, just as flowers flourish.

We flourish in a positive atmosphere, just as flowers flourish in proper amounts of sun and rain. I grew up in a negative home and it turned me into a negative person, which caused me to have a negative life. One of the things I have learned during my journey with God is that there is nothing negative about Him. God is always positive, and if we want to walk with Him, we will have to be the same way.

> God can make miracles out of messes and mistakes.

God can make miracles out of messes and mistakes when we have a positive attitude and believe all things are possible with God.

The Power of Hope

There's an old *Peanuts* cartoon that pictures Lucy and Linus sitting in front of the television set. Lucy says to Linus, 'Go get me a glass of water.' Linus, looking surprised, asks, 'Why should I do anything for you? You never do anything for me.' 'On your 75th birthday,' Lucy promises, 'I'll bake you a cake.' Linus gets up, heads to the kitchen, and says, 'Life is more pleasant when you have something to look forward to.'

Hope is the confident expectation of good, and we should all live with hope. Abraham hoped against hope. He hoped when there was no physical reason to hope. Looking at your circumstances won't always give you reason to hope. You must look beyond them to God's Word and remember what He has done for you and others you've known in the past.

Hope never disappoints us, according to the Bible (see Romans 5:5). This allows us to be filled with joy, now! We don't have to wait for our circumstances to change because, as long as our thoughts are hopeful, we will have joy in our hearts, which strengthens us and helps us live with passion and enthusiasm.

> You have the ability to make your life better by choosing to think better thoughts.

You have the ability to make your life better by choosing to think better thoughts. And no matter how good your life is, you will never enjoy it if you think sour, negative thoughts. Some people find something wrong with everything. All that is required to see a positive change is a decision.

If you have encountered a lot of disappointments in your life, beware of beginning to expect more of the same. Sometimes we think we are protecting ourselves from being disappointed if we don't expect anything good to happen. But all that really does is open the door for the devil to keep tormenting us and it closes the door for God to turn things around in our lives.

> Your life can count for something. You can leave a legacy!

Create an atmosphere God can work in. He wants to help you, He wants to lift you up and make your life significant! God wants to heal you and use you to bring healing and restoration into the lives of other hurting people. Doesn't that sound exciting? Your life can count for something. You can leave a legacy!

Promises or Problems?

> Have you ever spent any time thinking about what you have been thinking about?

If you will meditate on God's promises instead of your problems, you will reap a harvest of righteousness, peace and joy. Our minds are like soil in a garden and the seeds we plant in them will produce a harvest in our lives. If you don't like the harvest, ask yourself what you have been thinking. Have you ever spent any time thinking about what you have been thinking about? If not, try it. It is a good thing to do, because you just might locate the root source of some of your problems.

Every day we must choose the attitude we will face the day with. We can think of everything wrong or we can find something right. The bad things often seem to find us, but we might have to search for the good ones. We get into such a bad habit of being critical, we often forget all the good things each day brings.

We often forget all the good things each day brings.

Spend some time in the evening going over your day. Do it slowly and ponder each event. Could you walk when you got out of bed this morning? If so, that is a positive thing and probably something you just took for granted, since you have done it for so many years. Did you have someone to say good morning to? There are millions of people in the world who don't have that. Did you have something to eat? Were your cupboards and fridge filled with many choices of food, and did you perhaps stand there feeling confused trying to decide what you would pick? There are millions of people in the world who won't eat at all today because they woke up to nothing. Did you stand in front of your wardrobe and spend a long time trying to decide which of your many outfits you would wear to work? As you go over your day, hopefully you will remember some of the good parts: the smile from your elderly mother, the laughter of your child, the person who let you go in front of her in the queue at the supermarket, or the compliment your spouse gave you. How about that front-row parking space you got at the shopping mall in the rain?

Are all of these things only 'little things', or are they the real stuff life is made of? I believe it's the latter.

Let us develop an attitude of gratitude.

We should not make a big deal out of little inconveniences or disappointments, but we should make a big deal out of little blessings, especially in our thoughts. Let us develop an attitude of gratitude and it will glorify God and give us a better quality of life. I have found, along with millions of others who have decided to be thankful, there is plenty in our lives to be thankful for, if we will just look for it. Beginning and ending each day with thanksgiving is a good thing to do. Being generally thankful is good, but I believe voicing thankfulness for specific things is even better.

Whatever we meditate on is what becomes big to us. If we meditate or focus on our problems, they appear larger than they are. But if we focus on good things, even if we can only think of a few, those are the things that seem big to us.

> If we focus on good things, even if we can only think of a few, those are the things that seem big to us.

The Responsibility of Free Choice

God has given us the responsibility of choice. Choice is a freedom, but it is also a responsibility, and I am not sure everyone understands that. People often say they are free to choose, but that also means they are responsible for the outcome of their choices.

For example, a person might choose to have a sexual relationship outside marriage, but if she gets pregnant she doesn't want the responsibility of raising a child. She wants to exercise her right to have an abortion, but then she has the responsibility of knowing she ended a human life which, many say, will haunt her for the rest of her life. This does not mean a person cannot receive forgiveness, nor does it mean she can never overcome the outcome of bad choices. But it does mean we should think seriously about our choices and realise freedom comes with responsibility. There are some choices we should think long and hard about before making them.

> There are some choices we should think long and hard about before making them.

We have enjoyed freedom in the United States, but it comes with responsibility. Many have not embraced their responsibility and we are starting to lose some of our freedoms. It is sad when we lose the right to pray in school or have the Ten Commandments in public buildings. Yet, these were freedoms we lost because we did not stand up responsibly and speak out against those who moved aggressively to steal those freedoms. America was founded as a Christian nation and our forefathers never intended for it to be anything else. They paid a high price for us to have the freedoms we enjoy today; however, if we are not responsible to pray, vote and speak out against unrighteousness in the land, we can only expect to lose more and more. Silence is just quiet agreement! Stand up and be counted!

Silence is just quiet agreement! Stand up and be counted!

In the same way we must understand we are free to think whatever we want to think, because our opinion is ours and no one can keep us from having it. However, we will also bear the responsibility of the choices we make. I encourage you to think good thoughts. Think on things that are in agreement with God's plan. After all, it has been proven for centuries that His ways really are best!

i dare you

Be Positive!

Keep a journal or a running list of things you can look at from a positive viewpoint. Start with your family or your spouse. List specific qualities you love. Then move on to your present circumstances with your friends, neighbours, house, job – anything goes. Ask God to help you find the positive in each and every day.

Can People Feel Your Thoughts?

I believe people may be able to feel the thoughts we think about them. This idea developed from something that happened to me personally. One day, many years ago, I was with my teenage daughter, who'd been dealing with severe acne on her face – and on that particular day, hair problems as well. In general, she just wasn't looking her best. Throughout the day I kept thinking how bad she looked and as the day wore on, I noticed she looked as if she was depressed. I asked her if she was all right. She sadly looked at me and said, 'I feel like the ugliest person in the world!' Immediately, the Holy Spirit spoke to my heart and said, 'She can feel your thoughts.' Wow! What a lesson to learn. If we think good things about people, it can actually lift them up, but if we think bad, negative, critical things, it can make them feel discouraged or depressed. I think this is especially true if it is someone we have a close relationship with. I would hate to think that just anyone's thoughts could affect me, but I do think when our hearts are open to someone and we trust him, his thoughts could affect us as much as ours can affect him.

> It's very hard to think negative thoughts about someone you're taking to the Lord every day.

If nothing else, I know when I think negative thoughts about an individual, it causes me to treat him according to how I think of him. So, if he doesn't feel my thoughts directly, he does indirectly through the way I treat him. One of the best ways I know to correct my thoughts about someone is to pray for him. It's very hard to think negative thoughts about someone you're taking to the Lord every day. You'll be amazed at how God will change your heart towards that person; your thoughts and ultimately your actions could very well change the way he behaves.

God's Word says we should believe the best of every person. If we believe the best and think the best, it will help him be the best he can be. It has been said, if we treat people the way we want them to be, they will rise to the level of our confidence in them. It is amazing to realise the power of thoughts. Your thoughts can affect you, the people around you, your future, your finances, and literally every area of your life.

How could we ever hope to fulfil God's purpose for our lives without considering what His purpose is for our minds? Yes, God cares about what you think, so make sure to choose your thoughts carefully.

CHAPTER 13

Passion for Your Emotions

Did God give us our emotions? Of course He did; even God Himself has emotions. God sits in the heavens and laughs (see Psalm 2:4). 'Jesus wept' (John 11:35). Emotions can bring both pain and pleasure. As author Gary Smalley said, emotions can indicate changes you need to be aware of. When they move or turn on, pay attention to them, but do not let them control you! Passion for our purpose requires emotion, but not the fleeting or roller-coaster kind – rather, the consistent, intense and fired-up feelings that we need to pursue our calling.

> Why would God give us something with the ability to give both pleasure and misery?

Emotions can give the greatest feelings of pleasure one could imagine; they can also poison our lives and be a source of torment. Why would God give us something with the ability to give both pleasure and misery? Once again we see God gives us a choice. It is His will for us to enjoy our lives, but we can be miserable if we want to and the choice is up to us. However, God wants us to enjoy the emotions that bring delight, and yet we must resist being led by the ones bearing misery.

Does God Want Us to Be Happy?

Some Christians are not comfortable with the thought of people striving to be happy. It seems selfish, and we have the idea God is only pleased when we sacrifice. We measure the value of an act of service by how much we have to suffer and give up. It is sad so many Christians have been taught to suppress their desire for happiness and pleasure. Is it really wrong for us to do something for the sheer pleasure of doing it? I don't believe it is. One of the reasons God gave us emotions is so we can feel pleasure, happiness and delight. God Himself said if we would delight ourselves in Him, He would give us the desires of our hearts (see Psalm 37:4).

> We glorify God the most when we are the happiest in Him.

What would you say if I told you we have an obligation to be as happy as we can possibly be? I believe we glorify God the most when we are the happiest in Him. Look at Psalm 37:4 again: it says we are to delight ourselves 'in Him'.

I have striven for many years to learn how to do just that. Somehow I had the idea it was wrong to enjoy myself, until I saw that Jesus said He came so we might have joy in our lives and have it in abundance (see John 10:10, 16:24, 17:13). He wants our joy to be full!

> The belief that holiness and happiness are at odds with each other is tragic and is the main thief of our passion.

The belief that holiness and happiness are at odds with each other is tragic and is the main thief of our passion. God's purpose in giving us emotions was so we could feel life to the fullest.

The Bible says a lot about self-denial, but instead of being an end in itself, it is designed to lead us somewhere. Self-denial enables us to follow Christ, who always leads us to ultimately find all we desire. God promises a great deal of delight and pleasure if we will put Him first.

Don't Let Emotion Rule

Satan gains a lot of ground in the lives of believers through emotions. We constantly talk about how we feel, and unfortunately there are many people out there who let their feelings control them. It has been said that emotions are the believer's number-one enemy. Feelings are powerful tools that can help us or prevent us from fulfilling our real purpose.

> Feelings are powerful tools that can help us or prevent us from fulfilling our real purpose.

One thing we can depend on when we're talking about emotions is that we cannot depend on them. They are fickle, which simply means they are ever changing and frequently without giving notice. It is like the young man who played golf with his dad: each time he hit a good shot, he was excited and wanted to learn more about golf so he could play more with his dad, which would enable them to spend more time together. But when he hit a bad shot, he angrily banged his club on the ground and said the game was stupid and that he would never play again.

Emotions are fickle! We can go to bed feeling one way and wake up feeling entirely different. We may feel really good about doing something one moment and a few days later feel we don't want to do it at all.

I like to compare emotions to the law of gravity. What goes up eventually comes down! If I throw a book in the air, it will come down; and if I am riding on an emotional high, sooner or later I will either bottom out or level out, but I won't stay on that high for ever. Hopefully, we learn to level out and not bottom out because that is often when we get depressed.

The main reason for this book is to encourage you to live with more enthusiasm and passion.

There is nothing wrong with feeling excited. The main reason for this book is to encourage you to live with more enthusiasm and passion, and that includes feelings of excitement. But I must also encourage you to realise you will not always feel excited, and when you don't, you must continue doing what you know is right. Your feelings may change, but you must remain the same. The book thrown in the air goes up and comes down, but the person who threw it remains in the same place.

Be an Example of Stability

I grew up in a very unstable home. Everyone acted on his or her emotions all the time, and as a result I never knew from one minute to the next what to expect. My father was alcoholic, angry and emotionally unstable. My mother lived in fear of my father and her behaviour was co-dependent on his. She developed an anxiety disorder that prevented her from responding to stress in a normal way. My brother, who is my only sibling, was also emotionally driven and as a result made many seriously bad decisions in his life that took him down a wrong path. I came out of this atmosphere as an abuse victim with a strong personality and a bitter attitude. Since I never saw an example of stability, I allowed my emotions to become a dictator in my life; they gave the orders and I obeyed. If I woke up in the morning and felt depressed, I spent the day depressed. If I felt angry, I spent the day taking my anger out on whoever happened to step in my path. If I felt like saying something, I said it. If I felt like doing something, I did it.

I allowed my emotions to become a dictator in my life.

I had no idea there was any other way to live, until I met Dave and he became an example of stability to me. I watched him remain the same no matter what our circumstances, and after a while I began to believe stability was also available to me.

I think one of the greatest things we can do for people is to be an example of stability to them. We need to be steadfast, consistent and stable in our purpose. The world today is such an emotionally charged place, it seems ready to explode at any moment, but that is not God's will for His people. Jesus said we are in the world, but not of it. In other words, as believers in Jesus Christ we live in the world, but we must resist acting like it. We cannot respond the way the world responds to life's situations. Jesus is our peace; He is the supreme example of stability, and through Him we can enjoy lives of stability.

Perhaps you have convinced yourself that you are just an emotional person and you cannot help living with emotional highs and lows. If that is the case, I must respectfully say you are wrong. People are not 'just emotional'; they choose to be emotional, which means they are led by their emotions. Their emotions own them rather than them owning their emotions. God gave you emotions so you could feel good and bad things, but He never intended any of those feelings to rule you. You are to master your mind, mouth and emotions. God has given us free will and we must exercise it to make choices line up with God's will for our lives. When you're on a plane with a small child, the flight attendant will often walk by soon after take-off to remind you that you should put your oxygen mask on first before helping your child, if the need arises. Why is that? Because if you can't breathe, you can't help your child breathe. If you're overly emotional and lacking stability, you won't be any help to your child – or anyone else, for that matter.

Emotional Healing

A person's emotions can become sick just like any other part of his or her being. A person can have physical illness, mental illness or emotional illness. I believe emotional illness can result from imbalances in our chemical make-up, or it can be the result of a lifetime of allowing emotions to rule. When people experience years of emotional highs and lows based on their circumstances, they eventually wear out and they simply don't function normally. It's like your car's engine: operate it at full throttle without ever changing into a higher gear, and shortly you'll be buying a new car or taking the bus.

But thank God He is our Healer and any part of our being can be healed. Jesus can heal us everywhere we hurt! I needed emotional healing and received it through my relationship with Jesus. I learned new ways to think and respond to life. Jesus became the Anchor of my soul, my Rock, and my Hiding Place in times of trouble. I learned to dwell in the secret place Psalm 91 speaks of: it says if we dwell in the secret place, we will remain stable and fixed under the shadow of the Almighty, whose power no foe can come against. There it is, the promise of stability and a life solidly fixed on Him.

For many years the emotional wounds from being rejected during my childhood prevented me from responding properly in relationships, but Jesus healed me. I was unable to trust and therefore responded emotionally to every challenge life presented, but Jesus healed me. He healed me, and if you need emotional healing, He will heal you also. He gives us beauty for ashes (see Isaiah 61:3).

Years of emotional ups and downs can place so much stress on our systems that chemical imbalances occur. The adrenal glands are weakened and not able to allow enough of the right chemicals to enter our bodies to handle the stressors in life. We begin to respond to simple things in an out-of-balance way. For example, I can remember being so stressed mentally, physically and emotionally that even something simple like needing to suddenly brake in traffic would cause me to have shortness of breath and a suffocating feeling until my system calmed down. I would break out into a sweat and my heart would pound and I would want to run and simply get away from everything and everybody.

But God did not intend for us to need to hide from life; He has given us what we need to live life boldly and fully. If you feel you need emotional healing, I encourage you to realise Jesus can heal you emotionally the same as He can spiritually. He cares about every part of your being and intends for you to be whole and complete.

You Are Not Your Emotions

> Your emotions are not who you are – they are how you feel.

Your emotions are not who you are – they are how you feel. You are spirit, you have a soul, and you live in a body. Your emotions are part of your soul; they belong to you, you don't belong to them. Learn to stand back and look at your emotional responses as something that belong to you and over which you have control. I remember all the years of feeling I was out of control, and I hated that feeling. I didn't like to listen to my mouth saying stupid things and the feeling I had no control over it. I didn't like exploding in anger over petty things that really were not that big a deal, but I did it frequently. I was already angry and being out of control made me even angrier. Don't you hate the feeling of watching yourself do and say things you know are ridiculous, but you seem to have no power to control them? Well, if you hate it enough, you will do whatever you need to change. Start by believing it can change and you can be a stable person. God is no respecter of persons; what He does for one, He will do for another. He healed me emotionally and I have become a stable individual, and He will do the same thing for you – if you truly desire it.

Learn to Pass the Test

The Bible says God tries or tests our emotions (see Psalm 7:9). That means He permits things to come into our lives with the potential to move us emotionally in order for us to practise staying stable while using our faith.

The Bible actually says we are blessed when God disciplines us in that way and He does it so He may give us power to keep ourselves calm in adversity. Notice He does not keep us calm, but He gives us the power to keep ourselves calm (see Psalm 94:12–13). I believe we frequently expect God to do things for us He has given us the power to do for ourselves.

Why would God test us?

> Beloved, do not be amazed *and* bewildered at the fiery ordeal that is taking place to test your quality, as though something strange (unusual and alien to you and your position) were befalling you.
> – 1 PETER 4:12

> Good times don't bring the worst out of us, but hard times do.

Have you ever gone to the furniture store to buy a chair without sitting in it? Have you ever purchased a car without test-driving it? Of course not, and God also tests us to reveal the quality of our faith. No matter what we think of ourselves, we find out what we are truly like in times of difficulty. Good times don't bring the worst out in us, but hard times do. That is why God says these difficult times are good for us. They allow us to see what is in our character that needs to be changed. They also give us an opportunity to use our faith, and faith only grows through our using it. As we choose to learn to trust God instead of getting upset about something, we experience His faithfulness, which, in turn, increases our faith for the next time we need it. The more we use our muscles, the more they grow – and our faith is the same way.

Learn to pass your tests quickly so you don't have to keep taking them over and over. We never flunk out of God's school; we just keep doing re-sits until we pass. Even when we do pass, we often get refresher courses just to keep us sharp.

> We never flunk out of God's school; we just keep doing re-sits until we pass.

The Bible says we should no longer live by our human appetites and desires, but we should live for what God wills (see 1 Peter 4:2). That means we should not live by our emotions. We can have them and enjoy them when they are behaving, but we cannot live by them and also fulfil God's purpose for our lives.

Your spirit is the deepest part of you. It is the place where the Holy Spirit dwells after you receive Jesus Christ as your Saviour. God is calling all of us to deeper lives and that means following the Holy

i dare you

Choose to Be Calm in Adversity

Passion is doing what you do with all of your heart, no matter how you feel.

Emotion is doing the right thing until you no longer feel excited and then giving up.

Passion is doing what you do with excellence at all times.

Emotion does what it has to do and no more.

Passion never gives up, no matter how long it takes to reach a desired goal.

Emotion gives up easily and looks for something that is not difficult.

Spirit, who dwells in the depths of your being, not your emotions on the surface. Refuse to be a surface, shallow Christian who is carnal and controlled by ordinary impulses.

A Catered Affair

Have you ever hosted a celebration with outside caterers coming in? Everything is made easy for you, and all you have to do is sit and give orders and someone else makes everything happen. It is always fun until the bill comes and needs to be paid. The Apostle Paul told us not to cater to our flesh and to ordinary impulses (see Romans 8:8). That means we should not give in to every emotional whim we have. Our emotions would love to be the host at a 'catered event' where they give the orders and we cater to them. The only problem with that is when the bill comes, we will have to pay it – our emotions won't.

There is a high cost for the cheap thrills of life.

There is a high cost for the cheap thrills of life. By following our emotions, we can cost ourselves a good job, a great relationship, our health, our self-respect, and even our futures. Don't cater to your flesh – discipline it! Use self-control and you can master your emotions through God's help.

If we sow to the flesh, we will reap from the flesh (see Galatians 6:8) because we only reap what we sow and nothing else. Sowing to the flesh (giving in to emotional whims) sounds like fun, until we finally realise that what the flesh gives back at harvest-time is not something we desire to have. The Bible says the flesh produces ruin, decay and destruction. Is that what you want? I don't believe it is. We want abundant life and all the peace and joy it brings. Not only is it available, but it is God's will for you.

However, you must learn to sow to the spirit and not to the flesh.

The Apostle Paul said that when we are children we act like children, but that we need to mature and act like adults who are done with childish ways (see 1 Corinthians 13:11). Do you need to grow up? If you do, don't be afraid to admit it. You can never get where you need to be if you're not honest about where you are right now. I think it takes courage to be honest with ourselves. Cowards hide from everything, including the truth about themselves. But if you will dare to face truth, it will open the door to a brand-new life – the one you have been looking for.

Children typically cater to their feelings and they usually don't stop until they have to begin paying the bill (bearing the consequences). We hope they will learn from our words just as God hopes we will learn from His, but unfortunately very few learn that way. We usually need a mixture of the Word dealing with us from the inside and our circumstances dealing with us from the outside, and somehow our flesh finally gets crucified and we begin to submit to God's will instead of demanding our own.

> We are stubborn and want our own way even though our way often means destruction.

God tells us to obey Him and we will be blessed. It sounds easy enough, so why do so many take the long, hard route? Because, like children, we are stubborn and want our own way even though our way often means destruction. Just like children, we must learn, and we should thank God for being patient. He sticks with us all the way through our childish attempts at getting our own way and believes in us even when we have a difficult time believing in ourselves.

God has a great plan for your life and it is one that includes emotional stability and peace of mind. Keep learning and growing and you will eventually enjoy the fullness of all God intended for you.

Enthusiasm

I believe one of the reasons God gave us emotions was so we could be enthusiastic about Him and the life He has planned for us. Ralph Waldo Emerson once said, 'Nothing great was ever achieved without enthusiasm.' I recently saw a definition of enthusiasm that said it was a belief in special revelations of the Holy Spirit. I thought that was interesting simply because I am a big believer that people must have a revelation of God in their lives to live enthusiastically. One might become enthused about a thing or event, but those things will pass and enthusiasm often wanes. However, a revelation of God and a determination to keep Him first in one's life enables one to live with zeal, passion and enthusiasm. Passion is a synonym for enthusiasm.

We can enjoy all aspects of life simply because we enjoy God.

Feeling enthusiastic is great. It releases energy and an ability to enjoy all one does. The great thing about God is He enables us to be enthusiastic about all we do. We shouldn't just have enthusiasm about fun, but we can be equally enthusiastic about work. Through God, we can enjoy what others think might be mundane and boring. We can enjoy all aspects of life simply because we enjoy God. It's that plugged-in passion, that zeal and drive that never really go away, especially when we're tuned into the right goals and direction God is leading.

Paul said in Romans we should never lag in zeal and in earnest endeavour; we should be aglow and burning with the Spirit, serving the Lord (see Romans 12:11). We are God's servants and He wants us to serve Him with enthusiasm, passion and zeal.

How would you like it if you had a servant and he always had a sour, deadpan attitude? Or what if you had to provide something exciting all the time in order for him to be zealous? You wouldn't like it and neither would I. When our attitudes are sour and deadpan, God doesn't like it either. He is awesome and we should be enthused about Him and the privilege to serve Him, so don't spend your life waiting for something to excite your emotions before you live with passion. Instead, do all you do with an acute awareness that life is a gift and it should be celebrated.

Our emotions are connected to our thoughts and attitudes. Being thankful at all times in all things enables us to live enthusiastically. I have discovered that murmuring, complaining and fault-finding actually drain my energy and I start dreading everything. Nothing makes me happy. On the other hand, if I start each day with a grateful attitude and keep my thoughts right throughout the day, I have more energy and zest for life.

I get more done and I feel less tired.

When you feel your moods changing, take a moment and ask yourself what you have been thinking. You will discover that you can actually 'think yourself happy'. In the Bible Paul said, 'I think myself happy' (Acts 26:2 KJV), and if it worked for him, it can also work for us.

Enthusiasm is contagious and yours will rub off on other people. I'm sure you've noticed how enthusiastic people seem to make others enthusiastic. Stir yourself up so you can stir others up. One spark can set off a mighty blaze. The world needs to know God and be excited about serving Him. Will you dare to be a fire in a world that would love to quench your flame, especially if you're on fire for God?

> Will you dare to be a fire in a world that would love to quench your flame?

Use your emotions for the purpose God gave them, and don't let the devil use them for his purpose. Embrace life with passion and use your emotions wisely. God wants to use them to help you enjoy your life, but the devil wants to use them to prevent you from enjoying life. The good news is the choice is up to you.

CHAPTER 14

Passion for Your Finances

I once met a woman who was working in a department store when I was shopping in the area she was responsible for. We began to talk and I found out she had been a Christian for many years. As we continued our conversation, I asked if the employees working in the sales area were paid a salary or if they worked on commission. She told me that although they worked for a salary, they had to meet quotas in order to keep their jobs, and she admitted she was worried because she had not been meeting hers.

'Do you ever pray and ask God to give you favour with people so they'll come to you to ring up their sale?' I asked her.

Very sheepishly, she looked at me with raised eyebrows. 'Is it really all right with God if I pray about money?'

I assured her God cares about everything that concerns her and He wanted her to be bold enough to ask for anything she needed.

This was a woman who needed more business or she was going to lose her job, which she very much needed to keep. She needed to boldly pray that God would send her customers who wanted to make purchases, but she had no idea she could do that. Though she had been a Christian for most of her life, she was living with very little, because she had an erroneous idea that talking to God about money or material needs was not appropriate. It is a sad thing when people think that God only cares about the spiritual areas of their lives. He wants to be involved in our ordinary, everyday lives, and He wants to be involved all the time, and not just for one hour on Sunday morning. God is for all of life, not just for church! I frequently say we should let God out of the Sunday-morning box we try to keep Him in and allow Him to invade our Monday, Tuesday, Wednesday, Thursday, Friday, Saturday and Sunday too.

> We should let God out of the Sunday-morning box we try to keep Him in.

God's favour is a wonderful thing available to us. The Bible says in James 4:2 we háve not because we ask not. There is a great deal of help available to us from God we never receive, simply because we do not ask. Money is not something dirty or sinful we cannot talk to God about. We need it to do the things in life that we need to do, like pay for housing, food, clothes, and all the other things necessary to maintain a quality lifestyle. Money is not evil; it's the love of money that is evil. God is not against your having money as long as the money does not have you.

Our enthusiasm for the purpose God has for us can, unfortunately, be greatly affected by money – we may feel called to start some type of ministry but worry our own family's security will be put in jeopardy. There's a tension there, and until we understand money and the role God has designed for it to have in our lives, we will struggle with pursuing our passion and purpose. If we have a wrong relationship with money, it certainly can cause problems. If we follow the leading of the Holy Spirit in using and distributing our money, we not only can have all of our needs met, but we can also be a tremendous blessing to others in need.

Money!

What do you think money would say if it could talk? How about this:

'I'm depressed and sad because I am tired of people abusing me, using me for wrong purposes, fighting over me, stealing me, and lying, cheating and committing crimes to get me. I get blamed in some way for most divorces. I'm tired of fighting with greed all the time. I'm hoarded and I'm wasted. People think that I am their security and I'm not. They act as if I'm God, and I'm certainly not. I just wish people knew how much good they could do with me if they treated me right and how blessed their lives could be.'

To have or not to have money – that's one of the most important questions we wrestle with. At least it seems to be a big question among some Christians. There are sectors of Christianity that believe God wants everyone to be rich, and then there are those who believe poverty is a virtue and basically the only way one can serve God with a pure heart. And, for some strange reason, people who are not Christians always seem to feel that anyone serving God in full-time ministry should not have much money or a prosperous lifestyle. Almost every time I do an interview with a secular newspaper, TV station, radio station or magazine, I get asked what I call 'the money question.'

Recently, I was asked by *Time* magazine if I believed God wanted people to be rich. I told the interviewer that I could not answer his question with a direct yes or no because I believe we can be rich in many ways. Money is not the only way to be rich. Good health and being loved makes a person rich. Working at a job we love and enjoy is another type of riches.

I believe God requires that we be good stewards of our money. We must be careful not to let money crowd God out of our lives. We must keep Him first at all times. I believe that God watches how we handle our money. Once Jesus was standing in the temple watching what people put into the offering. He noticed that some rich people only gave a little, but a widow gave all she had (see Mark 12:41–43). What she offered was referred to as a 'mite'. It was worth less than our penny is today, but to God she gave very generously. Are we generous? Do we readily help those who are in need and less fortunate than we are? There are many, many factors that determine the level of financial success that a person has.

The Bible says in 3 John that God wants His people to prosper and be in health above all else, even as their souls prosper. What does that mean? To me, it simply means God wants us to have enough to meet our needs and plenty to help other people with besides. He also wants us to have what we are spiritually mature enough to handle. Money in the hands of a generous person can be a great blessing, but in the hands of a greedy person it can bring ruin.

Now, of course, we all think we are certainly among the spiritually mature, but I have come to trust that God knows more about me than I know about myself, and He gives me what He knows I can handle at the present time.

I am sure some are reading this book who immediately say, 'I'm spiritually mature and I don't have enough to meet my basic needs.' There could be any number of things causing that and we will discuss many of them, but one thing to keep in mind is that the hand of the diligent makes rich (see Proverbs 10:4). We live in a fast-paced society where people want instant gratification. Twenty-somethings are entering the workforce today with no previous experience, expecting to be paid the same amount as someone who's worked in their field for more than twenty-five years. Jobs aren't the only thing some younger people want to rush ahead with – when young married couples buy their first house, they often expect it to be similar to what their parents currently have, both in size and cost, not realising it took thirty years for their parents to reach that point. This attitude is certainly not a diligent one. Many people today feel they are *entitled* to things. They don't feel they need to wait for them and earn them, they expect them; in fact, their generation is sometimes called the 'Entitlement Generation'. The truth is God wants them to start at the beginning: work hard, be diligent, be patient, and *gradually* see an increase in their lives. It is God's way and I believe the best way for people to have true prosperity and the maturity needed to go along with it.

I like to put it this way: if a tree has more fruit than roots, it will topple over in the first storm it encounters. I believe human nature is much the same way. If we have a lot of material things and no depth of relationship with God, we can easily be destroyed. Money has a lot of power and can pull people in the wrong direction. That does not mean we have to be afraid to have money, as some religious denominations teach, but it does mean we should strive not to ever get a wrong attitude or let money control us.

Don't use people to get money and things, but be committed to using money and material goods to bless people. Rich people can do a lot of good for society if they are willing.

> Be committed to using money and material goods to bless people.

The Law of Gradualism

God's way is normally that people should increase, little by little, as they follow the principles in His Word. I like to call it 'the law of gradualism'. There are always the few who inherit money or win the Lottery, but the majority of people will have to work, save, and learn how to properly manage all their resources. This does not happen overnight, but often takes many years. Continuing to be diligent to do what is right during those years is very important. This is where passion with purpose can really help.

In 1976, I had an encounter with God that changed my life for ever. I had been a Christian for many years prior to that, but not a very serious one. Suddenly, God became the most important person in my life. I wanted to know what He wanted me to do and I studied His Word incessantly so I could learn. One of the things I discovered was the law of sowing and reaping, which the Bible clearly teaches.

While the earth remains,
Seedtime and harvest,

Cold and heat,
Winter and summer,
And day and night
Shall not cease.
   — GENESIS 8:22 NKJV

For he who sows to his own flesh (lower nature, sensuality)
will from the flesh reap.
   — GALATIANS 6:8

Give, and [gifts] will be given to you; good measure, pressed
down, shaken together, and running over, will they pour into
[the pouch formed by] the bosom [of your robe and used as a
bag]. For with the measure you deal out [with the measure you
use when you confer benefits on others], it will be measured
back to you.
   — LUKE 6:38

Wanting to obey God, we began to give more and more, and for a
while it seemed we had less and less. God often tests us to see if we
are obeying Him just to get something from Him, or if it is because
we love Him and are committed to doing what is right just because
we love righteousness.

I was in a unique time in life and ministry. I had been teaching a
small Bible study at home, which began shortly after my encounter
with God, and I quickly realised I was not having the time to prepare
for the ministry I believed God had called me to. I had a full-time
job, three children, a husband, a house to take care of, and was
heavily involved at my local church.

God began dealing with me to step out in faith and give up my job
so I would have time to prepare for what He had for me in the future.
This was frightening to me, and at first I didn't obey Him. Instead,
I did it my way, convincing myself I could be obedient by giving

up my full-time job and getting a part-time job. I quickly learned that part-time obedience is not obedience at all. I finally ended up at home trying to learn to trust God for finances and provision.

> Have you ever obeyed God expecting to be blessed and yet it looked as if you went backwards instead of forwards?

For six years we needed financial miracles almost every month just to be able to pay our bills. New clothes, car repairs, entertainment and other stuff were extras we only had when God supernaturally provided. I am glad to say He always made provision, but I would not have considered myself prosperous. We never had anything over and above our basic needs, and I will admit it confused me because I felt we were giving more than ever and yet our finances were not as abundant as they were before I obeyed God and gave up my job. Have you ever obeyed God expecting to be blessed and yet it looked as if you went backwards instead of forwards? Those times are certainly testing times.

However, as we remained diligent and grew in our walk with God, *little* by *little* we increased. I want to strongly encourage my readers not to decide what God's Word means based on their experience. Sometimes when people are not experiencing something they were expecting, they decide God must have meant something else. They place their own interpretation on Scripture to get it to match their experience, but that can be a serious error, shutting the door to their ever receiving the best God has for them.

Even though I did not have prosperity in my finances for many years, I still believed I could, should, and would because I saw it in God's Word. Yes, I had to wait longer than I thought was fair, but I also look back now and realise how valuable those years were to me. They trained me to believe God for finances we now need in abundance to run our worldwide ministry. Those years of total dependence upon God brought me close to Him and allowed me to see His miracle-working power displayed over and over in providing for us beyond ordinary means.

Does God Want People to Prosper?

What does it mean to prosper? When I think of being prosperous, I think of success, not failure. People who prosper are people who are helped along their way or who can see circumstances of different degrees of prosperity and success, week after week. Small successes add up to big ones.

The word 'prosper' can also mean *to be whole*. In other words, a truly prosperous person is one prospering in all areas of life. His spirit is prosperous, which means he knows God's Word and has a great relationship with Him. His mind is at peace, and he has joy no matter what his circumstances are. He has good health, good relationships, and is generally successful in every area of life.

I believe God wants His people to prosper. He is good, and whom would He rather be good to than His own children? He's a Father, and just like most earthly fathers, He enjoys providing for those who depend on Him. God told Joshua that if he would obey His commands and go boldly forward, he would prosper and have good success (see Joshua 1:8).

The first Psalm says that if we delight in the law of the Lord, everything we do shall prosper and come to maturity. In Psalm 118:25, the psalmist boldly prayed and asked God to send prosperity 'now'. He sounds to me as if he needed a breakthrough quick! Ever prayed a prayer like that? In Psalm 35:27, the Bible says God delights in the prosperity of His people.

God told Abraham He would bless him with an abundant increase of favours, make his name famous, and make him a blessing to others if he would obey Him. Abraham did obey and the Bible records that Abram (who later became Abraham) was extremely rich in livestock, in silver and in gold (see Genesis 12:2, 13:2).

The Bible is filled with examples of people God prospered in amazing ways – Joseph, Ruth, Esther, David, and Solomon, and the list goes on. In the New Testament, the early apostles did not seem to have a lot of material goods, but they were the ones who taught people to give so they could reap an abundant harvest. Paul wrote in his letter to the Ephesians that God was able to do exceedingly, abundantly, above and beyond all they could dare to hope, ask or think. That certainly doesn't sound as if He wanted His people to barely get by! God tells us to be daring in our asking, and He did not say we could only ask for spiritual things.

> God tells us to be daring in our asking, and He did not say we could only ask for spiritual things.

Matthew writes that if we seek first the Kingdom of God, all the other things will be added besides (see Matthew 6:33). I believe there is sufficient evidence just in the few scriptures I have mentioned to safely say that God wants His people to prosper, for surely we don't believe God wants sinners to prosper while the righteous live in poverty.

> God wants His people to prosper.

Quite often people say, 'I know a lot of wonderful, godly people who are poor. How do you think the prosperity message makes them feel?' I believe, if anything, it gives them hope for their future. Poor people can certainly be godly, but that does not mean that poverty is godly. Who would not want to improve their situation if they knew there was a way to do so? I would think any poor person would be tremendously excited to learn anything that might improve his situation.

Have a Good Attitude While You Are Waiting

Just like a good farmer, you should sow your seed, release your faith, and be patient while you wait for the harvest. Just as I did, you may, and probably will, go through some testing times, but I believe if you are diligent in doing what God instructs you to do, you will see increase in your life.

> If you are diligent in doing what God instructs you to do, you will see increase in your life.

There's a story about F. B. Meyer, one of the most prominent English Baptist ministers of his time during the late nineteenth and early twentieth centuries. He once preached in London, while other well-known preachers such as Charles Spurgeon and G. Campbell Morgan were preaching there too. All three men were wonderful preachers, but Spurgeon's church and Morgan's church were both bigger than Meyer's church. And he admitted to being a bit envious of them.

So he prayed, asking God to tell him what to do because he was jealous of them, and he didn't want to be. God instructed him to pray for both Spurgeon and Morgan, that their churches would prosper, and that more and more people would come to them.

This certainly wasn't the answer F. B. Meyer was looking for.

'I don't want to do that, Lord!' he protested. But, after thinking about it, he thought it best to obey the Lord. So he prayed diligently that Spurgeon's church and Morgan's church would grow and grow. In re-telling this story, he said, 'Their churches grew so much in answer to my prayers that they overflowed. And,' he said, 'the overflow came to my church.'[1]

F. B. Meyer could have sulked. He could have whined and complained and done everything in his own power to grow his church, but nothing would have helped. Instead, he kept a good attitude and waited on God, and most importantly he did what God asked of him. And his church prospered.

It's often a lot easier to be obedient and have a good attitude when things are going well, but it usually requires a little bit more from us when God is asking us to do something tough and things aren't going so well.

> It usually requires a little bit more from us when God is asking us to do something tough and things aren't going so well.

Here is a list of things I would recommend that you avoid if you want to be truly prosperous.

1 Never be greedy or have money and material things on your mind excessively. (1 Timothy 3:8)
2 Do not love the world or the things in the world. (1 John 2:15)
3 We are never to gain money or material goods through questionable means, but we should work hard and learn to manage what we have well. (1 Timothy 3:3)
4 Respect money and never waste it. (John 6:12)
5 Be thankful for what you have while you're waiting for what you want to have. (Philippians 4:6)
6 Trust God and don't get confused if things don't happen when you want them to. (Proverbs 3:5)
7 Never, never be jealous or envious of what someone else has. (Proverbs 14:30)

Keeping a good and godly attitude while you wait shows you are ready for promotion.

How We Should View Money

Money should be viewed as a tool, or equipment, to be a blessing to others. God told Abraham He would bless him and make him a blessing, and His plan is the same for each of us. We should not view money as our security because riches do not provide true security (see Proverbs 11:4). They can be abundant one day and gone the next. Our security is in God. Even when riches increase, it is unwise to set your heart on them (see Psalm 62:10).

I believe we need to view money as a possible problem if it is not handled correctly. Money has the ability to deceive people. We can easily begin to think that we'll be happier if we have more money, but money actually has no power to provide true happiness unless God is being served with it. The world is filled with rich, miserable people. Money can also cause people to begin to compromise and go against their consciences. It can actually take people away from their relationships with God. They become so busy taking care of all their possessions, God gets crowded out of their lives.

> Money actually has no power to provide true happiness unless God is being served with it.

Money can also do a lot of good and be used to bring comfort, ease pain, put smiles on faces, relieve pressure, help people live better lives, and bring thanksgiving to God. For example, our ministry had the opportunity to fully fund a hospital in India that services a 100,000 people in villages with little or no medical care. After going to the hospital and seeing how much better it made the villagers' lives, Dave and I personally wanted to do our part to help fund another hospital in Cambodia. I get a lot of joy out of helping relieve the pain of other people.

Paul told the Ephesians they were to work with their own hands so they would have resources to give to others (see Ephesians 4:28). Now, that would certainly be a novel idea – work so you can give it away! Only recently, Warren Buffett, who is the second richest man in the world, and worth approximately $44 to $46 billion, decided to do just that when he made the announcement that he would start giving nearly 85 per cent of his wealth away, mostly to the Bill and Melinda Gates Foundation. In an interview with *Fortune* magazine, he shared that he and his late wife, Suzie, had always agreed with Andrew Carnegie, 'who said that huge fortunes that flow in large part from society should in large part be returned to society.'[2] We work so we can give back.

> While you are asking God to help you prosper, make sure you also learn how to be an aggressive giver.

According to the Bible, it is more blessed to give than receive, so while you are asking God to help you prosper, make sure you also learn how to be an aggressive giver.

What Is God's Attitude Towards People Being in Debt?

I don't believe being in debt is a sin that will cause someone to lose his salvation, but it isn't the wisest way to live. Debt causes pressure and is frequently the root of divorce. Approximately 71 per cent of Americans say debt is making their home lives unhappy. They live from pay cheque to pay cheque, and their debt steals their freedom and ultimately their real joy. In 1980 there were a half-million bankruptcies, and in 2005 there were 2 million.[3] Most of those people were middle-class, educated baby boomers with large credit card debt.

> People living off the plastic are living in an illusion.

People really should discipline themselves to live 30 per cent below their means if they ever intend to be financially secure, but most people live way beyond their means. The majority of people today regularly spend more than they make and credit cards have made this possible. However, these people living off the plastic are living in an illusion. Experts say it takes about five years before it catches up with you, but sooner or later reality comes crashing in. Any time you borrow, you're spending tomorrow's prosperity today – but what happens when tomorrow comes?

> Any time you borrow, you're spending tomorrow's prosperity today – but what happens when tomorrow comes?

It is best not to use credit cards, unless you get into the habit of paying off the balance at the end of each month. Considering that over 60 per cent of Americans have outstanding unpaid balances on their credit cards,[4] you may want to think long and hard about how you will handle a credit card before you get it. A better choice may be a debit card, which accesses your bank account. It is so easy to run around all month and put all your purchases on your credit card, but when the bill arrives, the shock of realising just how much was spent during those thirty days is jolting. Don't be talked into the lure of Air Miles or cashback or other perks that the credit card companies offer these days. More times than not, they are not worth it.

The only way to use credit cards and not get into trouble is to use them responsibly. That means that you should not buy things you cannot pay for.

People perish for a lack of knowledge (see Hosea 4:6). Do you know the state of your finances? Can you tell me how much you have in your bank account and savings? How much you're spending on bills each month as opposed to extras? Do you know what bills you can expect in the next thirty days, or will you be shocked when they arrive because you forgot all about them? Did you know that when something is advertised 'ninety days interest free', most of the time the interest is built into the price of the purchase? People sign contracts all the time without understanding what they are signing.

Most students graduate with a lot of information they will never use, but very few have any idea how to manage money. They simply go off to college or university, where they will be offered credit cards on a regular basis. One major credit card company spends $10 million a year advertising credit cards to high-school and college students in the United States. Some colleges even get paid to let credit card companies advertise on campus. It's obviously working – in 2004, 76 per cent of undergraduate college students in the United States had at least one credit card in their name with an average outstanding balance of $2,169; 32 per cent of students had four or more credit cards, and the average graduate had six credit cards; and one in seven owes over $15,000.

Everyone's a target by credit card companies, and the elderly are no exception. My mother is eighty-three years old. We regularly supplement her income because she does not have enough money to live on, and yet she gets letters and phone calls all the time offering her credit cards. She even receives credit cards in the post that she can begin using immediately. Why would any sane society offer credit to someone who already cannot pay her bills? They do it because they don't care, they are greedy, and if they can make a little more money, that is all that matters to them.

> We must develop the patience to wait for things and we will enjoy them even more.

Greed is the root cause of a lot of debt. We must develop the patience to wait for things and we will enjoy them even more. I recently told my mother I was going to give her a cash allowance each month, and when she wanted to buy special things they needed to come from that allowance. I told her I would provide for all of her needs and would buy her gifts from time to time, but when she just 'wanted' something, she needed to save for it out of her allowance. At first she didn't like it at all, because she was accustomed to spending whatever she wanted. However, her system was not working for me and, in reality, I knew that it wasn't good for her. It is always easy to spend someone else's money!

So, after about two weeks, she shared with me how much she loved the new system and said she was excited about saving for what she wanted. She even said, 'If I have to save my money to get things, they will mean more to me.' Credit cards allow people to have instant gratification, but I don't think people enjoy what they have as much as they would if they had to wait a while and save for it.

I also believe the availability of credit cards drives all of us to buy things we would not buy if we waited even one day. Emotions run high when we are in the shopping centre with a credit card. I have found when I am emotional, things look much better than they do after my emotions calm down and I am home. It doesn't hurt to buy things, in fact it often feels good; but will it still feel good when you have to pay the bill?

God does not want you to have the pressure of debt. Being in debt is not prosperity. According to God's Word, the borrower is a servant or a slave to the lender (see Proverbs 22:7). Debt can sap your passion and block your purpose. Never forget that Jesus died so you could enjoy freedom, not bondage.

Work, Give, Save and Spend

Learn to work, give, save and spend all within your current limits.

It's important you learn to work, give, save and spend all within your current limits. When you do that, God will increase your limits (financial ability) and you will make more money, be able to give more, save more, and spend more.

If you spend all of your money, you won't have anything saved when you have an emergency. My daughter recently had a car accident that was her fault, so she and her husband had to pay the $1,000 excess on their car insurance in order to be able to claim. She said, 'I am so glad we have that emergency fund, because now we don't feel pressured to try to come up with the thousand dollars.' I have watched them over the years live on a budget and save for the things they wanted. I have watched them say no to things they wanted to do, but knew they could not do and be properly prepared for the future. A little bit of discipline now will save you a lot of pressure and anxiety later on.

> A little bit of discipline now will save you a lot of pressure and anxiety later on.

God wants you to prosper and be blessed, but He does not want you to get into debt for extras you could wait to buy. You might ask what you should do about a house or a car. Is it all right to have a loan for large items such as that? Most people will have to take out loans and mortgages for things like that, but your goal should be to get to the point where those debts are paid off and you can live debt-free. Does it sound impossible? Well, it isn't! Making extra payments on loans instead of buying another thing that can wait will help you to pay off your debts really quickly. You can be debt-free if you want it badly enough! Start praying for it, believing it will happen, speaking it out loud, and seeing it in your heart. Remember, God is able to do exceedingly, abundantly, above and beyond all that you *dare* to hope, ask or think (see Ephesians 3:20). Be daring in your asking and passionate about your giving.

Six Reasons for Lack

I realise that when we decide to believe God wants to prosper us, we sometimes have to deal with the reasons some people don't prosper. As I have already stated, there are many reasons for lack, or going without, in the lives of various individuals. I mentioned that sometimes we are being tested and just need to be patient and diligent, but there are other things worth considering that we should look at.

1 Having a Poverty Mind-set. So many times our enthusiasm for what God wants to do with us is dampened by the feeling that we can ask for too much from God. We lower our expectations to the point that when God is ready to use us, we miss the opportunity because we're still thinking we can't ever have what we really desire. We don't ask for the best and we settle for much less than God wants to give. It's like the time a so-called fortune-teller studied the hand of a young man and told him, 'You will be poor and very unhappy until you are thirty-seven years old.' The young man said, 'Well, after that, what will happen? Will I be rich and happy?' The fortune-teller said, 'No, you'll still be poor, but you'll be used to it by then.' Of course we don't believe in or recommend fortune-tellers, but this example makes a good point. We can get used to living a certain way and accept it as the way things are without ever searching to find out if there is a better way.

God does not usually give you what you cannot see yourself having. He told Abraham He would give him all he could see (see Genesis 13:14–17). Some people have experienced a lifetime of poverty handed down from other generations, but they should not refuse to believe they can be prosperous just because they have not experienced it yet. Remember, God takes pleasure in the prosperity of His servants (see Psalm 35:27).

Some Christian denominations actually oppose any kind of teaching that says God wants His people to have prosperity. People who teach prosperity are often referred to as 'prosperity preachers'. I frequently get asked in interviews if I am a prosperity preacher, to which I reply, 'Well, I am not asking God for poverty!' I don't encourage people to be poor! I want to enjoy my life and help other people, and from all my study of God's Word, I believe that is His will also. I want to give people hope that every area of their lives can improve.

My parents never had much when I was growing up. We were not poor, but I left home at the age of eighteen with the 'I can't afford it' attitude. I heard that all of my life and so that is what I believed. Most people probably say thousands of times in their lives, 'I can't afford that.' I finally learned to say, 'It would not be wise for me to buy that right now, but some day soon I will be able to.'

Because of my mind-set, I always bought the cheapest of everything. I would not buy anything unless it was reduced, until I finally realised I was wasting more money on petrol looking for something on offer than I would have spent had I bought it at the standard price. I felt deprived, yet even when I had money, I was not willing to spend it to have nicer things. God had to really deal with me about my attitude. He actually told me I had a cheap attitude and it took some bold, daring steps of faith for me to change.

I wanted nicer things, but I was always afraid to spend the money. I didn't buy what I really liked, and instead bought the cheapest item. My husband was the exact opposite. If we had the money, he would buy what he truly wanted and encouraged me to do the same thing.

If you suspect you have what I call a 'poverty mind-set', I encourage you to change your thinking, change your confession, and start believing the day will come when you can have the best life has to offer. The Bible says you are the head and not the tail, above and not beneath, and you can lend to many nations and yet never have to borrow (see Deuteronomy 28:12–13).

> Should our Bible teaching be fear-based because some people make wrong choices?

Some who feel it's wrong for Christians to have a lot are afraid that people will become selfish and get out of balance. There will always be people who handle money wrongly, but should our Bible teaching be fear-based because some people make wrong choices?

I don't believe it is possible to do a thorough study on the subject of money in the Bible and say God does not want His people to have it. Jesus said more about money than heaven and hell. Some 15 per cent of His sermons include teaching about money. About half of the parables mention it, and there are approximately two thousand verses in the Bible talking about money. I'd say money was a pretty important topic to Him!

It is very interesting to me that nobody seemed to have a problem with people being rich in the Old Testament. They lived under the Old Covenant, which clearly included material blessings for those who followed God's commands. The New Covenant was said to be better in every way, and yet when we get into the New Testament, we begin to see that people were accusing even the apostles of being money-hungry because they received offerings. I always wondered about that until God showed me it was only in the New Testament that Jesus said, 'Go ye into all the world and preach the gospel to every creature' (Mark 16:15 KJV). 'Go ye' *is expensive!* Non-believers are not going to finance the preaching of the gospel, so if Christians don't have what they need to survive, much less any left to give, who is going to do it? This explains to me why the devil fights to keep people from having enough.

It is God who gives us the power to get wealth that He might establish His covenant (see Deuteronomy 8:17–18). God certainly does not want the world (whom He is trying to draw to Himself) to think He cannot or is not willing to take good care of those who belong to Him. God is not stingy and small-minded; He is generous and more than enough for everything we need.

God does not just give people wealth, He gives them the *power* to get it. There are godly principles we have to apply before God can multiply us. Being able to *see* ourselves as prosperous is one of them.

2 Having a Poverty Mouth. What is in your heart comes out of your mouth. As long as you cannot see yourself having abundance and prosperity, you will say things that hinder God from blessing you and help Satan keep you poor.

What is in your heart comes out of your mouth.

If Jesus were walking the earth today, I don't think we would ever hear Him say, 'I can't afford nice things', or 'I'll never drive a new car or be able to buy my own home.' Do you? I'm pretty sure Jesus would speak positively and confidently and His entire attitude would be one of expecting His Father in heaven to take good care of Him. We cannot expect *life* (good things) if we are going to speak *death* (negative things).

God gives life to the dead and calls those things that are not as if they already existed (see Romans 4:17). We are to imitate our heavenly Father in all things (see Ephesians 5:1). Therefore, we should talk the way God talks. In other words, we should say what the Word of God says. Don't say things like: 'I can't afford that', 'I could never live in a house that nice'. 'I could never shop at that store'. 'I will probably never have a brand-new car'. 'I guess I will never get to take a nice holiday'. 'This job doesn't pay anything and I'll probably never be able to get another one'. 'I would like a steak, but I'll be eating burgers all my life'. 'Every time I get some money, I have some kind of disaster that takes it away'.

Don't talk out of your emotions. When you are upset, be prudent and restrain your lips (see Proverbs 10:19). Begin to say what God says you can have, not what you have right now.

3 **Jealousy and Envy.** There's an old story of two shopkeepers who were bitter rivals. Their shops were directly across the street from each other, and they would spend each day keeping track of each other's business.

If one got a customer, he would smile in triumph at his rival. Day and night they taunted each other as each one strove to outdo the other. Pretty soon it got to be more than a game; it became a match in jealous hatred and anger. One night an angel appeared to one of the shopkeepers in a dream and said, 'I will give you anything you ask, but whatever you receive, your competitor will receive twice as much. Would you be rich? You can be very rich, but he will be twice as wealthy. Do you wish to live a long and healthy life? You can, but his life will be longer and healthier. What is your desire?' The man frowned, thought for a moment, and then said, 'Here is my request: strike me blind in one eye!'

Don't be jealous of people who are more prosperous than you.

Don't be jealous of people who are more prosperous than you. Until we are truly happy for others when they are blessed, we will always be in need. The Bible says jealousy is a waste of time (see Titus 3:3). Don't make jealous statements like: 'Did you see that ring she wears? I would never wear anything that gaudy. She cannot really afford a ring like that anyway. It must have cost a lot of money'. 'I would never buy my clothes there. It is ridiculous what they cost. I cannot believe how people waste money'. 'There is no reason for anyone to drive a car that expensive'. 'I don't care how much money I had, I would never pay that much for a meal'. 'Did you hear, they are taking *another* holiday?'

'I would never' is one of the most ridiculous statements people can make because they usually end up doing what they said they would never do.

When you see or hear of someone else's blessings, pay attention to how you respond in your heart and with your attitude. You might locate the reason for lack in your own life. Instead of being jealous, pray for people to be blessed even more than they are. Just look at them and say, 'I'm in that line!'

If you know a godly, prosperous person, watch how he lives, talks, gives, treats people, and handles his money. Let him be a college course for you in 'how to prosper'. Jealousy causes strife. We should ask God for what we want and trust Him to give it at the right time. If our motives for asking are wrong, we won't receive what we ask for. Being jealous is not a godly motive (see James 4:1–3).

4 Not Giving All God Tells You to Give. God said we should bring *all* the tithes into the storehouse (see Malachi 3:8–12). A tithe is the first 10 per cent of all your increase. Instead of saying, 'I'm tithing on my salary so do I really have to tithe on that bonus, or the profit from the sale of my house, or that inheritance?' we should be excited about giving *all* God asks for. He never tries to take anything away from us, but He is putting us in a position to be able to bless us more.

Jesus asked a rich, young ruler for a special sacrifice, and he was not able to give it. The Bible says the young man went away sad because he was very rich (see Mark 10:21–30). I believe if that young man had given his all, as Jesus asked him to do, he would have later received even more than he gave.

Ananias and Sapphira only gave part of what they committed and dropped dead. Yes, that is rather severe, but perhaps God is trying to let us know how important obedience is by using their example (see Acts 5:1–10). Abel gave an acceptable offering, but Cain did not. Cain gave *something,* but it was not what God asked for. God was pleased with Abel, but He was not pleased with Cain. As a result, Cain became jealous and killed Abel and ended up living with a curse all of his life. It was all because he was not willing to give God his best (see Genesis 4:3–8).

Just the opposite, the Macedonians begged for the opportunity to give, even though they had problems of their own (see 2 Corinthians 8:1–4). Whose attitude do you think God liked the best? Who do you think put themselves in a position for promotion? It isn't hard to work out, so I strongly encourage you to give *all* God asks and you will never be sorry. Your flesh might not like it at first, but you will reap rich rewards later on.

Give *all* God asks and you will never be sorry.

5 Having Strife (Bickering, Arguing, Bitterness, Resentment and Unforgiveness) in Your Life. The Bible says in Psalm 133 that where there is unity, God commands the blessing. Wow! That tells me I will be a maker and maintainer of peace and that I will be blessed. I think there are a lot of people who are expecting God to enable them to prosper, they may even be giving, but they are angry and offended most of the time. God cannot bless that kind of attitude.

Are you praying and believing in God for increase in your life? If so, you must remember that faith works through love (see Galatians 5:6). We can pray in faith for abundance and prosperity, but if we are not walking in love, our faith has no energy behind it. When you pray, if you are holding anything against a person you should drop it, leave it, and let it go. You must completely forgive in order for prayers to be answered (see Mark 11:25–26). Are you praying for a promotion and a pay rise at work, but you're mad at your boss who will need to approve it?

Jane was a single parent who worked hard for five years at the local electricity company and she really needed a big pay rise to help her support her family properly. Jane was still bitter at her ex-husband, who cheated on her and rarely paid his child support. She had also been angry at her boss for two years because a colleague was given the position that Jane wanted. Every opportunity Jane got, she talked unkindly about her ex-husband and her boss. It was so bad that her friends were starting to dread being around her. Even her children had noticed how negative and bitter she had become.

Jane was praying and, according to her terminology, 'really believing God' for the pay rise, but it still didn't come. Then one week her church had a guest speaker who revealed how strife prevents people from being blessed, and she realised she had taken Satan's bait and fallen deeply into his trap. She recognised her sin, asked God to forgive her, and started praying for her ex-husband and boss to be blessed. She was amazed when after only three weeks went by, she was called into the boss's office and offered a position that would give her an increase of $8,000 a year and an extra week of paid holiday. Jane prayed for something and blocked the answer to her own prayer by allowing her heart to be filled with strife. I wonder how many other hundreds of thousands of people are doing the same thing and feeling confused about why they don't prosper in life.

Wisdom leads us to riches, honour, and promotion (see Proverbs 4:8, 8:18). But true wisdom is peace-loving (see James 3:17). If we are not peace-loving, we are not walking in wisdom and, therefore, we will not walk in riches, honour, and promotion.

6 Not Saving Money. God commands the blessing upon the storehouse (see Deuteronomy 28:8). Do you have a storehouse? Do you have a piggy bank, a savings account, a sock you hide money in, or anything you could call a storehouse? When my husband, Dave, was a teenager he had a sock in one of his drawers where he saved money. He actually saved enough money in his sock to pay $1,000 in cash for his first car, and that was a lot of money. Dave's family did not have much in the way of money, but he determined that he would work hard and save. He believed if he did, God would bless him and it happened.

> Start a storehouse to honour God's principles and watch Him bless it.

Try it out – start saving for something you want to buy instead of putting it on a credit card. Start a storehouse to honour God's principles and watch Him bless it. God can give you all kinds of ways to earn extra money. Dave got to work a lot of overtime at his job during the time he was saving the money for his car. Who knows, perhaps had he never started saving he would not have had an opportunity to work overtime?

If people don't learn to save and have a storehouse, they will never live beyond their next salary cheque. They will always be one cheque away from poverty. If you think you cannot save, then you are deceived. Start taking an honest look at what you waste money on and begin saving it instead. You will probably be amazed at what it will amount to over time.

i dare you

Keep a Right Relationship with Money

It's OK to enjoy money, but we don't want to love it, just as we never want to mistreat anyone to get money nor be dishonest in our pursuit of it. Don't ever desire money for selfish reasons. Certainly, it's natural to want to be blessed, but we can actually learn to enjoy blessing others even more than we do being blessed.

Here is a biblical test we can all take frequently to see if we are keeping a right relationship with money. If we have the money or goods to sustain life, and we see our fellow believer in need and yet close our heart of compassion to that person, then we do not have a right relationship with money. It is not wrong to have money as long as we do not allow the money to have us! The Bible says that the love of God cannot live and remain in us if we see our fellow believers in need and refuse to help in any way (see John 3:17).

I don't believe God wants us to always be doing without. After all, He is the God of 'more than enough', not just 'barely get by', or 'do without'. Follow God's principles set forth in His Word, and if you're patient, I do believe you will prosper in all you lay your hand to. I am not suggesting that everyone will be a multimillionaire, but I do believe everyone can have his or her needs met and have an abundant supply left over to help those in need.

CHAPTER 15

Get Physical

This book is about daring to live with purpose and passion, and having a strong, healthy body is part of what enables us to do that. We all know when we feel bad physically that everything becomes more difficult. When we're tired, run-down and depriving ourselves of exercise and good, nutritious meals, problems can seem three times as bad. It's harder to focus and devote the necessary attention to what we need to be doing. I'm here to tell you, though, God can enable us to do anything and He frequently gives people supernatural strength to accomplish amazing things even when they are ill. It is not God's desire that we struggle continually with poor health.

Jesus was and is a healer. As I said earlier, Jesus can heal us everywhere we hurt. Our healing was bought and paid for in the atonement, the same as our sins. Atonement means reconciliation, and it means *at-one-ness*, which I love to ponder. Jesus died for our wholeness – body, soul and spirit, mind, will and emotions. He shed His blood so our sins and all of their effects could be forgiven and overcome.

Surely He has borne our griefs (sicknesses, weaknesses, and distresses) and carried our sorrows *and* pains [of punishment], yet we [ignorantly] considered Him stricken, smitten, and afflicted by God [as if with leprosy].

But He was wounded for our transgressions, He was bruised for our guilt *and* iniquities; the chastisement [needful to obtain] peace *and* well-being for us was upon Him, and with the stripes [that wounded] Him we are healed *and* made whole.

  – ISAIAH 53:4–5

These beautiful scriptures prophetically describe or foretell the amazing thing that Jesus did for us when He died and shed His blood on the cross of Calvary.

I believe many people mistakenly believe Jesus died only to solve their spiritual problems. They believe He forgives sin, but they don't necessarily believe He does anything about the results of sin. They acknowledge the gift of eternal life, but as one woman put it recently, they also believe we must 'white knuckle' it until we get to heaven. In other words, heaven is great, but life is something we must endure and try to get through. Heaven is the reward, but life is the test. Put another way, heaven is our favourite amusement-park ride and life is the queue to get there.

Sin still exists in the world, but God has provided a way through Jesus Christ for our sins to be continually forgiven. Sickness exists in the world, but we can ask and believe for healing from God.

Is Physical Healing God's Will?

Some people believe God wants them to be ill. If that is the case, then I wonder why they go to the doctor and try to get well. If God wants people to be ill, why did Jesus heal people? It is important we know God's will; otherwise we cannot release our faith to receive it.

In Matthew 5, 8, and 9, Jesus cleansed a leper, healed the centurion's servant, Peter's mother-in-law, a paralysed man, and a woman who had been bleeding for twelve years. He cast demons out of a man who was possessed and raised a girl from the dead. He opened the eyes of two blind men and gave a dumb man the ability to speak.

And Jesus went about all the cities and villages, teaching in
their synagogues and proclaiming the good news (the Gospel)
of the kingdom and curing all kinds of disease and every
weakness *and* infirmity.

– MATTHEW 9:35

If we are going to believe the Word of God, we must believe God's
nature is to heal and make whole. I mentioned 3 John 2 in our previous chapter which says, 'Beloved, I pray that you may prosper in
every way and [that your body] may keep well, even as [I know] your
soul keeps well *and* prospers.' It sounds as if it is important to God
that we have a prosperous life in all areas, including good health.

How Can We Receive Healing from God?

James said we have not because we ask not. There may be thousands
of people reading this who have never asked God to heal them
physically, simply because they did not know it was His will. If that
is the case, you need to ask.

Ask in faith with no doubting, hesitating, or wavering (James 1:6)
and be certain about what you are asking God to do for you. Don't
let your circumstances cause you to doubt. Believe that God's healing
power is working in you, even if you don't feel or see any change yet.
Isn't that what we do when we take medicine? We go to the doctor,
get a prescription, and start dutifully taking our medicine. Sometimes we take an entire bottle of pills and need a repeat prescription
because we are still having problems, but we continue to take the
medication because we believe in our doctor when he says it works.

> God's Word is like medicine – it has inherent power that
> heals.

God's Word is like medicine – it has inherent power that heals. God's Word states that we should be attentive to God's words, for they are life to those who find them, healing and health to all their flesh (see Proverbs 4:20–22).

The Hebrew word for 'health' is 'medicine'. In Exodus 15:26, Isaac Leiser's translation says, 'I am the Lord thy Physician.' By putting Proverbs 4:20–22 and Exodus 15:26 together, we could translate them as: 'I am the Lord thy Physician, and the medicine I prescribe is My Word.' Powerful!

I always encourage people to confess God's Word out loud and meditate on it frequently to help them in any kind of situation. Psalm 107:20 says, 'He sent His word and healed them.' When people phone our office for prayer when they are ill, we often send them a list of healing scriptures we recommend that they confess out loud. We tell them to do it as diligently as they would take medicine, and we have had some fabulous reports of people receiving healing.

To receive healing from God, we often have to be patient and steadfast. Miracles often occur instantly, but healing is frequently a process that takes time.

> Miracles often occur instantly, but healing is frequently a process that takes time.

A very good friend of mine named Pennie suffered for twenty years with a back problem that kept her in a lot of pain. She did everything there was to do, short of surgery, which the doctor didn't recommend. She finally reached the point where she knew she needed a miracle! I consider Pennie to be a godly woman and she is definitely a woman of prayer. She prayed often over the years without seeing her circumstances change, but she continued looking to God for her healing. Though God did not immediately remove her pain, He did strengthen and enable her to cope with bringing up her children and perform all of her duties as a pastor's wife.

One day as Pennie was praying about her situation, which seemed to be getting worse, God impressed these words on her heart: 'Run to your miracle.' She was not sure what He meant, but the first thing that came to her was to run a marathon, which, of course, was impossible for her in her condition. She went to her doctor, who looked at her and said, 'It is impossible.' Pennie said, 'Good, then God will have to do it.'

She began to train to run a marathon, and when she began she could only endure running a short distance. She continued with a trainer for six months and finally it was time to run her twenty-six-mile marathon. A few days prior to the race, her knee began to hurt, and the pain was so bad she was limping. Every bit of reasoning told her she could never run the race, but her faith was so strong that she told her husband, 'I am going to run in this race even if you have to carry me to the starting line.'

The day of the race, she limped to the starting line, and as she stood there, her back stopped hurting and has never hurt for a day since then, which at the time of writing was over three years ago. God still heals and does miracles today!

> God still heals and does miracles today!

So why did Pennie have to wait so long? Why did God have her run to her miracle? We don't have the answers to those questions, but we are told to be patient, obedient, diligent, determined, steadfast and full of faith. Faith sees what it does not have yet, but believes it can have, based on God's Word.

> Faith sees what it does not have yet, but believes it can have, based on God's Word.

We receive the promises of God through faith and patience (see Hebrews 10:35–36). So, if you are in need of healing, I encourage you to pray and not give up.

Should I Take Medicine?

Questions about taking medicine often come up. Some people have said if we are standing in faith for a healing, we should trust God alone and not take medication. God may say that to someone in a specific situation, but for me, I don't believe that is a requirement we must meet in order to receive supernatural healing. As a matter of fact, I think there might be times when it would be downright foolish not to take medication. I am fond of Proverbs 18:9: 'He who does not use his endeavors to heal himself is brother to him who commits suicide.'

Some medicines probably should be avoided, because the side effects are worse than the original disease, but these areas are ones we must pray about and receive direction from God.

Many people today are opting to use alternative healing methods, which include nutrition and other health treatments done without harmful medications. I believe that any time we can help ourselves naturally, it is much better than introducing a chemical into our bodies. I do take medicines, but I don't take them if I can avoid it. The best policy is to seek God about what you do before you do anything. Following His lead is always going to work much better than anything else.

Seek God about what you do before you do anything.

Why Do People Get Ill?

Before sin came into the world, there was no illness. Man was so healthy and strong that Adam lived 930 years before he died. Today the expected lifespan in the United States is 77.6 years and worldwide it is 64.2. Illness can be, but is not always, caused by personal sin. It is often the result of the sin principle and the decay sin brings, which is at work in the world today. We are in the world, sickness is in the world, and sometimes we collide with one another.

> Illness can be, but is not always, caused by personal sin.

The Bible often links sin and illness together. God forgives all your iniquities and heals all of your diseases (see Psalm 103:3). 'The prayer of faith will save him who is sick, and the Lord restore him; and *if* he has committed sins, he will be forgiven' (James 5:15, emphasis mine). Jesus forgave the paralytic's sins before He healed him (see Matthew 9:2).

In the Bible we read of a man born blind, and when the Pharisees questioned Jesus about whether his blindness was the result of his own sin or his parents', Jesus replied it was neither: He said he was born blind so God's power might be displayed through him.

There is probably more illness and disease in the world today than at any other time. Our food is often depleted of vitamins and minerals, our water and air can be polluted, stress levels are too high in most individuals, and some people don't get enough sleep or exercise. In general, I think it is safe to say most people don't take care of themselves as they should. Their bodies are in a run-down condition, and when germs and viruses come around, it is very easy to catch whatever illness they represent.

Take Better Care of Yourself

> You are being selfish if you don't take care of yourself.

Are you being selfish if you spend time and money taking care of yourself? Absolutely not! In fact, I believe you are being selfish if you don't take care of yourself. Your body is the temple of the Holy

Spirit (see 1 Corinthians 6:19). God lives in you. He once lived in the tabernacle or the temple, but now He dwells in those who believe in Him and have accepted Jesus as their Saviour.

The Bible actually says that God makes His home in those who receive Jesus as their personal Saviour (see 1 John 4:15). This is a privilege, but it is also a responsibility. We need to take care of God's house! He has invested Himself in us and we should invest also. Take time to take care of yourself. If you wear out the body you have now, you cannot go to the department store and buy another one.

Take time to get educated about good nutrition and make healthy food and lifestyle choices. Some people get ill all the time merely because they don't respect themselves enough to take care of themselves. In my book *Look Great, Feel Great,* I wrote that I believe people in the United States are in a self-respect crisis. What I meant was that a lot of people feel bad about themselves because they have been devalued by others, and their own opinion of themselves hurts them more than anything else.

> People must love themselves in a balanced way or they are in for a lifetime of misery.

People must love themselves in a balanced way or they are in for a lifetime of misery. You never get away from yourself for even one moment, so learn to love and appreciate yourself, because God does. He loves you with an everlasting love and, you know, He even likes you. We get all freaked out about our funny-shaped toes or our freckles, but God thinks they are cute. He thinks we are wonderful. You may have felt in life that you were picked out to be picked on, but the good news is God has picked you out to pick you up. He will pick you up and make your life significant.

> God has picked you out to pick you up.

If you need healing or you don't want to become ill, then make a commitment to take better care of yourself. If you do what you can do, God will do what you cannot do. Would it be better to receive healing or live in divine health? Of course divine health would be better. If that is what you want, you will have to learn something about preventative medicine, and that means taking care of yourself before you become ill. Just eliminating excess stress in your life can prevent illness, so why not start today by making better choices? The Apostle Paul had a colleague who became so ill from overworking in the ministry that he almost died. None of us can consistently break God's laws of health and get away with it. The time is now! Be proactive rather than reactive. Be passionate (have a strong desire) to take care of your body and then follow through with lifestyle choices that will help you reach your goal. Get educated in health and the benefits of exercise and good nutrition.

Avoid Clogging Your Body with Stress and Negative Feelings

Often when we become ill, the culprit can actually be anger and unforgiveness. The Bible tells us that both of these negative emotions open a door for the devil to bring harm to us (see Ephesians 4:26–27; 1 Corinthians 1:10–11). 'A calm *and* undisturbed mind *and* heart are the life *and* health of the body, but envy, jealousy, *and* wrath are like rottenness of the bones' (Proverbs 14:30). Beware of negatives and remember that negative feelings buried alive simply never die. They stay in us, eating away like a cancer at our spiritual, mental, emotional and physical health.

> Negative feelings buried alive simply never die.

The Apostle Paul said a wide door of opportunity opened unto him and with it many adversaries. Sometimes the devil attacks us with illness simply because we are doing good and he wants to distract us.

I have experienced various health challenges in my life and I know by experience it is much more difficult to be kind, desire to pray and serve others when we are focused on the pain or misery in our bodies.

The day before I left for a mission trip to Rwanda, I became ill. Not so ill I couldn't go, or wasn't able to function, but ill enough to make it difficult. Unfortunately, I become even more ill after I left and headed for the former Soviet Union to minister there. A mosquito bit me on the side of my eye and it swelled shut, which had *never* happened to me before from a mosquito bite. I had stomach trouble, sores on my tongue, a sinus infection, and a very sore throat – all of which made it very difficult to preach, but God enabled me to do all I needed to do.

During those times when it's just plain hard, I try to stand steadfast and keep doing what I believe God is calling me to do. I also try to think about how I became that ill and then I attempt to learn how I can take better care of myself in the future.

Don't take illness and claim it as your own.

Don't take illness and claim it as your own. I frequently hear people say things like, 'My allergies' or 'My ulcer'. The least we can do is not take illness in like a family member and refer to it the same way we would a relative! It may be visiting, but we should be determined not to let it take up permanent residence.

Jesus is your Healer and He wants you to feel energetic, strong and healthy. Don't settle for anything less. Do all you can to co-operate with the Holy Spirit as He works to bring you to a place of divine health.

i dare you

Say No to Stress!

One of the things that can steal our health and happiness the fastest is stress. It starts with being so busy we don't have time to exercise, and then it moves into not taking time for a healthy lunch but grabbing whatever is in the vending machine (if you grab lunch at all). Drinking caffeine drinks to give us energy and ignoring our bodies' cry for water, and having so many commitments that we don't get enough rest or sleep – pretty soon our bodies are run-down from lack of good nutrition and hydration, and going full-throttle with no time for rest. Our performance either at work or whatever day-to-day commitments we have start to suffer, and then our anxiety and worry heat up. It's a ruthless cycle, but it can be stopped before it gets that far. Here are some quick tips:

1 *Prioritise.* Always be intentional in prioritising what's most important. Make the time to plan out what you want and need to do each day. By taking ten to fifteen minutes out of your day to plan, you'll save yourself a lot of wasted time and energy later.

2 *Maintain balance.* We want to pursue our purpose with passion, but let's not pursue our dreams at the expense of our family, our relationship with God, and other areas of our lives. Ask God to help you keep the right things in the right places.

3 *Take time out.* You may feel pressurised to take care of everything and everyone else's needs but your own. Realise you are not the Energiser Bunny – take time to unwind. Read, have a bubble bath, go for a jog, play a game of golf. Do something that will allow your mind to recharge and your spirit to refresh.

An Independent Spirit

Sometimes God uses illness as a halter to pull an individual into His will. Watchman Nee, F. F. Bosworth and others agree on this point. Watchman Nee said, 'May I put it bluntly: many are sick simply because they love themselves too much.' Unless this unbalanced self-love is removed from their hearts, God cannot use them. I mentioned we should love ourselves, but I don't mean we are to be in love with ourselves, having ourselves and our desires as the centre of our lives. God and His will must always come first.

> We should love ourselves, but I don't mean we are to be in love with ourselves.

I don't believe God makes people ill, but I do believe He uses it at times to chastise a disobedient individual, especially if he refuses to listen any other way. He can also use illness to slow us down in order to get our attention, if we refuse to slow down ourselves. God would love for us to listen to His Word and obey Him, but we usually don't submit that easily. We are often stubborn and independent and both of those must be weeded out of us.

> He can also use illness to slow us down in order to get our attention.

One minister told me that God had been dealing with him for a long time about getting the stress out of his life and living a more balanced lifestyle. He had been ignoring God's warnings and finally became very ill. While he was recuperating, he went for a walk in a park and eventually lay down on the grass to think and pray. The Holy Spirit reminded him of Psalm 23:2, which says: 'He makes me lie down in green pastures' (NIV). The minister said that since he refused to lie down and rest on his own, God *made* him lie down. In other words, he became ill and had no choice but to rest.

When Jesus was having what is commonly called the Last Supper with His disciples, the Bible says He *broke* the bread, *blessed* it, and *gave* it to them. Think about that: broken, blessed and given. God has to break us, He blesses us, and then He gives us to the world to help it. An independent, self-confident person is not one that is broken. When we are broken, we are dependent on God, our confidence is in Him, and we are pliable and mouldable in His hands.

The story of the prodigal son in the Bible starts with his saying to his father, '*Give me* my inheritance.' But, after losing everything and ending up eating with the pigs, he returned to his father and said, '*Make me* as one of your hired servants' (see Luke 15:11–24). We must make the transition from 'Give me' to 'Make me' before God can do much with us. He wants us fully committed to Him so that He can do whatever He has to do in order to accomplish His purpose.

Ask God to break you, bless you, and give you to the world as a blessing. Ask Him to break your heart with the things that break His.

> Ask God to break you, bless you, and give you to the world as a blessing.

Dream Big and Never Give Up

Sean Swarner is the first cancer survivor to climb the world's highest mountain – Mount Everest. At the age of thirteen, he was diagnosed with Hodgkin's disease and given three months to live. Two years later, at fifteen, Sean was diagnosed with Askin's sarcoma. The prognosis was much worse than the previous diagnosis and the doctors gave him only two weeks to live. But, just like the first time, Sean survived.

Being the only person in the world to have ever had both of these cancers – and live to tell about it – Sean set out to share his story to motivate others and influence lives. On 16 May 2002, at 9.32 a.m., he became the first cancer survivor to stand on the top of Mount Everest.

Since then, he has reached the summits of three more of the world's seven highest peaks and has spoken all over the world about his life and adventures to countless people and organisations. At the top of Everest, and essentially the world, he left a flag adorned with names of people affected with cancer, forever commemorating the struggle of cancer patients worldwide.

Sean did the same at the highest points in Africa and Europe and, just recently, through his climb of the 23,000 foot Aconcagua in South America. He says his ultimate goal is to climb the highest mountain on each continent and trek to the North and South Poles. His passion is to 'cover the globe with inspiration'. He wants to carry out these climbing expeditions not just for himself, but to inspire those affected by cancer and anyone else to dream big and never give up.[1]

If Sean could do what he has done, surely we can be a bit more daring, adventurous and passionate about life. We don't all have to climb a mountain (at least I know I don't), but we should all dream big dreams and never give up.

When we think about our physical well-being, we need to keep in mind that how we feel physically will affect how we feel emotionally. Our excitement and drive for following through with God's plan for our lives can only grow when we maintain a healthy lifestyle, but it can certainly weaken and be hurt if we don't make the effort to take care of ourselves. Be intentional in your pursuit of a healthy body, and I believe you will see a positive difference that will help you have a better quality of life.

CHAPTER 16

Never Give Up

I recall hearing a story about a little boy who kept standing up in church, even though his mother repeatedly told him to sit down. After a serious warning from his mother about what would happen to him if he did not sit down, he finally complied. After a few minutes of sitting in the church pew, the little boy looked at his mother and said, 'I may be sitting down, but I'm standing up on the inside.'

> We cannot always control all of our circumstances, but we can control the attitudes of our hearts.

This is what we all have to do if we are going to see our destinies fulfilled. We all experience disappointment in life and endure many things that try to convey the message we are not going to make it or we won't get what we had hoped for. We cannot always control all of our circumstances, but we can control the attitudes of our hearts. A person who refuses to give up will be successful! His circumstances may have him 'sitting down' for a while, but if he keeps standing up on the inside, he will outlast his circumstances and eventually see his dreams come true.

Our attitude must be: *I will never give up!*

Overcoming Your Past

We all have a past of some sort that tries to keep us trapped. Our past mistakes and disappointments scream loudly that our lives will never change, but that is absolutely not true. Our past only has the power we give it and no more. God's Word is clear about what to do about the past – *let go of it!* That means we should believe it has no power to harm us or affect our futures. This is a new day and God has a plan for all those who are willing to let go and press on. Are you ready?

Stop thinking about what you lost and start seeing what you have left. Even if it doesn't seem much to you, God can use it to do great things. Your future is not based on what you have, but on who God is and His promises to you.

> Your future is not based on what you have, but on who God is and His promises to you.

How long will you mourn over what did not work out in your life? When will you let go of what you lost? When will you move on from what has been stolen from you, your past sins, failed relationships? Are you ready to release everything in your past and have a new beginning? God is ready, but if you're not, He has to wait until you get the right attitude. He has to wait until you have an attitude of faith, which has everything to do with now and always leaves the past in God's hands, believing He is big enough to work something good out of it. Faith always works in the now. It believes right now that God is able to take care of the past and the future. Faith says, 'Today is God's gift to me and I will live it fully.'

> Faith always works in the now.

The past will prevent you from moving into the future God has planned for you. If you keep holding on to what is over, you will never experience anything other than grieving and mourning over something you cannot do anything about. Don't hold on to something old just because it is familiar. Dare to take a step of faith and say, 'I will try again!'

Chuck Colson is a great example of getting over the past. Here was a man who, at one time, was one of the most feared men in Washington, DC. As legal counsel and an aide to Richard Nixon, the President of the United States, he was sent to jail for his role in Watergate, but as a result of his experience as a convicted felon, he went on to start Prison Fellowship, now the world's largest Christian outreach to prisoners and their families, with more than fifty thousand volunteers working in hundreds of prisons in dozens and dozens of countries around the world. This ministry, now blessing millions of people, was started over thirty years ago and it's all because Chuck took his past and turned it into something good, something fruitful, and something eternal. God's eternal purposes for that man were accomplished in spite of the sin that sent him to prison. It was a part of God's plan from the very beginning.

> Your past might be something from ten years ago or it could be something from ten minutes ago.

Your past might be something from ten years ago or it could be something from ten minutes ago. Either way, it is the past and needs to be left with God, who is able to bring something good out of it. Don't settle for something mediocre that is not fulfilling and satisfying. Press on to the next level and be determined to never give up.

I believe determination and a refusal to give up are the key ingredients to success in any area of life. Anyone who is now enjoying fulfilment and contentment has already made the decision, possibly thousands of times, not to give up. I couldn't even count the times in my own life when I had to make that decision. Believe me, there were plenty of times when I felt like calling it quits. Quite often I felt I would never overcome the results of my abusive past. It seemed to me everything in my life was affected by it and quite often I felt overwhelmed. I felt as if I had so far to go that I would never get to my destination. Have you ever felt that way, or do you perhaps feel that way right now? If so, I can assure you nothing in your past is greater than God, and if you refuse to give up, you will enjoy complete victory. I shudder to think about what I would have missed in life had I given up years ago when everything in my life seemed so hard.

I can assure you nothing in your past is greater than God.

Decide right now that you will not miss the best God has for you. Do your part by having an aggressive 'I will not give up – I am determined' attitude.

Don't look back – you've already been there, there's nothing new you need to see in the past. Instead, look ahead to the new, exciting and challenging adventures God has in store for you – tomorrow, next month, and in the years to come. Maybe you're thinking you don't want another challenge, but the truth is you were created for it. It's similar to how airlines train their pilots. First they put them in a simulator programmed to test the pilots with a variety of possible problems to make sure they can handle any emergency. They start the pilots off with simple challenges, which eventually lead up to disastrous situations they must navigate. It's interesting to note the pilots are only given the more difficult problems after they master the easier, less-serious ones. The result is that once these pilots have completed these courses, they are ready to handle any problem they encounter.

Maybe you're thinking you don't want another challenge, but the truth is you were created for it.

This is similar to God's method of working with us. God teaches us how to handle the problems of life, but never gives us more than we can cope with. He teaches us through each situation, so we can be fully prepared and mature people, ready to handle any challenge in life.[1] After all, if God removed all the challenging things from our lives, we would not develop properly. We need the struggle to survive.

I once heard a story about a bee taken on a trip into space. The atmosphere in the spaceship was weightless, so the bee floated around with no effort at all. When the crew returned and gave their report on how the weightless atmosphere affected the bee, the report was as follows: 'The bee enjoyed the ride, but died!' I am concerned that may be what happens to a lot of people. They search for something that won't require much effort on their part, they shrink from challenges and difficulties, but in the process they die inside because God did not create us to live that kind of apathetic life. He made us to look for and experience passion and enthusiasm day by day.

Getting over the past and pressing into the future may require an effort, but you have what it takes! Don't ever be convinced of anything else. As long as you believe you can, you can. As soon as you begin to believe you cannot, you won't, and it will be even harder to convince yourself you can.

Arise!

The word 'arise' simply means to get up and get going. That may be the answer you have been looking for. Sometimes we make overcoming our difficulties a bigger problem than it needs to be. You might be asking God, 'What do You want me to do?' 'How can I survive, how can I overcome?' God's answer to you may well be what it was to many other people in the Bible who experienced disappointment with life: Arise!

For forty years Moses led the Israelites in the wilderness. These people were very dependent on him. For four decades, they'd looked for him to take them into the Promised Land, but he died before they got there. The people were in mourning, they were confused, and they were uncertain of what to do next. So God spoke to Joshua, who was to be their new leader, and said, 'Moses is dead. Arise and take these people over the Jordan into the Promised Land.'

Joshua and the people already knew Moses was dead, so why did God say, 'Moses is dead'? I believe it was an emphatic statement intended to wake them up to the fact that they only had two choices: to sit there and die, or get up and press on!

When Jesus encountered a crippled man at the Pool of Bethesda who was waiting for a miracle, He asked the man how long he had been in that condition. The man replied, 'Thirty-eight years.' Did Jesus say, 'OK, well, keep waiting and maybe something good will happen'? No! He said, 'Get up!'

We read in Micah 7:8, 'When I fall, I shall arise.' To get up, to stand up, is a decision we have to intentionally make, not something that just automatically happens. We must choose to get up and not be trapped in the past.

There are days I feel discouraged and as if I cannot go on. When those feelings come, I read the following Bible verse:

> Arise [from the depression and prostration in which
> circumstances have kept you – rise to a new life]! Shine (be
> radiant with the glory of the Lord), for your light has come,
> and the glory of the Lord has risen upon you!
> – ISAIAH 60:1

All the promises given in this verse are predicated on the instruction to arise. If we refuse to do that, God will not do His part either. We must have enough faith to get up and keep going.

Decide today: are you giving up or getting up? It is easy to give up, but those who are strong in the Lord will always get up!

> It is easy to give up, but those who are strong in the Lord
> will always get up!

Has Your Brook Dried Up?

The prophet Elijah was a great man of God, but just like the rest of us, he experienced difficult times in his life. One of those challenges was during a famine when no rain fell on the land for many years. God instructed Elijah to go to the brook Cherith and dwell there because there was a supply of water. He also fed him daily by having ravens bring him food. Everything was going well until suddenly the brook dried up (see 1 Kings 17:1–9). We all have times just like this when all is well and then suddenly, without warning, something we did not expect happens and everything falls apart. During these times we should remember God has another plan. When one door closes, another one always opens. We may be too upset to see it, but God always makes a way for His people.

When the brook dried up, God told Elijah to *arise* and go to Zarephath, where He had already commanded a widow to provide for him. God had a plan, but Elijah had to arise. We must arise inside our hearts before we will ever arise physically.

> We must arise inside our hearts before we will ever arise physically.

i dare you

Press On

I am challenging you to press on. I am asking you to keep moving forward. Will you get up and get going? Will you press forward even if everyone you know is discouraging you and telling you to give up and face reality? We can face reality, but that doesn't mean we have to give up. Reality is facts, but the promises of God are truth. Facts are not final, they can be altered, but God's Word stands firm and sure, and it is unshakable and unmovable. God's Word is the Rock on which we are encouraged to build our lives.

There are certain times in life when we are more tempted to give up than at other times. Knowing how to recognise them ahead of time may help us overcome them. Let me share with you what I believe some of them are and perhaps you can add to the list from your own experiences in life.

If you are discouraged and depressed, you probably won't even see God's new provision. Faith sees what is not even visible to the naked eye, but doubt and unbelief are blind to God's provision. Be like the little boy in church, and when your circumstances have you sitting down on the outside, refuse to sit down on the inside. Have a determined attitude and refuse to be defeated when your brook dries up.

When You Have Waited Longer Than You Thought You Would Have to Wait

Things almost always take longer than we thought they would. We enjoy instant gratification and aren't happy when we don't get it. Receiving the promises of God requires both faith and patience, so we must be determined not to give up if things take longer than we hoped they would.

God told Abraham that Sarah, who was barren and past child-bearing age, would become pregnant and give him an heir from his own body. This was Abraham's passion, it was his dream, and he rejoiced when he was told his dream would come true. Isaac was the child of promise, but he was not born for another twenty years. I cannot even imagine what Abraham thought during those years, but I am sure he had thousands of times when he felt like giving up or thought, *What is the point in believing? This is never going to happen!*

After all, he was an old man, Sarah was an old woman, and they were both getting older every day. I have had that conversation with God. 'God, do You remember my age? I am not getting any younger, You know. If You are going to do what You said You would do, don't You think You better get on with it before I am too old to do it?' It is, of course, a foolish conversation, because age means nothing to God. We are never too old or too young to be used by God. If God has to do a miracle anyway, why not make it a good one?

When Lazarus was ill, Jesus was called to come and help, but the Bible says He waited two more days until Lazarus died, and then He went to help. Jesus wanted to do a miracle, but He had to wait until Lazarus had a big enough problem to need one. Jesus raised Lazarus from the dead and God received the glory (see John 11).

> Sometimes God waits just so our breakthrough will be even more amazing.

When we are waiting longer than makes any sense to us, we should remember that sometimes God waits just so our breakthrough will be even more amazing and no one can possibly get the glory but Him. Fighting the good fight of faith, which includes refusing to give up, is one of the things that makes the victory sweeter. Abraham gained strength as he gave praise and glory to God. During times of waiting, be sure to keep a positive attitude, spend time with positive people, and refuse to give up. Every day you wait is one more behind you, one you won't have to wait through again.

> Every day you wait is one more behind you, one you won't have to wait through again.

When Everyone You Know Seems to Be Against You

I know how hard it is not to give up when you are the only one willing to keep going, but it is possible and most of us will find it necessary at some point in life. Jesus was left alone during His most difficult time, there in the Garden of Gethsemane, and He had to make the decision not to give up.

The Apostle Paul was left alone at his first trial. He said no one acted in his defence. All forsook him, but the Lord stood by him and strengthened him (see 2 Timothy 4:16–17).

When I answered the call to preach the gospel, my friends and extended family turned against me. I remember feeling so lonely that I thought I would die.

I am sure you have had lonely times, times when you felt no one believed in you, everyone had forsaken you. You may not realise it, but those times were actually very good for you because they were intended to teach you not excessively to rely on others, because you will always be devastated if you do. We cannot put our confidence in human flesh, but in Christ alone. Andrew Murray said in *God's Best Secrets*, 'For the only thing that ever hurts us is an expectation of something when we should only expect that something from God.'

That does not mean we should be suspicious of people and expect them to let us down, but it does mean we must realise all we really need to succeed is God! God will never give up on us and we should keep our eyes on Him and decide we will never give up either.

All we really need to succeed is God!

Having people who encourage us is important, but we must not allow it to be more important than it should be. Anything we have to have besides God to keep going is something the devil can use against us. For example, if I have to have compliments from people in order not to get depressed and give up, the devil will make sure I don't get any. But if I refuse to give up and I trust God for everything I need in life, then the devil has no power over me.

I enjoy having encouragement from people, and when I need it, I always ask God for it. But I determine that I will not give up in the meantime. Refusing to give up is one of the most powerful decisions you will ever make in your life.

When You Are Tired

People's moods and attitudes can change drastically when they are tired. The more tired they are, the more their commitment level wavers. It is very easy to say what we will do when all of our circumstances are good, our feelings are supporting us, our friends are on our side, and we have not been waiting very long. However, physical, emotional or mental tiredness can quickly cause us to want to give up. We say things like, 'This is just too hard', 'This is too much for me', 'How much can a person be expected to endure?' or 'Maybe I didn't hear from God after all'.

It took me many years to learn it was very important for me to live my life in such a way that I don't get so tired that I am no longer thinking right. When we feel desperate, we sometimes do desperate things we regret later, when we feel better.

Everyone gets tired. Maybe sometimes you feel like the business-man who dragged himself home, barely making it to his chair before he dropped, completely exhausted. His sympathetic, sweet wife was right there with a tall, cool drink and a comforting word.

'My, you look tired,' she said. 'You must have had a hard day today. What happened to make you so exhausted?'

'It was terrible,' her husband said. 'The computer broke down and all of us had to do our own thinking.'

Though it may not be quite to that extent, we certainly are going to have times when we have to stretch ourselves beyond what would be comfortable. A job has to be done and we have to do it.

When things don't go right and it takes longer than we thought it would, we'll have to hurry to finish, which adds more pressure. We can't avoid getting tired, but we can try to avoid exhaustion, and we can realise that what we think or feel when we are tired is not what we are going to think or feel when we have rested. When you're tired, don't try to make important decisions, because you might not make the right one.

> We can't avoid getting tired, but we can try to avoid exhaustion.

When I go to Third World countries and have an opportunity to minister to people who are so desperately needy, it always thrills me. In 2006, we hosted a conference in India where 1.3 million people attended in four days. More than 250,000 people gave their lives to Christ. We fed the hungry, built homes for widows and orphans, gave toys to children who had never had one – it was awesome! I am always ready to commit to ten more such trips when I feel so excited. But, by the time I have travelled fifty hours in a plane, have looked at food I am not sure I want to eat, and have jet lag, I have been known to say, 'This is just too hard on me. I don't know if I can do this any more!'

Our son David, who is the CEO of our world missions and is responsible for planning and managing any trips I make outside of the United States, merely laughs at me and says 'Here we go again, folks. She is excited, so she wants to go all the time, but in a few days she will be tired and never want to leave home again.' He neither adds nor cancels anything until I have rested and we talk again. By then, I have balanced out and am able to make wise decisions rather than emotional ones.

So remember to be careful about following your feelings, especially when you are really tired. You may give up on something that you will regret later in life.

When You Experience a Variety of Trials

The Apostle Paul said that we encounter a variety of trials and tribulations (see Acts 14:22). If we have just one thing, we can often deal with it, but when one thing after another happens, it gets a little harder. When we have to focus on our problems instead of our purpose, our dreams we were once so passionate about seem to fade into the background and sometimes they seem so dim that we just give them up.

Theresa had big dreams and plans when she was eighteen years old. She felt a call to world missions and wanted to do all she could to further the gospel of Jesus Christ. Then she met Jack, who also felt a call to the mission field. They fell in love, got married, and Theresa got pregnant right away at the age of nineteen. They loved each other, but neither one of them was prepared for a serious commitment, like marriage and a family. They had financial pressures, they argued a lot, Theresa got pregnant again and had another baby, and she started having some stress-related health problems. Jack had to take two jobs to support the family, so he and Theresa spent very little time together. Theresa resented being left alone a lot and Jack resented her complaining about it, since he felt he was doing all he could do to make her happy and provide for his family.

Ten years went by and it would be safe to say Theresa and Jack merely existed, and the goal was just to get through each day. One day, a friend of Theresa's asked her what she wanted to do with her life. Did she have any aspirations other than being married and bringing up her children? Had she thought about what she wanted to do when her children left home? What about Jack? Did he want to manage the fast-food restaurant he worked at all of his life, or were there other things in his heart?

The questions shocked Theresa into realising she did have dreams at one time, but all of life's trials and tribulations squeezed them out. She and Jack never talked about missions; in fact, they had not talked about it in years, even though they went to church. They would sometimes feel a little twinge when missions were mentioned in a service, but that was as far as it went. Theresa assumed what she felt as a young person was just a young girl's fantasy and she made too many mistakes anyway to ever be used by God. She never asked Jack about his dreams because she was too busy resenting him.

Unfortunately, this story is repeated over and over in society. The names may not be Theresa and Jack; you could replace their names with your own, or the names of people you may know, but the story is the same. The cares of this world, the anxieties of the age, crowd in and the Word of God is choked and bears no fruit (see Mark 4:19). People lose their focus; they get distracted, and they forget God has a purpose for them and that He wants them to live with passion. God has much more for us than mere existence, but we have to be determined to have it. We must arise and say, 'I will not give up!'

We can't avoid trials, but if we keep our dreams alive, it will make the trials more bearable. Rather than giving up during trials and tribulations, talk about your dreams and the things you believe God has in His plan for you. Have the attitude James talks about in the Bible: *Be exceedingly joyful when you fall into various kinds of trials, knowing that the trying of your faith works patience and when patience has had her perfect work you will be lacking in nothing* (see James 1:24).

> If we keep our dreams alive, it will make the trials more bearable.

Actually, the trials you experience are preparing you for the fulfilment of your dreams, so don't despise them because it only makes them seem worse. Have a positive attitude and keep saying, 'I will never give up!'

Being Too Intense About Your Faults

We all have faults and weaknesses and we all make mistakes. Yes, I said we *all* make mistakes. If we did not, then we would not need a Saviour. We want to desire change, pray about change, and face the truth about ourselves so God can change us into His own image, but we don't want to be too intense about our faults. If we are, then the attitude of guilt, condemnation and shame we carry will pressurise us and make us want to give up.

Guilt is like a treadmill—you just keep running and never go anywhere. Sometimes when you get on the guilt treadmill, it is hard to get off just as it is when you are on an exercise treadmill that is running quite fast.

> When you get on the guilt treadmill, it is hard to get off.

As I have said before, don't just look at how far you have to go, look at how far you have come. You may not be where you would like to be, but I am sure there are some positive changes you've already experienced through your relationship with Christ. However, you won't see the positive changes if you are too self-critical or too intro-spective about all of your faults. You must have a healthy attitude towards yourself, or your negative feelings will wear you down and make you want to give up. Have you ever heard this one? 'You will never change anyway, so you might as well stop trying.' Remember the devil is a liar, and if you believe him rather than God's Word, you will always experience defeat. Never stop trying, never stop moving forward. Never give up.

> You won't see the positive changes if you are too self-critical or too introspective about all your faults.

CHAPTER 17

Be Determined

Throughout this book we have talked about various ways to use passion in all areas of your life, which jointly coexist with your purpose. You can only be as passionate as you are determined. Determination essentially means the same as the notion of refusing to give up. They are both winning attitudes that all winners have – people who have dreams and overcome obstacles in order to see the fulfilment of their dreams. These individuals are not just lucky or born with a silver spoon in their mouths; they have done what they needed to do in order to enjoy what they enjoy.

> You can only be as passionate as you are determined.

Weak-willed people who carry apathy and indifference like weights around their necks won't get very far in life. God . . . gave us the fruit of self-control and a free will, but we must use it. The less people use their wills to make decisions they know are right, the more weak-willed they become. Being determined is the decision to do whatever you need to do in order to have what you say you want to have.

The Power of Diligence

Doing what is right one or two times or even a few times won't always bring victory. However, diligently doing – consistently doing – what you know you need to do over and over, sometimes for years, is the key. Benjamin Franklin said, 'Diligence is the mother of good luck.' But it's more than luck, isn't it? It's about having a determined attitude that says, 'I will do this for ever if that is what I need to do. I will not quit, I will not give up, I am determined!'

Real winners don't put time limits on their commitments. They are committed with no conditions, and when they begin, they have made up their minds they will finish, like the marathon runner who is concerned more about his endurance and finishing than how fast he can run.

The Bible says the *diligent* man will bear rule and he will be rich (see Proverbs 10:4, 12:24). God told the people they must *diligently* keep His commandments (see Joshua 22:5).

> Determination is a mind-set and diligence is the work that goes with it.

Diligence is a refusal to give up and a decision to keep doing what is right, until you get the desired result, and then continuing to do right in order to maintain what you gained. One cannot be diligent without being determined, just as one cannot be determined without being passionate. Determination is a mind-set and diligence is the work that goes with it. It's like the gears on a bike – you can have state of the art mechanics, but without the feet that step on those pedals, those gears will never move. There are many people who decide to do something, but their decision is not a quality decision. They may do it for a little while, but when the first sign of trouble appears, they fall by the wayside (see Mark 4:17). It is easier to think we will do right than it is to actually do it. Doing requires diligence!

We talked earlier about how diligence in properly handling financial affairs will produce good results. The same principle works in any area of life. If we do our part, God will never fail to do His part. He tells us what to do in order to have a good life and gives us the enabling power of His Spirit to equip us to do it. However, the decision is ours and no one can make it for us. Each of us will face midnight hours in our lives when we feel we just cannot go on. Some people give up and then others reach down deep inside and find a holy determination I believe God has placed in all of us. If we want victory, we must live deeper than how we feel, or what we think, or what other people say. We must be determined!

The Soul of the Diligent Shall Be Fat

According to Proverbs 13:4, the soul of the diligent man shall be made fat. Huh? You may hate the 'fat' word so much you have never pondered what this scripture means. What does it mean to have a fat soul?

I believe it means we will have an intense satisfaction and contentment in our souls. Our minds, wills and emotions will be at rest and we will be fulfilled and feel complete. Do you have a skinny soul or a fat one?

> Do you have a skinny soul or a fat one?

I think a lot of people overeat because they are not satisfied in other areas of life. If more people had fat souls, perhaps fewer people would be overweight and unhealthy. They wouldn't feel as if there was an emptiness there that needed filling. Pursuing your purpose with diligence and fervour is the way to fulfilment. Anything else will

i dare you

Be Determined!

1   Look at your problems as challenges and ask for God's help in meeting them.
2   Trade your fear for faith and your comfort zone for a desire for adventure.
3   Don't dwell on your past, but look ahead to the future. See the possibility, not the improbability.

leave you feeling empty and end up being the root of many problems in your life.

Don't Faint!

Many years ago a man hired an experienced guide to lead him on a hike into the Swiss Alps. After many hours they came to a high and remote mountain pass. To the man's dismay, he saw the path had almost been washed away. What could he do? To the left was a sheer rock cliff; to his right, a crevasse that dropped nearly 1,000 feet. Looking down, he felt his head growing faint and his knees beginning to buckle. At that moment his guide shouted, 'Do not look down or you are a dead man. Keep your eyes on me, and where I put my feet, put yours there as well.'

The man did as he was instructed and soon he passed from danger into safety.

The Bible says we are not to faint during chastisement or difficulty (see Hebrews 12:5). To 'faint' means to give up or to cease doing what you know you should do. That man could easily have let his realisation of the danger he was facing consume him and essentially help him fall to his death. Instead, he kept his eyes on his guide to lead him out of harm's way and back to the path he was pursuing.

> God has a plan for you, but He must prepare you for the plan.

All of us must be willing to grow up spiritually, but we should also be determined not to give up during the maturing process. This subject is covered very well in Hebrews 12. It says when we are chastised (taught and corrected) by God we should keep a good attitude and not give up (faint). We are to remember God only chastises those whom He loves. God has a plan for you, but He must prepare you for the plan, and He will lead you as long as you keep your eyes on Him.

I can well remember going through times in my walk with God

when I felt no other human being on earth could have as many faults as I did because it seemed as if God was continually showing me yet another thing that needed to change. It took a while, but I finally learned to thank God for dealing with me instead of wishing He would leave me alone. I realised only the truth would set me free. God's Word is truth, but we must accept it for ourselves if it is going to do us any good. Facing truth is often painful, but it is a pain that will eventually produce pleasure. It's like having a baby. You go through the pain, but once you have the baby, you are willing to do it again – and sometimes even again and again.

Don't faint in doing right; be diligent in your passion and purpose and you will reap the rewards of your diligence.

Shattered Dreams

Most of us are determined until something happens that shatters our dream. At that juncture in life, what we do and how we respond will make all the difference. The Western world often responds by trying to eliminate their pain through 'self-indulgence'. People party, drink excessively or take drugs. They hope pills will make them forget their ills. A young man in the Bible named Joseph had a dream he thought was shattered, but he eventually discovered that the very circumstances he thought to be stealing his dream were leading him to it.

It is important to remain positive and not get a wild spirit and start counteracting with lack of restraint. Some people eat excessively, others spend excessively, and some stop taking care of themselves and what belongs to them. They sink into a passive state where they 'wish' things would change and resent the fact that they don't. A lifestyle of doing whatever you want to do is not going to eliminate your pain. The only thing that will eliminate it is being determined to have God's will in your life and nothing else.

Larry Crabb, in his book *Shattered Dreams*, says that shattered dreams are never random:

They are always a piece in a larger puzzle, a chapter in a larger story. Pain is a tragedy. But it's never only a tragedy. For the Christian it's always a necessary mile on the long journey to joy. The suffering caused by shattered dreams must not be thought of as something to relieve if we can or endure if we must. It's an opportunity to be embraced, a chance to discover our desire for the highest blessing God wants to give us, an encounter with Himself.[1]

If God has truly given you a dream of something better for your life and your loved ones, it cannot be shattered. It may seem broken due to the circumstances around you, but God often leads us the long, hard way along paths we would not choose on our own. Even though we don't understand the purpose, we can be assured God has one. He is never purposeless!

> Even though we don't understand the purpose, we can be assured God has one. He is never purposeless!

Another way people deal with their pain and disappointment is through withdrawal. If they get hurt in a relationship, they decide not to enter another. If they get hurt at church, they decide not to go any more. They become introverted and they pull out of everything and close themselves off at home to nurse their wounds. They wall the world out, but don't realise they are walling themselves into a lonely existence that will eventually take its toll. Though at the time they are thinking they're just protecting themselves from being hurt, in reality they are making their problem much worse. Anything we hide from or run from has power over us. God wants us to confront life, not withdraw from it.

> Anything we hide from or run from has power over us.

There are actually times when people withdraw and refuse to face reality to such a degree they go insane.

Denial and Withdrawal
Are the Way of Madness

We can completely ruin our lives and, as I said, even lose our minds through refusing to deal with reality. If you have been hurt, learn what you can from it, forgive and go on. Don't hide or run! It is one of the most useless things you can do. We don't get rid of anything by hiding or running, because the problems are still there chasing us and they will never go away until we face them.

> The true Christian must be both an idealist and a realist.

Joseph had a dream that God gave him, but his brothers were jealous and hated him so much that they sold him into slavery. I don't think he sat there on the slave cart thinking, *I am not really in a slave caravan and my brothers really did not do this. This is not happening!* The true Christian must be both an idealist and a realist. We must have dreams and visions for better things in the future, because that is what faith demands. However, at the same time we cannot ignore the reality of what is taking place right now. The key is not to let what you see now steal what you believe for the future!

Joseph kept his dream, even though I am sure he did not see how it could be fulfilled. He dreamed he saw his brothers and father bowing down to him and now they were not even in his life.

But Joseph didn't sink into fatalism and just resign himself to being a slave. He decided to be a diligent slave and God gave him favour with his master and he got promoted. Things were looking up when he was suddenly accused of something he did not do and went to prison. Once again he did not change his outlook on life. He simply found ways to serve God in prison. He asked people to remember him when they got out and eventually someone did. An ex-prisoner knew Joseph was gifted in interpreting dreams and when Pharaoh needed one interpreted, they told him about Joseph.

Joseph went from the pit to the palace through applying the same principles I am teaching in this book. He became the assistant to Pharaoh, and during a severe famine he was able to provide food for his father and brothers who came to him bowing down and begging for help and forgiveness. What he saw did come to pass, but God took him the long, hard way. He was young, he had a lot to learn, and he wouldn't learn by having everything in life made easy. God loves us enough to apply tough love if He has to. We can look at Joseph's example and realise through good times and bad, we must stay the course, being diligent and enthusiastic about what God brings. If He brings you to it, we must remember, He will bring you through it as well.

> If He brings you to it, we must remember, He will bring you through it as well.

All Shook Up!

It seems some people are always 'all shook up' about something. They never remain stable in the storms of life and they allow themselves to be blown 'hither and thither', as the Bible says, by many things (see James 1:6).

We need to live by the Word of God, not how we feel or by the way things look to us. In order to do this, we must be willing to live a 'deeper life'. What I'm talking about is a life where we are so purpose driven and passionate about God's will that we refuse to let circumstances rule our lives. We deny the devil the chance to trip us up, and we press forward with intensity to follow the course that our Creator has set before us!

The Apostle Paul had many trials, but I don't envision him as a man who got all shook up every time he had a challenge he wasn't expecting. Jesus certainly remained the same no matter what He encountered. Going back to the example of Joseph, we see he was determined to be stable in his situation, which was clearly so unstable much of the time, and there are many others in the Bible we could look at and take lessons from on stability. Stability requires determination because you must remain on track and focused on God's will, no matter what is going on. That does not mean we don't tend to get flustered or emotional in an emergency or unexpected situations, but it does mean we don't let those feelings control us.

> Stability requires determination because you must remain on track and focused on God's will, no matter what is going on.

Do you ever get tired of spending all your time putting out fires the devil starts? Yes, I said the devil. People don't like to talk about the devil, but he is real and ignoring him won't make him go away. That's like pretending the mould in your fridge isn't really there; eventually, you're going to have to deal with it before it contaminates everything you eat and drink! When we have trials, Satan's purpose is to use them to destroy us, but God's intention is to use them to mature us and make us stronger than we have been previously. The devil is your enemy and he doesn't just lie to you. He will do everything he possibly can to keep you emotionally distraught. He wants you emotionally unbalanced, like one of those spinning tops that wobbles on a table, threatening to fall off. He wants you all shook up, making unwise choices and giving up on the promises of God. Be determined not to let the devil win!

> When we have trials, Satan's purpose is to use them to destroy us, but God's intention is to use them to mature us.

Make a decision that with God's help you will outlast the devil. He can come against you one way, but God's Word says he will flee before you seven ways (see Deuteronomy 28:7). Stand firm and watch him run!

Stability Requires Suffering

Remaining stable in hard times, when everything in you wants to scream and run, is hard. Some of you cringed when you read the word 'suffering' in the heading above. It's no fun to suffer, I know! But in order to be stable, and motivated, and moved towards the things of God, there will be times you must suffer in the flesh to do it. However, I promise you, each pain you feel is helping you towards your goal. It is no different than beginning an exercise programme or taking an existing one to a new level. Even as I write this chapter I am very sore from working out with my trainer at the gym this week (something I never thought I would do). He took me to a level of weights and gave me some more difficult exercises and it hurts, but I have grown to actually enjoy that feeling because it means I am getting stronger. I always say, 'New level, new devil!' It is my way of saying you will have to be determined if you want to make progress in any area of life, because Satan will always bring opposition.

Once again I want to remind you that you have what it takes. You

> Each pain you feel is helping you towards your goal.

can do whatever you need to do through Christ, Who gives you strength. Stand strong against fainting in your mind and be willing and ready to experience the enabling power of God. Keep believing and you will see God's glory (see John 11:40).

As you build new stability muscles, you will experience some discomfort, but the pain will be your gain and you will have a victory no one can ever take away. The Bible tells us in Romans 8:17–18 that if we want to share Christ's glory, we must also share His sufferings. We don't have to go to the literal cross like He did, but we do have to live a crucified life in which we decide we will give up the lower life in order to have the high life. We will have God's will and nothing less!

> Give up the lower life in order to have the high life.

I sense many of you just need a good dose of determination, a spark of passion that will ignite a steady stream of hope, enthusiasm and commitment to keep going. That is the only thing standing between you and real victory. Make up your mind regarding what you believe, have God's words to back it up, and don't ever back down. Say daily, 'I am determined to be all God wants me to be, do all He wants me to do, and have all He wants me to have.'

Shaky People in Shaky Times

The Bible teaches us God will continue shaking all that can be shaken until all that remains are those things that cannot be shaken (see Hebrews 12:26–29). God shakes things until we are no longer 'all shook up' by the shaking things. We're not talking about an Elvis tribute here, we're talking about radical, incredible change that will move our hearts and our minds forward!

Through some very difficult circumstances, God showed me I could not afford to be closely linked to people in ministry who let fear rule their lives. He assured me that He had some things He wanted to do, but the fearful could have no part in it.

When God called Gideon, he told him the same thing. He told him to get rid of all the soldiers who were fearful before he went into battle (see Judges 7:3). Why would God do this? It makes sense when you think about it – people who are fearful, excessively timid and cowardly will always lose their composure when the unexpected or the difficult occurs. They shake with whatever is shaking! People who are fearful use fear as an excuse for the problems they cause through their lack of stability. I have discovered everyone feels fear, but not everyone lets fear rule them. To be sure, it is an area we all must go through and grow through, but not one we should perpetuate all our lives. I had to learn to feel the fear and do what was right anyway. That is what courage is. It is not the absence of fear, but pressing forward when fear is present.

> Everyone feels fear, but not everyone lets fear rule them.

If I have employees working closely with me who are fearful and insecure, they can be nursing hurt feelings when I really need them to be strong for me. I finally had to realise that although I am a minister God has not called me to be surrounded by employees who need ministry. I need people who are able and stable. People who can stand firm, be determined, and not focused on how they *feel* about everything that happens. I need people who trust me and don't second-guess everything I say wondering if there is some hidden meaning. I am respectful, but I am also a straightforward person and I need people around me who are the same way. I don't have time or patience for pretence, game playing or offence.

I try to say what I mean and mean what I say. Like most of us, I sometimes say things based on my current knowledge and find out later I cannot do what I said because I really did not know what I was talking about, but I do try to be sincere and honest in my dealings with people. I do not like to, nor am I willing to, work with people who pretend one thing while something entirely different is in their hearts. Fearful people often do that. They say what they think every-one wants them to say instead of being honest.

> Sometimes we have to be shocked out of our willingness to
> just put up with a problem.

I know there are probably people reading this right now with many fears in their lives, and I don't mean to sound unfeeling or tough. However, sometimes we have to be shocked out of our willingness to just put up with a problem. I have an employee who was afraid of everything. We loved her and wanted to make use of her skills, but she spent more time crying and shaking than moving ahead. I finally called her into my office and said, 'We cannot continue with this any longer. Either you make a decision to get over this or we will have to let you go.' Later, she told me she went home and got very hurt and angry at me for being so unsympathetic, but after a few hours she settled down and felt God impress on her, 'Joyce is right, you have to face your fears.' That woman is one of our top-level managers today, and I can tell you I would not have done her a favour by just patting her on the head and telling her I knew how she felt and it was OK. I loved her, but I hated the spirit of fear operating through her. When Peter tried to get Jesus not to go to Jerusalem, He rebuked Peter and said, 'Get behind me, Satan.' He realised the devil was using Peter's weakness to get to Him, and He was not going to allow it.

You will have to learn to be a lionhearted lamb if you want to defeat the devil and enjoy God's best for your life. I am not unkind to people, but I am learning that I cannot let their weaknesses control my destiny. I cannot let their apathy affect my passion for life. I have a God-ordained destiny and I am going to fulfil it. I am determined and I am asking you to join me in being determined to live with purpose and passion, and to never give up, but be determined to do all God has called you to do.

Remember to do all He has called *you* to do, not what He has called *someone else* to do. If you do what you are meant to do, you will be doing something heaven calls amazing and great.

Martin Luther King Jr once said that 'if a man is called to be a streetsweeper, he should sweep streets even as Michelangelo painted, or Beethoven composed music, or Shakespeare wrote poetry. He should sweep streets so well that all the host of heaven and earth will pause to say, here lived a great streetsweeper who did his job well.'

Be Determined to Know God

The Apostle Paul said he was determined to know Jesus (see Philippians 3:10). Don't ever be satisfied to know *about* God, but get to know *Him*. Develop a deep, intimate relationship with Him for yourself and not through someone else. Too many people in centuries past have only known God through their priest, spiritual adviser, pastor, mother, father or friend. You need to know Him yourself and you can.

To know God should be our first and foremost determination, for He is our life. In Him we live and move and have our being (see Acts 17:28). He is our righteousness, peace and joy (see Romans 14:17). Actually, He is everything and we are nothing without Him. If you are not *determined* to know God, it will never happen. There are many things in the world that will crowd Him out of our lives unless we make knowing Him a top priority.

> Don't settle for a secondhand relationship with God.

If there is one thing I want you to understand at the end of this book, it's this: don't settle for a secondhand relationship with God. That's not the life of passion He is calling you to. Knowing God will keep you stable in hard times. It will make you secure and enable you to press beyond fear. It will cause you to know He is always with you whether you feel His Presence or not. You can know His forgiveness and mercy, His restoration and favour; truly knowing God will fuel your passion for life. When we see how beautiful and wonderful He really is, and realise all He has done for us in love, how can we not pursue Him and His will passionately?

Every success requires determination, even in the process of getting to know God. Paul said he was determined to know God. Will you be determined also? Determined to know God intimately, to know His will, to do your best, to be excellent, to fulfil your purpose, and to live with passion? Will you be determined to be a light in a dark world? Will you dare to be one of those rare individuals who are enthused, passionate and thoroughly pumped up about God and serving Him? Will you dare to be all you can be, and the best you can be? Will you dare to be daring for the rest of your life, and to never live one more day without zeal, passion and enthusiasm? I dare you to make the commitment and I pray you sense the Presence of God stirring within you as you reach for a life worth living!

NOTES

Chapter 1

1 'The *Apollo 8* Christmas Eve Broadcast', Dr David R. Williams, NASA Goddard Space Flight Center. Greenbelt, MD. www.spds.nasa.gov/planetary/lunar/apollo8_xmas.html.

Chapter 2

1 James Emory White, *Rethinking the Church* (Baker Books, Grand Rapids, MI, 1997), pp 27–8.

Chapter 3

1 John C. Maxwell, *The Success Journey* (Thomas Nelson, 2004), p. 17.
2 'Out of the Red: Holiday cheer without financial fear', by Amy Baldwin, *The News-Sentinel*, 21 November 2006. http://www.fortwayne.com.

Chapter 4

1 'Kids find a purpose, with Gavin's help', by Joe Depriest, *The Charlotte Observer*, 26 November 2006. http://www.charlotte.com/mld/observer/news/local/states/north_carolina/counties/gaston/16100399.htm.
2. National Center for Injury Prevention and Control, *Suicide: Fact Sheet*, 9 September 2006. http://www.cdc.gov/ncipc/factsheets/suifacts.htm.
3 Barna Research Online, 8 October 2001.
4 Bly, Nellie (2006), in *Encyclopædia Britannica*, retrieved 2 December 2006, from Encyclopædia Britannica Online: http://www.britannica.com/eb/article-9015794.
5 Carver, George Washington (2006), in *Encyclopædia Britannica*, retrieved 2 December 2006, from Encyclopædia Britannica Online: http://www.britannica.com/eb/article-9020575.
6 Barton, Clara (2006), in *Encyclopædia Britannica*, retrieved 2 December 2006, from Encyclopædia Britannica Online: http://www.britannica.com/eb/article-9013546.
7 http://www.drdino.com/articles.php?spec=32-15K, last accessed 15 May 2007.

Chapter 6

1 According to the most recent Bureau of Labor Statistics data. Gallup Poll news summary. 'Empty Seats: Fewer Families Eat Together', 20 January 2004. http://www.galluppoll.com/content/?ci=10336&pg=1.

2 'Empty Seats: Fewer Families Eat Together', by Heather Mason Kiefer. Gallup Poll. 20 January 2004. http://www.galluppoll.com/content/?ci=10336&pg=1.

3 Taken from SermonCentral.com.

4 Author and source unknown. Taken from InspirationalStories.com.

5 Malcolm Gladwell, *The Tipping Point*. (Little, Brown and Company, New York, NY, 2000), p. 163.

Chapter 7

1 www.motivational-inspirational-corner.com.

2 http://www.brainyquote.com/quotes/authors/c/charles_r_swindoll.html, last accessed 15 May 2007.

3 By Larry Harp. www.inspirationalstories.com.

4 www.quotationspage.com.

5 Rodney Buchanan in 'An Attitude of Gratitude' on www.sermon central.com.

Chapter 8

1 Jim Rohn's Weekly E-zine, © 2001 Jim Rohn International.

2 http://nerfew.org/MountainNewsMay2006.pdf, last accesssed 15 May 2007.

3 Ibid.

4 Ibid.

Chapter 9

1 *Discipleship Journal*, November/December 1992.

Chapter 10

1 *Today In The Word*, August 1989, p. 33.

2 Charles R. Swindoll, *Laugh Again: Experience Outrageous Joy* (Word Publishing, W Publishing Group, Nashville, TN, 1992), p. 19.

3 http://www.corexcel.com/html/body.humor.page3.htm, last accessed 15 May 2007.

4 http://www.sermons.org/sovereignty.html, last accessed 15 May 2007.

Chapter 11

1 S. J. Hill, *Enjoying God: Experiencing Intimacy with the Heavenly Father*. (Relevant Books, Orlando, FL, 2001).

2 From *Twilight over Burma: My Life as a Shan Princess*, by Inge Sargent, (University of Hawaii Press, 1994).

Chapter 12

1 Dr. Richard Swenson, *Margin: Restoring Emotional, Physical, Financial, and Time Reserves to Overloaded Lives* (NavPress Publishing, Colorado Springs, CO, 2004).
2 *Failing Forward* by John C. Maxwell (Thomas Nelson, 2000), p. 38.
3 Author unknown. Taken from http://www.inspirationalstories.com.
4 Lucinda Norman, 'An Atmosphere of Calm'. *Lookout* magazine, 15 December 1996.

Chapter 14

1 The Wycliffe Handbook of Preaching & Preachers, W. Wiersbe, p. 193.
2 'A conversation with Warren Buffett', by Carol J. Loomis, *Fortune Magazine*, 25 June 2006. Accessed online at: http://money.cnn.com/2006/06/25/magazines/fortune/charity2.fortune/index.htm.
3 'Bankruptcy law backfires on credit card issuers', MSN Money. http://articles.moneycentral.msn.com/Banking/BankruptcyGuide/BankruptcyLawBackfiresOnCreditCardIssuers.aspx
4 'Credit Card Industry Facts and Personal Debt Statistics', CreditCard.com.

Chapter 15

1 'Climb Every Mountain' by Sean Swarner, www.motivational-inspirational-corner.com

Chapter 16

1 http://www.cancer.org/docroot/COM/content/div_OH/COM_1_1x_Cancer_Survivor_Makes_Trek_to_Mc last accessed 15 May 2007.

Chapter 17

1 Larry Crabb, *Shattered Dreams: God's Unexpected Path to Joy.* (WaterBrook Press, Colorado Springs, CO, 2001).

JOYCE MEYER is one of the world's leading practical Bible teachers. A *New York Times* bestselling author, she has written more than seventy inspirational books, including *The Confident Woman; Look Great, Feel Great,* the entire Battlefield of the Mind family of books, and many others. She has also released thousands of audio teachings as well as a complete video library. Joyce's *Enjoying Everyday Life®* radio and television programmes are broadcast around the world, and she travels extensively conducting conferences. Joyce and her husband, Dave, are the parents of four grown-up children and make their home in St Louis, Missouri.

To CONTACT THE AUTHOR IN THE UK:
Joyce Meyer Ministries
PO Box 1549
Windsor
SL4 1GT
Great Britain
+44 (0) 1753-831102

Please include your testimony or help received from this book when you write. Your prayer requests are welcome.

To CONTACT THE AUTHOR IN THE UNITED STATES:
Joyce Meyer Ministries
P.O. Box 655
Fenton, Missouri 63026
+1 (636) 349-0303
www.joycemeyer.org

To CONTACT THE AUTHOR IN CANADA:
Joyce Meyer Ministries-Canada, Inc.
Lambeth Box 1300
London, ON N6P 1T5
+1 (636) 349-0303

To CONTACT THE AUTHOR IN AUSTRALIA:
Joyce Meyer Ministries-Australia
Locked Bag 77
Mansfield Delivery Centre
Queensland 4122
+61 (0) 7 3349 1200

The Battle Belongs to the Lord

The Secrets to Exceptional Living

Eight Ways to Keep the Devil Under Your Feet

Teenagers Are People Too!

Filled with the Spirit

Celebration of Simplicity

The Joy of Believing Prayer

Never Lose Heart

Being the Person God Made You to Be

A Leader in the Making

'Good Morning, This Is God!' (gift book)

Jesus – Name Above All Names

Making Marriage Work (Previously published as *Help Me – I'm Married!*)

Reduce Me to Love

Be Healed in Jesus' Name

How to Succeed at Being Yourself

Weary Warriors, Fainting Saints

*Be Anxious for Nothing**

Straight Talk Omnibus

Don't Dread

Managing Your Emotions

Healing the Brokenhearted

*Me and My Big Mouth!**

Prepare to Prosper

Do It Afraid!

Expect a Move of God in Your Life . . . Suddenly!

Enjoying Where You Are on the Way to Where You Are Going

A New Way of Living

When, God, When?

Why, God, Why?

The Word, the Name, the Blood

Tell Them I Love Them

Peace

If Not for the Grace of God[*]

JOYCE MEYER SPANISH TITLES

Las Siete Cosas Que Te Roban el Gozo
(Seven Things That Steal Your Joy)

Empezando Tu Dia Bien (Starting Your Day Right)

[*]Study Guide available for this title

BOOKS BY DAVE MEYER

Life Lines

JOYCE MEYER

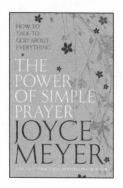

The Power of Simple Prayer

For the first time, Joyce focuses on the bestselling topic of prayer and how it can transform your life.

978 0340 943885   £10.99   Paperback

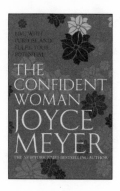

The Confident Woman

Joyce's most personal book yet, *The Confident Woman* shows how you can live with purpose and fulfil your potential.

978 0340 943816   £10.99   Paperback

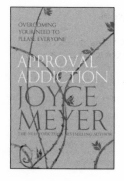

Approval Addiction

Selling nearly 400,000 copies in the US to date, *Approval Addiction* can help you overcome low self-esteem and the need to seek approval from others.

978 0340 943847   £10.99   Paperback

www.joycemeyerthebooks.com

JOYCE MEYER

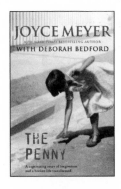

The Penny

Joyce Meyer's first ever novel, inspired by her own childhood. Set in the summer of 1955, 14-year-old Jenny Blake makes the decision to pick up a penny. The chain of events that unfolds changes her life forever.

978 0340 943878   £6.99   Paperback

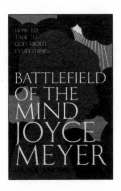

Battlefield of the Mind

In the US over 1 million copies have been sold of this book, which teaches how to banish damaging emotions like worry, depression and anger.

978 0340 943830   £10.99   Paperback

Look Great, Feel Great

The *New York Times* bestselling guide to physical, emotional and spiritual well-being.

978 0340 943823   £10.99   Paperback

www.joycemeyerthebooks.com